spent

EXPOSING OUR

COMPLICATED

RELATIONSHIP

WITH SHOPPING

edited by kerry cohen

SEAL

SPENT

"Where Nothing Bad Can Happen" by Monica Drake was previously published in The Rumpus
(therumpus.net).

"Let's See How Fast This Baby Will Go" by Gloria Harrison was previously broadcast on
"This American Life."

"Shopping for Breasts" by Wendy Staley Colbert was previously published at Salon.

"The Book Money" by Aryn Kyle was previously published in *More* magazine as "How I lost
$500,000 for Love."

A portion of "Mother Lode" by Nancy Rommelmann was previously published in *LA Weekly*.
ISBN 978-1-58005-512-3

Library of Congress Cataloging-in-Publication Data
Spent : exposing our complicated relationship with shopping / [edited by] Kerry Cohen.
pages cm
ISBN 978-1-58005-512-3 (paperback)
1. Shopping--Humor. 2. Women consumers. I. Cohen, Kerry. II. Title.
PN6231.S5467S66 2014
813'.01083553--dc23

2014009455

Published by Seal Press
A Member of the Perseus Books Group
1700 Fourth Street
Berkeley, California
sealpress.com

Cover by Elke Barter Design
Interior Design by Kate Basart/Union Pageworks
Printed in the United States of America
Distributed by Publishers Group West

spent

"He's always asking: 'Is that new? I haven't seen that before.'
It's like, Why don't you mind your own business?
Solve world hunger. Get out of my closet."

—MICHELLE OBAMA, from "Mrs. Obama Speaks Out About Her Household,"
The New York Times

contents

S ometimes I joke with my husband about how he has four pairs of shoes in our closet: his fall and winter shoes, his spring and summer shoes, his running shoes, and his biking shoes. When one of these gets worn into shreds, which they do each year, he buys new ones to replace them. But he never has more than those four. I have approximately seventeen pairs of boots and sandals and wedges and heels. I probably also only need four, but I'll dance on the blacktop with anyone who tries to take them away. And, still, I comb for more.

Do you know Old Gringo boots? If not, I might have changed your life just now. You are about to go broke. I have three pairs. After every purchase, I came home and announced to my family that now I would be complete. I would finally be happy. It was a joke. I was kidding. But there was a small prick of hope inside me each time I bought that new pair.

Lots of men shop. I don't mean to suggest they don't. But let's face it: shopping is a woman's thing. Bitches gonna shop, it's just what we do. And, yet, the more I talk to people, the more I find that it's not that simple. Women's relationships to shopping can be intensely complicated. Because the entire shopping industry is geared toward women. Those marketing people know what they're doing.

When I walk into the makeup counter section of Nordstroms or Saks, I get a tickle in my throat. The colors! The textures! Even those little boxes the mascara comes in! Sometimes I don't throw them out. They're so damn pretty with their sleek black gloss and scripted font. I'm the biggest pushover for that kind of marketing. I can't help it. Something new feels so good and solid in my hands. It's so lovely and untouched, like a hope.

There's something stitched within the world of shopping and buying. Shopping isn't just about the worth and value of the things we buy. It's about our own worth, our own value. Just the act of shopping makes us feel good. The things we buy are costumes. They are disguises. They are evidence of who we might become, if we were someone else. Better, perhaps. Or at least different.

As women, we tend to underestimate ourselves. We believe that we are less than, and nothing is more heavily marketed toward women than things that will make us better. The implication is that we aren't okay, that we will never be okay. But the right face cream, the right scarf, the right set of plates will perhaps make us better. We will improve, if we just had that thing.

The stories in this collection take us through various takes on this notion. Mel Wells attempts to fill her loss through stealing. Kristin Thiel recovers from a similar sort of loss through a single pair of sneakers. Robin Romm sorts through the extensive items her mother bought after she dies too young, too soon, from cancer. The sorting is also a sorting of her grief, a realization that the things her mother bought were a way to stay "tethered to the physical world." The writers here buy clothes. For Emily Chenoweth and Monica Drake, one sweater, one blouse, could modify everything. Susan Senator and Randon Billings Noble contemplate the ways in which the experience of shopping alters when our bodies change. The writers also buy kitchen items, dishtowels, mattresses, tools, cars. The things these writers buy take on illumination through their words. A mattress isn't just a place for Rachel Sontag to sleep; it's the home she can't seem to create. The Kitchen Aid isn't just a tool Candace Walsh can use to make baked goods; it represents the ways in which she has finally found her true self.

Some writers see humor. Traci Foust, who hates shopping, raises three sons who love shopping in ways she can't fathom. Ophira Eisenberg tries to come to terms with the fact that she buys shoes she can't afford for a dinner at the White House. Other essays, like Abby Mims' about her dying mother's relationship to clothes, are heart wrenching. Jennifer Finney Boylan's essay about how life with her family continues with ordinariness and love since her transition from a man to a woman expands our understanding.

All of the essays show that shopping is about much more than we realize. These women illustrate that when we are overwhelmed with work, or more commonly, when our bank accounts are dangerously low, our minds often turn to shopping. Because that new sweater or plush towel or suede boots, with its sweet tag dangling, is a promise for redemption.

WHERE NOTHING BAD CAN HAPPEN

Monica Drake

there was a winter when I was obsessed with a certain green sweater. Love is too big a word. I was deeply interested from a distance, the way it's easy to be intrigued by a stranger. The sweater was in a catalogue. I carried the catalogue in an old leather bag, along with paintbrushes, rags, oil paints, and a hardback copy of *The Mandarins*, by Simone de Beauvoir, that I'd found at Goodwill for fifty cents.

That's how I shopped: used, cheap. Books.

It was 1985. *The Mandarins* was forty years old. If you don't know it, it is a novel with a Marxist view, filled with serious, dark, and dramatic sentences, like this: "Eating to live, living to eat—that had been the nightmare of my adolescence. If it meant going back to that, it would be just as well to turn on the gas at once."

Reagan was president, the rich/poor split creaked open, my home state, Oregon, was deep in a recession, and I didn't believe in conspicuous consumption. To not shop was political: buying new petroleum-based clothes was about buying into the whole Military Industrial Complex. Selling the hours of your life to a job to pay for the trinkets of your life was a consumer trap.

So I was broke but had conceptual, theoretical, sociopolitical reasons for opting out of a financial world I had never really entered, yet.

I was into painting, and friends. I wanted time to hang out and paint. My big plan: if you don't earn much, don't spend much.

But the catalogue migrated around my apartment, with the pages turned open to one thing: a photo of a woman walking beside a man down a country road in what I guessed was a New England fall.

A New England fall was essentially as foreign to me as de Beauvoir's postwar Paris. In Oregon, leaves turn brown, soggy as milk-soaked raisin bran with the first fall rain.

In the catalogue, the woman frolicked in red and yellow leaves and wore the green sweater. A stack of five other colors, charcoal to cherry, were displayed fanned out in an insert. I studied it until I came to feel the generous thickness and weight of that wool in my hands.

The sweater would be only scratchy enough to show its natural fiber integrity. Mostly, it would be soft. It could be called *moderately priced* by somebody else. For me, it was a fortune. Bottom line: I was broke, with oil paint–stained cuticles. I was twenty years old, trying to find my way through a dark northwestern winter. Mostly, I was freezing.

I had one sweater from St. Vincent de Paul—a men's V-neck, with three buttons down low and two shallow pockets, grandpa-style. The rest of my clothes came out of free boxes that showed up in apartment basements: rhinestone necklaces, old silk dresses, perfectly broken-in 501s.

People leave things when their lives change—when they move, gain weight, break up. I was rail thin and didn't mind baggy clothes, so I made a perfect candidate for cast-offs. And I liked a fashion risk, a good joke, an ironic, moth-chewed dead mink coat that was so tattered it had turned itself into a premade antifur commentary. I wasn't *invested* in getting dressed.

The catalogue showed up curled in the dark of my little aluminum mailbox down the hall. The sweater looked pretty in a practical way, thick, warm, and plain.

It was a straightforward, conservative sweater!

To buy that sweater, in the politically informed, punk rock heyday of Portland, would be as out of step as dating a Conservative Christian, a Young Republican. It wasn't my thing. So why did I keep looking at it, assessing the value, the price, the possibility?

I was involved with a man, a *philosopher*, fifteen years older than me, but other than a gray hair in his insane pile of dark curls, the age difference didn't register in the slightest.

We rode bikes, everywhere. We wore black coats, black turtlenecks, old jeans. I had more going on in the way of work than he did—there were places around town where gallery owners liked me and let me step in. Sometimes my shift in an art gallery lasted only as long as the owner's lunch. Other times, it might run all day.

He and I were both enrolled at Portland State University. He hovered between undergraduate status (one course short of graduating?), a master's degree (enrolled), and a PhD (also enrolled). He took classes out of state, registered for two schools at once. He'd forged an academic liminal no-man's-land, a no-student's-land, free of linear progression.

Who needs a graduation date? Why should learning end?

With my random paychecks I rented the first apartment I ever had with a bathroom actually *in* the apartment—part of the apartment. I didn't have to keep shampoo and soap in a basket to carry down the hall. I could step out of a shower without wrapping myself in a robe, didn't need to dress to cut through communal spaces lined with junkies, runaways, poker players, anorexics, pizza chefs, and punks.

See the kind of rented rooms I'd come from?

I was proud of my apartment.

These were the things I wanted: a good sweater, and a bathroom of my own.

My rooms were on the ground floor where windows opened onto an empty lot I called a yard. In that lot, whole parties would spring up—early morning poets, scavenging crews out counting their cans, homeless loners sleeping off a binge.

One night, in a heavy rain, an older woman I worked for gave me and my six-dollar coaster bike a ride home. It was a good bike, with only one bent crank, and the truth is I got it for free. My brother paid the six dollars, because it was his bike for a while first. As I got out of my employer's car, she leaned to peer through her window and up the front steps of the building. The bare bulb of the entry afforded a welcoming glare. It illuminated raindrops, granting each drop a halo, a downpour of cheap jewels.

My boss pushed her glasses back on her nose, cleared her throat. She said, "Dear, do you feel safe here?"

It was a brick building, freestanding and solid.

She was hesitant to leave.

My apartment door had a lock that was more secure than the front door of the house I grew up in. The building's main entry had a buzzer system. My key was already in my hand. Inside, the manager would be wandering our grease-scented halls, smoking, adjusting her wig, sometimes rubbing lotion over the terrible eczema that bothered her arms. Her two little dogs would grunt and scoot their bottoms on the worn carpet runner.

In the empty lot, shadows—people in thick coats, and what looked like a few doubled-up stocking caps—shuffled through the bushes. My neighbors.

Not all neighbors have houses.

I said, "Of course." I was fine. I thanked her, wiped rain off my forehead, and then closed the door of the warm car and moved to hoist my dear old bent bike from her spacious trunk.

On a Sunday morning just after that, waking up, I pulled back the curtain in my tiny kitchen, and there was a man with a compound bow outside. It was a complicated sort of power bow. The sky was gray and heavy. The man wore a camouflage-print rain slicker. It was as if he'd crawled out of the woods, or been dropped from another planet, or maybe he'd just come from a shopping spree at Andy and Bax, Portland's military surplus store. He drew back an arm, released, let an arrow fly. *Thunk*. It was a solid sound when the arrow hit a hay bale he'd clearly carted in for that purpose.

I don't know if he was trying to threaten somebody, in particular.

The important detail is, he shot *parallel* to the windows that lined my rooms, not toward the building. That's a huge distinction, one I was willing to give him credit for; on my part, it was the difference between witnessing a spectacle and sure death.

He hit a hay bale! That was all. People have hobbies. In a city, it takes tolerance to live side by side.

I dropped the curtain, ran water in an old pan I'd found in the basement, and put it on the tiny gas stove to boil for coffee.

Beside me, on a narrow tile counter, the woman in the green wool sweater laughed, kicked her way through the leaves, and lightly held her boyfriend's arm. Her boyfriend had fabulous teeth. Actually, they had matching teeth! Sun dappled her hair. She was happy. To look at that catalogue was like looking out a window, maybe my own window, only into a tidier sort of world. I reached for a chipped china coffee cup, a Goodwill special, and put a stained drip cone on top.

Thunk.

A second arrow hit. I spilled the hot water, scalded my wrist, and swore that whatever came next, today or any day, I wouldn't jump again.

The man I was seeing had two sisters, identical twins. They were gorgeous, dark-haired, and busty, and moved in a cloud of Nordstrom: perfume, leather, new clothes, lip gloss, hair spray; formaldehyde, nylon, urea, petrochemicals, arsenic, lead, and cadmium, if cadmium has a smell.

Their brother and me? We weren't smokers but hung out with people who were; we ate cheap gyros and drank dollar pitchers of beers. I'm sure we smelled all too often like a tavern.

One of the twins married the kind of man whose name you'd see high over the city, on the side of major construction projects. The other married into possibly more suspect sources of money, though I didn't ask and so don't know. Don't take my word on any of that.

One was straight-up Nordstrom, the other a little more Nordstrom Rack. Both looked stunning, all the time.

When I think of them now, I see them with their Nordstrom's bags, always with those bags.

Along with *The Mandarins*, I had a battered paperback of *Breakfast at Tiffany's*, another book from the mid-1950s that I'd rescued at a garage sale. While de Beauvoir, in France, was busy being a serious and sometimes gloomy theoretical Marxist,

Truman Capote, in that very American way, mainlined the as-of-yet-unnamed existential angst of retail therapy.

The character Holly Golightly begins her story resisting ownership of anything, even a stray cat. She says, "I don't want to own anything until I know I've found the place where me and things belong together. I'm not quite sure where that is just yet."

I understood. I wasn't sure, either. I was making my way.

But she describes her love of Tiffany's as fending off despair. She says, "The blues are because you're getting fat or maybe it's been raining too long. You're sad, that's all. But the mean reds are horrible. You're afraid and you sweat like hell, but you don't know what you're afraid of. Except something bad is going to happen, only you don't know what it is. . . . What I've found does the most good is to get into a taxi and go to Tiffany's. It calms me down right away, the quietness and the proud look of it; nothing very bad could happen to you there, not with those kind of men in their nice suits, and that lovely smell of silver and alligator wallets."

Some say the psychological source of compulsive shopping is rooted in a lack of love. Maybe it's true. Holly Golightly, a young woman on her own, is a portrait of a compulsive shopper ready to launch.

As I saw the two twin sisters, with their Nordstrom bags, I wondered if they felt the mean reds, the soothing sense of commerce, Nordies as a place *where nothing very bad can happen.*

I wondered if they felt a lack of love.

Their mother plucked her eyebrows like a 1940s starlet into high, thin arches. She curled her lashes, put mascara on, and painted her lips coral. She set her hair in pin curls, and kept her blinds closed.

In all the years I knew her, I saw her leave the house exactly once. I never saw her put a foot into the tended yard.

Their father, her husband, quite the patriarch, owned buildings downtown. He'd buy, sell, and trade over breakfast with the guys. Shopping—dealing—on a big scale, was his business. His motto? *Get a Brooks Brothers.*

Put on a good suit, go out with the guys, and the money would come.

Once, he moved the family into the most expensive house in Portland's real estate market, at the foot of the West Hills. The family showed me a fragile, yellowed newspaper clipping, their names, the address, the price. By the time I saw it, the girls had moved out, were raising families of their own. The father moved in with his mistress. The big house had long been sold. He stayed married, though, and bought his wife a modest ranch home tucked farther back in quiet, empty, curving streets, in the hills.

In my apartment, one day my old, curved refrigerator quit working. I asked the manager for help. She offered a new one, though it'd be a while. A very long while. Months. After that, my guy and I rode our bikes across town, from one side of the river to the other, every evening. We rode miles, through the city, just to eat cheap Vietnamese food.

And we got thinner, and thinner, and we were happy.

The only time I knew his mother to leave her house, the ranch house, was after the new fridge was finally in. She came to my apartment for dinner.

I cleaned the apartment. I moved an easel and put a few freaky paintings out of the way. I roasted a fat chicken that barely fit in my tiny, enameled oven. I made a salad.

If I'd bought the green sweater, I would've worn it. I looked at the catalogue, touched the image, chided myself for not having something reasonable to wear in a drafty apartment on a cold, dark night. I put on a little stained silk dress, and turned up the heat.

When she came over, her grown son, her rock-and-roller, her long-haired anarchist, her anticorporate man-boy, came in at her side. He went for a beer. She clutched her clutch purse in both hands, as though somebody threatened to take it away. She lifted the stiff material of a sallow roller blind to look out one window, over the dark side yard, turning her head one way, then the other, and asked, "Do you feel safe here?"

There it was, that question again.

I said, "Completely!" and put a little quiet jazz station on the old stereo, hoping she'd relax. "Wine?"

Her body language showed me that she was terrified, but of what? Germs? Maybe. Neighbors, crime. I could only guess. She was Holly Golightly, as far as I could sort it out: "You're afraid and you sweat like hell, but you don't know what you're afraid of. Except something bad is going to happen, only you don't know what it is."

Nothing bad would happen!

I've always been a good cook. My guest sat uneasily on one salvaged wooden chair. I put dinner dishes on a rickety table, and then brought out the roasted chicken. My catalogue was on the couch. The New England woman and boyfriend, in their sweaters, with their matching teeth, were practically having dinner with us, laughing and having a good time. It was a party. I said, "I'm so glad you could be here—"

And then we heard a sound, *pop, pop, pop*. Three rounds, in quick succession. It was almost a party sound, like champagne corks popping, and almost blended in with the jazz playing, except *almost* isn't close enough and we all knew what it was—a gun—and ducked. I moved fast, looked out over the edge of the window in time to see a bottle fly, glass break, a car drive away.

There, in two spotlights angled to light up the welcome sign for a retirement facility, was a man on the ground. He moaned, then hollered, swearing. I recognized his voice. I knew him, through the local bar scene.

I called 911. When I went out, two friends were with him. He was bleeding from his calf. We were only a handful of blocks from a major hospital, there in the heart of the city. An ambulance, squad car, and fire truck all showed up at once, crowding our narrow street.

When I gave the police my version of events, I used the man's name. Let's say his name was Craig Schmeg. Let's say it was Joey Poey. Looney Balloony. I won't use his real—or real-ish—name here, but the name I gave the cops? It was a simple, silly rhyme.

The man I was involved with, at my side, out in the street, said, skeptically, "Really? That's his name?"

I nodded yes, it was true. The police wrote the name down.

We stepped away together, aside from the cops, and my boyfriend asked, quietly, "What did his parents speak, Pig Latin?" More seriously he whispered, "That's not a real name." Maybe it wasn't. I'd never given it thought. It was a street name.

We went back to my apartment, where the woman who would never actually be my mother-in-law raised her fine eyebrows. Together the two of us told her the story—that we knew the man, that he'd be fine, that nobody got the license plate, but it was some kind of drive-by. It was random. The victim threw a bottle after he was shot. We finished each other's sentences. We told the story, in unison. We'd been helpful, we'd called the police, we'd done things right.

She held on to her clutch. I saw, in the way her eyes met mine, all disappointment, judgment, and fear. What I saw, mostly, was blame: I was somehow responsible for all this.

I shouldn't have said I knew the victim. That didn't go over. I shouldn't have told her the neighborhood was safe. But it was!

With the blinds up now, as the flickering lights of emergency vehicles played over our faces, she said, "I think I should go."

I said, "We haven't had dinner."

She asked her son to see her out. That was fine, he'd be back. He'd be around a good long time.

I poured myself more wine and watched through the window. She climbed back in her car, drove up the hill, off to a place where she could lock her own door, *where nothing very bad would ever happen.*

Maybe it wouldn't, didn't. What did I know? I was twenty.

Once they were outside, it was just me and the catalogue, and a big dinner. There was the smell of roast chicken along with a whiff of turpentine in the air, the paintings put aside.

I tore the page out of the catalogue.

What did I see in that sweater? It was a basic cable knit. Looking back now, I can imagine I saw an easier life, in the pretty photo, but I don't think that's quite it. If I really ever thought that sweater could improve my existence, I would've ordered it.

It was the plainest, most sensible sweater in the world. It was practically dull!

It was a thing beyond judgment. Who could be judged, draped in such a practical sweater? It was a justifying sweater, the reasonable thing. It would work as a costume, to say that I, the owner of such a sweater, made solid choices.

The truth is, everything I did, all the choices I made, invited easy criticism: I wore the same clothes days in a row. I wore free clothes. I dated an older man, an unemployed man, and I didn't let that bother me. I could make my own money. I wasn't looking for marriage. I went out to the bars too often, knew the drinkers, the hoodlums, the locals. I lived in a funky old building and liked it. I was so skinny that once even a homeless drunk with unsavory stains on his pants, lying at the curb, felt entitled to shout out, "Gain some weight!" as I cruised past on that same six-dollar bike. There was always somebody encouraging me to get in deeper with food, cars, clothes—with corporate America.

Fifteen years after *Breakfast at Tiffany's*, the *Chicago Tribune* reported, "We've become a nation measuring out our lives in shopping bags and nursing our psychic ills through retail therapy."

Of course, *retail therapy* isn't therapeutic any more than drinking is medicinal—maybe less so.

Some call it "promiscuous spending," a term designed to link shopping and sex, a carelessness to it, and a feminization. Capote saw that coming. There's a reason he made Holly a call girl, an escort, a powder room whore. We're all supposed to buy into the system, but buy in too much, and you're judged there, too.

At the end of *Breakfast at Tiffany's*, Holly Golightly shops: "she acquired a stag-at-bay hunting tapestry and, from the William Randolph Hearst estate, a gloomy pair of Gothic 'easy' chairs; she bought the complete Modern Library, shelves of classical records, innumerable Metropolitan Museum reproductions (including a statue of a Chinese cat that her own cat hated and hissed at and ultimately broke), a Waring mixer and a pressure cooker and a library of cook books. She spent whole hausfrau afternoons slopping about in the sweatbox of her midget kitchen. . . ."

I had that midget kitchen.

Holly says, "I don't have [the mean reds] much any more, except sometimes, and even then they're not so hideola that I gulp Seconal or have to haul myself to Tiffany's: I take his suit to the cleaner or stuff some mushrooms, and I feel fine, just great."

She's given in.

It turns out that even Simone de Beauvoir, that Marxist, was a serious shopper. It's in her memoirs. She spent her book advances on nylons and furs, chocolate, oranges, and everything or anything else she wanted. Sartre was having affairs, she was having affairs, and she was shopping.

Was that a lack of love, too?

Shopping is strange terrain; the act of desire is both soothing and agitating, what looks distant can be brought close, and money rides shotgun to consumer lust. The nation's "consumer confidence index"—the confidence, and willingness, to spend instead of save—is so psychologically misguided: we've all learned by now that overspending is an indicator of consumer despair, not confidence at all.

It's the "consumptive" aspect of the economy. Consumptive? That couldn't sound more like an illness.

I'm still not an easy shopper. I avoid big box stores like mad—the despair of the hot, sprawling parking lots alone makes me want to stop for a drink halfway across. But I have a house, and a family, and somehow our house grows crowded with things.

My old apartment stands, across town. Once in a while I drive past it and nod. That place and I? We went through a lot together. I think about how spare the space was, and how many people came through.

I'm not in touch with that man, or his family. Sadly, it's a part of my life that's gone in a free box somewhere, cast off.

I never ordered the sweater.

Owning that sweater wouldn't have made my ragged, lovely life any more explicable to people who made other choices—people who prioritized jobs, real yards, dry cleaning, savvy career moves, and chasing the big bucks. Owning that sweater wouldn't have gentrified the neighborhood. It wouldn't have changed anything. In my heart, I didn't really want it to.

THE THINGS SHE CARRIED

Robin Romm

a fter my mother died, my father could not bring himself to empty out her closets. My mother had been sick for a decade, dying slowly throughout my twenties. She had plenty of time to feel all the things people feel when they understand that they are dying, when it no longer feels like an abstraction, but rather a fact. She felt alone. She felt afraid. She felt able to appreciate the sun on her face, the velvet of a cat's ear. She felt out of control. She felt grateful for her friends. She felt air hunger. She felt like something in her was against her, was eating her alive. Though I lived this with her, in my way, I did not live it the way she did. Trying to imagine what she felt to be diagnosed at forty-seven stirs up a fear too bright and alive to sit with. She must have felt like she was trapped in a burning building with no means of escape, except the burning was inside her.

I was passing through Eugene a few years ago when my father told me he needed me to go through the closets and empty them of my mother's things. She'd been dead five years by then, her patterned blouses long out-of-date, the boxes of shoes covered in a sheen of dust. I had no interest in this task. It felt overwhelming. And I'd already cleaned out so many dead people's closets—his father's, his mother's, my mother's stuff from our cabin. It was getting strange, as if I could add a line to my CV: the only one with the stomach for the closets of the dead. My father still slept in that bedroom, still cuddled the dogs there and read the paper. Couldn't he just drink a few glasses of wine and do it? But when I showed up at the house and saw the way his back curved when he mentioned it, the reserved and closed-off look in his pale blue eyes, I knew the answer was no. He could not.

The closets were filled with expensive clothing—clothes to wear to the theater, out to dinner, to the courtroom (my mother was a trial attorney). That alone would not be strange. My mother loved clothes. She loved saturated color (magenta, maroon, royal blue). She loved silks and linens and leather. She spent hours getting dressed up or *farpitzed*—her rings glittering, her shirts shining, her lipstick in concert with her eyeshadow and probably her handbag. She had secret fashion knowledge I do not possess. She was vain, in other words, but a lovely, self-respecting kind of vain. Reflecting back on it, I admire this about her. Vanity, kept in check, is a weapon against despair. But what felt strange, unsettling, about emptying my mother's closets was not the clothes themselves, but the price tags on almost all of them. These clothes, with their yellowing tags, were objects I would never have permitted myself to buy. But my mother, sick with cancer, had bought them knowing she would die. I imagined her, walking alone in the big city after a consultation at Sloan-Kettering, entering the hallowed halls of Saks. And now I filled garbage bags with her unworn purchases—these out-of-date, too-big-for-me fancy outfits. At least ten garbage bags.

Judgment filled me as I shoved the clothes into the bags. I loved my mother, but this was ridiculous. Expensive, wasteful, and maybe a little insane. What was she doing? My mother was a civil rights attorney. She fought, at least a lot of the time, for the greater good. She made me do volunteer work from the time I could make a phone call—sex education, tax reform, environmental work. She had principles and values and would permit nothing less from me. Why was she spending gobs of cash on cropped suede mini-coats with jeweled buttons? Coats that she bought, apparently, on a whim, with no occasion in mind? Or five different versions of cream-colored blouses? How many cream-colored blouses does a mom need? And elastic pants? When did she ever consider wearing elastic pants? They were all the way elastic, sort of like jodhpurs made out of seat belts. And don't get me started on the flowing overcoats: black, charcoal gray, matte black, beige, shiny black, dark red. . . . The shelves of shoes. Though the shoes, at least, fit her friend Martha and my friend Deborah and could easily be given good homes.

I dragged the bags downstairs, annoyed and upset, churning with feelings. This often happens to me in my childhood home. I churn and churn, and then emote, but though I pride myself on being emotionally perceptive, the emotions are too quick a fish for me and I can only just grab their tails before they slip from my grasp.

I'm upset! I thought. *This is unfair!* Unfair, a leftover and useless idea from my mother, the attorney. Nothing is fair. But still, it made me brood. It made me dark-feeling and furious. It was terrible stuff, these Neanderthal feelings, leaking up from my lizard brain.

I lugged the bags across the wood floors near the kitchen where I knew they would sit for months while my dad figured out where to donate them. He sat at the kitchen table. "Why did she buy all this shit?" I fumed. "It's wasteful and crazy. It's irresponsible." I lifted a bag up like a gavel and banged it down, except bags don't bang, they just silently settle. Very unsatisfying! What else could I bang? I eyed the teakettle in the kitchen, the toaster. Bang!

My father looked at me from his cluttered and dirty post-mom kitchen, the handmade plates now cracked and chipped in a greasy cupboard, hinges loosening. His hair was more white than ever, cut dignified and short. He wore, as he always wore, his torn orange hiking shirt. See? Here he was with plenty of places to go, and yet he only needed one shirt! Why couldn't she have donated money to things she cared about? More money to loan repayment scholarships for public interest lawyers? Money to help with cancer research? Money to save the environment, to give microloans to poor communities? Or whatever! To buy thousands of dollars worth of clothes was downright gross and insane and shameful and consumptive! So materialistic and capitalist and—! I shoved a bag toward a window, then another bag. My father turned his most fierce stare on me. "She hoped to wear them, Robin," he said. "She hoped she might get better and live and wear them."

And then I felt despair. A cool hand on my throat, then the tightening of tears. Because that statement, although complicated, felt more true than not true. The operative word: hope. My mother hoped to wear this stuff, these bags of designer clothes. She hoped to be around. She hoped to live even though she knew she would not live. And don't we all hope for that? She hoped for a future free from pain and full of theater, dinners, and meaningful work. She hoped that buying things would cause this to be so. The clothes were an offering to an angry God. Or maybe they were an act of defiance.

Before this, though, I had my own irrational foray into the world of emotional shopping. My mother had a prized object, a red leather Italian purse that she would not let me borrow, and, when she got too sick to use it, I stole it. By this time, she had brain damage and couldn't ask for it back, but still I hid it, squirreling it away in my car. I wanted the bag. I wanted my mother to want the bag. I wanted to be the things she carried. I wanted to shine with an expensive grace. I wanted my mother. I didn't know what I wanted. I wanted to beat up death, slice its balls off with a sharp blade, and cut them up so tiny they disappeared—death crouching, death asking for mercy. I wanted to blow it up. I couldn't do what I wanted, so I took the bag. But after she died, I didn't want the red bag. I only wanted that red bag when she was alive, when it still belonged to her. I wanted a new red bag now, in my different orphaned life. I wanted my own bag. A bag for the future, for a different future, this weird and alien future that was not about dying, that was suddenly about my own living. I couldn't explain to anyone why I needed this bag.

I looked obsessively for this red fantasy bag—in stores in Eugene. In Berkeley where I lived. Online. I didn't know what I was looking for exactly, but I looked for hours. For days. For weeks. I looked at every red bag available in America. I assessed their merits and shortcomings, the inches of their handles, the metal of their zippers, their stitching. I examined them, imagined them flung on a table, draped on my arm. I imagined getting a tenure-track teaching job and storing my papers in it. I imagined that the bag would be there for me, championing me to shape a life that made sense, now that this other life had ended—the life of watching my mom die. I could not move forward without this bag. But I couldn't commit to any of the bags that I saw. The hunt for the bag became a quest. It felt like a riddle, complex but solvable. When I searched for the bag, I felt that I was moving forward. The search also took me away from myself, from my grief. It gave me a project, and, better yet, a project that no one else could care about or relate to. It was all mine.

It took me years to unravel the shopping obsessions that overcame me in the year following her death. Red bag, briefcase, shoe with a certain toe box. I would pore over these things, obsessively comparing traits of like objects. I would make a purchase after months of research and then the whole thing would start over. I could gather things, exactly the right things. I could accumulate objects even if the people and life I loved and wanted more than any object were stripped from me ruthlessly, brutally.

Mine was different from my mother's hopeful shopping, but not completely. She shopped to say "Fuck you!" to death. I shopped to create a distraction, but also to reengage with some part of me left reeling, a seeking and searching part of myself. I could not find my mother. My mother, she was gone. But how do you comfort the unsettled part of you, the part that won't stop looking for what is lost? These other searches that I created—the search for a perfect object, and later a perfect job—were difficult, absorbing, taxing, and yet they, unlike the other quest, had possible happy endings.

Some of you will tell me to meditate, to find a relationship with creativity or spirituality that fills this searching maw. You are surely right. But I will continue to hunt for things, I think, despite all the advice you give me.

Why does that feel so embarrassing to say? I know that I should have deeper, better pursuits. I mean, of course I *do* have better pursuits, but they share their time with these fairly shallow ones. That time I spent looking for a bag could have been used to mentor a child or donate blood or volunteer with a literacy organization and better the world. But the fact of the matter is, I, too, succumb to it—the idea that shopping gives us a sense of hope. A hope that we will find something we've looked for. Shopping, in the developed world, in a world in which we do not need a hunk of candle wax so as to read by lamplight on the plains, is frequently a metaphoric act. For my mother, and for me, it represents that simple wish: that we might stay invested in and tethered to the physical world.

When I finally found the bag—used, on eBay (I had it for years and it just fell apart last month), I paraded it around, happy I had it. It had a more youthful look than my mother's boxy one, and it matched a pair of my shoes. But within a month, I remembered a pair of my mother's earrings from the 1970s that I could not find. I needed earrings like that, I decided. And the whole thing started again. And again.

And frankly, I'm fine with that.

THE SHOEBOX

Mel Wells

the twisted metal hardware of the door at Anthropologie is cool under my sweaty palm. I'm passing between the alarm towers, wrapped in lace and crochet like some bohemian art installation instead of antitheft devices, and the meaty bird of my heart is already banging against its cage when the ringing begins.

Fuck.

I turn slowly, feigning confusion, trying to block out the knowledge that I've got a two-hundred-dollar dress under my clothes. A short brunette with glasses and an elfin face approaches me.

"Excuse me," she says, her voice barely audible over the blood rush in my ears.

"Maybe it's my phone," I say, pulling it from my pocket and offering it up. Portland is Apple Mecca, and my old, chunky Android is heavy in my palm. "It makes my car radio beep when I get texts." That is true. I'm even convincing myself.

She raises an eyebrow, so I unbutton my coat, pull it open. I hold out my other empty palm, all innocence and surrender.

"That skirt looks familiar," she says.

"Yeah, I bought it here," I reply. This is not entirely true. I stole it a couple of months ago from this store. The alarms have stopped and I step between the towers again. Silence. I shrug. The girl shrugs, her red-glossed lips part, then close. I push through the doors into free air.

This moment is the closest I ever come to being caught during my two-year stint as a shoplifter in my late twenties. Instead of scaring me straight, I feel reassured—the alarms went off and I still escaped. And until I write down and share these words, only four people know about my brief affair with crime. Only one, my therapist, knows how much I enjoyed it.

Before this spree, I'd stolen once in my entire life. I was a junior in high school and had just made the tennis team. My coach informed us that everyone needed athletic shorts with pockets. I knew without asking that my parents would not buy them: my stepfather refused to pay for anything but the barest essentials—socks, underwear, a winter coat—and even those meant a fight. I had a job at the local Tastee Treet making milk shakes and swirl cones and running the cash register, but my 1978 Dodge Challenger's clutch had just gone out. The repairs left me with about ten bucks, and that was after I dug under the floor mats and checked the pockets of all my jeans. I also had a half-empty gas tank and another week before payday.

I drove to Shopko and tried on a pair of black Nike shorts that made a rustling noise when I walked. They had pockets. They were $18.99. I stared in the mirror at my winter-white legs, feeling my anger rise. I knew my teammates' parents would buy shorts for them. They would also buy new tank tops and expensive shoes, and be stoked that their kids had made the team.

I surprised myself by yanking my pants on over the shorts and buttoning them up. I examined myself again in the mirror. Not too bulky. The empty hanger swung on its hook. The dressing room wasn't monitored. I put on my jacket and browsed around casually for a minute. I didn't want to beeline for the door—that seemed obvious. Finally I took a deep breath and walked out of the store. Nothing happened.

At practice the next day, I slipped tennis balls in and out of the pockets, ignoring the pricks of guilt until they faded. I never told anyone; I was too ashamed.

A few weeks later, two of my classmates were arrested for shoplifting from that same Shopko. They lived in my neighborhood—a wealthy area we'd moved into before it was bourgeois, where our neighbors spent Christmas in Sun Valley on new skis while I based my wish lists on my mom's whispered budget, debating how to parse the hundred bucks. I remember wondering, why would *those* guys steal?

After my close call at Anthropologie, I yank off my clothes in my bedroom and stand in my underwear, inspecting the soft folds of the dress for security tags. I had removed one in the dressing room; were there two? But I can't find anything. Finally I do a Google search on the company's antitheft measures and find out they've got chips hidden in their price tags.

I hold the tag up to the light. Sure enough, I see the dark outline of multiple thin squares. I pull out a pair of scissors and slice it down the middle. It cuts easily. My online source says this is how to disable them. I wonder if I can believe them. I slip the tag into a shoebox half-filled with price tags that I keep on the floor of my closet. Each one holds a little thrill of victory. I begin carrying my hair-cutting scissors in my bag.

Sometimes I wonder what my family would think if I died suddenly and they came across the shoebox. Would they figure it out? I try to think up a good lie, especially in case my boyfriend, Russell, ever finds it.

Russell buys all his clothes at Goodwill and still manages to look dapper. We have fancy dates, where he wears a vest and tie and I wear a garter and stockings under my dress, and by the end of the night we're kissing and unbuttoning and tugging and laughing as if we can't undress each other fast enough.

"I love that you dress up for me," he says, and I hear, "I love you." I use my credit card to buy corsets imported from Europe. I finally understand black lace and push-up bras and stiletto heels. But we also argue over clothing, specifically which of us is more oppressed by fashion.

"I will never get as much respect as you in a suit," I tell him. "I'm either a slut in a skirt or a bitch in pants."

"Menswear is more restrictive," he counters. "Men are attacked for wearing women's clothing, while you get to wear anything you want." We argue about power versus freedom until, finally, we agree to disagree. He doesn't give any ground, and I'm left simmering.

I never win any of our debates, and I feel mounting guilt for buying brand-new clothes. I feel guilty for having credit card debt and tens of thousands in student loans when Russell uses only a debit card and is quickly paying off one small student loan. Sure, my credit score is great and I pay all my bills, but I wonder if the sensation I have—this distinct feeling that Russell has one foot out the door—is because of my debts. He takes me to Goodwill and I flip through rack after rack. He finds long slacks and suspenders and then browses kitchen gadgets while I try on a pile of dresses. They all look tired and slack in the fluorescent lights. Nothing smells new. I fight tears of frustration and leave empty-handed.

It was about a year and a half into our relationship that I began shoplifting. At the time, the nonprofit I worked for was housed in the Wieden + Kennedy ad agency. Every morning when buying coffee, standing next to über-swanky hipsters oozing cool, I felt embarrassed by my ill-tailored, cheap wardrobe. When I left the building to get lunch, I walked past Anthropologie's soaring display windows. One day I went in.

As a bookish, urban white girl in her late twenties, I was doomed to love Anthropologie. I checked a price tag and nearly fled, but I felt a bold, reckless rush as instead I gathered items and headed to the dressing room. In that well-lit private space, I put on a soft purple shirtwaist dress that I could never afford. I longed to wear it, and this longing was tied to a fifth-grade memory of the popular girls asking, "Why are there holes in the knees of your jeans?" as though I was simply being perverse—as though I hadn't begged my parents for new ones and been offered patches (which I refused, knowing that only the poor kids came to school with visibly repaired pants). Grunge came to Idaho too late to save me. I was never cool.

My heart began to pound as I pulled my clothes on over the dress. This wasn't Shopko. I put on my wool coat and cinched the waist. My cheeks flushed and I took a few deep breaths.

There is nothing under your clothes, I told myself. *You came in to try on a few dresses and didn't find anything.*

Eventually I calmed down enough to leave the dressing room, squeeze past the line of women with armloads of soft, vibrant fabrics, and force myself to walk normally out of the store. Nothing beeped. I made it halfway down the block and my breath burst from my lungs into laughter. It was easy. Too easy. So I did it again.

I got several compliments on that purple dress the first time I wore it. Each one was a little tic of validation. I *did* look good in nice clothes. I *did* have good style—I just never had the budget to express it.

In addition to being a compliment whore, I'm a glutton for information. I begin researching security systems, store policies, and devices to remove security tags. When I scroll through top-ten lists of why people steal, none of them resonate. I keep telling myself, *See? You're different. Better.* But one catches my eye: "rebellion/initiation: to break into one's own authentic identity." What if my authentic identity is deviant? What if I have some pernicious need to buck conformity—to break the rules without retribution?

More than anything, I fear becoming one of those out-of-control stereotypes in magazine articles with headlines like "Confessions of a Kleptomaniac." But those women stole recklessly, compulsively. I am different. Careful. Discerning. I never steal anything I wouldn't wear.

Wait, that's not true. I stole a silk dress from Banana Republic that was a size too small but easy to stash in my tall boots—I wrapped it around my ankle under my sock and zipped the boot, thanking god for skinny calves. Two days later I sold it at Crossroads Trading, but the girl gave me a curious look. Was it because this dress was clearly never worn? Because it was still in the display window at Banana Republic? In any case, I took the measly thirty bucks for a hundred-and-forty-dollar dress and concluded that the payoff wasn't worth the risk. Thievery wasn't going to pay the bills.

To further convince myself that I was *not* a cliché destined for jail time, I set some rules:

1. No stealing from people. Only stores.
2. No stealing from local, independent stores. Only corporate.
3. No stealing with other people around. I don't want them to be implicated.

The first rule is easy, but sometimes I contemplate breaking it, just to feel the reassuring gut-plummet of guilt. I know I'm still trustworthy with my friends, but I can't tell them. Who would trust a thief?

Russell certainly has his own secrets. We pass our three-year anniversary and I've hung out with his friends only a handful of times. He isn't on Facebook; he doesn't tweet. I give him space—so much that we can go days without talking. I trust him completely, tell him more about myself than I've told anyone, and give him an all-access pass to my heart and my body. But the vulnerability of such openness makes me tremble, especially because I can't shake the sense he's holding back.

Everything I read about shoplifting says I should feel intoxicated, erotically excited, a "monomania of possession." Instead, I feel like I'm onstage. When I'm in Nordstrom, I'm a woman who doesn't need to look at price tags. I breezily flit between sale and designer racks. A little giddiness bubbles up when I realize, for the first time in my life, that prices have become irrelevant.

When the store employees approach me, I hand over my piles with a smile and a false name. When they offer to help, I say I'm simply *so* bored with my wardrobe. "First world problems, right?"

They always laugh. I thank them profusely for grabbing extra sizes (a good technique to help them lose count), ask their advice, and commiserate over body woes. I try on bright-colored dresses and parade in front of mirrors so they'll remember me as the fuchsia maxi girl and forget about the slinky blue sweater that I'll stuff under my layers.

"That is gorgeous on you," the saleswoman says.

"Aw, you are so sweet," I reply. "I love your style."

We talk and laugh and for this brief moment I'm the person I've always wanted to be: gregarious and witty, confident in my body, and, above all, totally unconcerned about money.

At first I tried to be unnoticeable in dressing rooms, but my body is not built for discretion, as I am six feet tall with blond hair. Attention is unavoidable; I've learned that my only choice is to direct that attention, to make it flow in ways I want. To control it. I am always in performance mode.

I am also a low-tech thief. Most security tags can be ripped off and leave only a tiny hole. This means I rarely steal denim, corduroy, or other material that is difficult to tear. Ironically, expensive materials rip easily, and I'm a good enough seamstress that I can repair them perfectly with fifty cents of thread.

One day Russell is driving us home after a couple of hours of browsing aisles at Goodwill and he asks if he can tell me something. I cringe. The last time he told me "something," it was that he just couldn't commit to me and we took a six-month break from dating. But this time, he simply pulls a small metal item from his pocket.

"The matchbox?" I ask.

He hands it to me. I palm its weight. He'd showed me the small metal box when we were sifting through junk and I'd shrugged. It was nothing special, and it was five dollars.

"You took this?" I ask, avoiding the word *stole*.

"Yup," he says, grinning. "I nicked it."

"You would do that?"

He shrugs. "It's small. And I buy things there all the time."

"Your mother would be so disappointed."

He rolls his eyes. "I can get away with anything."

I slide the lid open and shut, worrying the latch with my thumb.

"What?" he asks, still grinning like the Cheshire Cat.

I shake my head and swallow the urge to laugh. Russell regularly sparks my competitive side, to the point at which we cannot play tennis or basketball and can barely handle Scrabble because he always wins and is *infuriating* about it. Now here he is, so pleased about a goddamn matchbox. The urge to tell him, to outshine his pathetic little victory is so strong that I choke a little.

But I just say, "I'm surprised." I reach over and place my hand on his thigh. He puts his hand over mine, his wide palm completely covering my narrow one. My secret sits in my gut and, instead of guilt, I feel safety. My boyfriend is unknowable but so am I, and this makes me feel less exposed. I relax a little.

"Really," I say, flipping my hand under his and squeezing, "it's the most anti-capitalist crime, right? Screw the system?"

He smiles and his eyes crinkle. He is so adorable. "Right. Like Robin Hood."

I resist pointing out that we're hardly misers. He owns his house and drives a new car. I'm much more impoverished. But still, I worry this won't quite justify my own shoplifting, not for him. Russell cringes sometimes when I swear. Our first real fight happened at a friend's thirtieth birthday party when I, dressed in a fluffy pink prom dress from the 1980s, jokingly gave him a lap dance. He pushed me off, saying I was making other people uncomfortable. I got angry and walked away but later apologized and promised to be more appropriate. If swearing and lap dances make him uncomfortable, I'm sure being a thief would get me dumped.

When I get home that night, I pull the shoebox out of my closet and dump its contents on the bed. I use my phone as a calculator to add up the tags, giddy as Mr. Scrooge and his gold coins. The total is nearing four thousand dollars. I vow to quit. I tell myself this is enough. But the words don't feel true.

A few months later, after I've taken Russell home to meet my family, after I'm in his family photos, I discover the secret I've been sensing for months: He cheated. Just before I began stealing, he had a three-month relationship with a friend of a friend, telling her I was an ex. When she pressured him for a commitment, he broke up with her, but now he's been pursuing her again.

The news guts me. It carves out every appetite, every pleasure, every emotion and leaves me robotic. I stop shoplifting. I stop caring about compliments, just wearing whatever is professional enough to get through work until I can come home and stare at the ceiling until the tears rise again and wring me out.

For a while, I think I am cured of my deviant behavior. But along with my appetite, my libido, and my ability to laugh, the urge to take something seeps back into my body. I'm in a dressing room and realize there's no security tag on the shirt I'm trying on. My fingertips twitch. I bolt out of the store and, panicked, decide to puncture my little secret. My best friend is visiting the next week and I decide to tell her, thinking this will make shoplifting less appealing.

When I go over my closet and show her how much of it is stolen goods, she just laughs at me, saying, "Damn, girl, steal something for me next time!" I don't quite know if she's serious, but nothing changes between us. I love her for treating me like her funny, crazy friend—for still trusting me.

I decide to tell Russell. We're still in touch, attempting to forge a friendship from the wreckage. I realize there's no use in keeping this secret, in trying to be invulnerable anymore. I've already learned that a few stolen dresses are not insurance against betrayal.

When he comes over that evening, he sits stiffly on my couch. It's awkward that we no longer touch. I hate it all: the way desire still sharpens my senses in his presence, the way touching him would only make me cry, the way he ruined us.

I bring over the shoebox and dump its contents. "You're not the only one with secrets," I say calmly. "I'm a very, very good thief. Over four thousand dollars in two years." I wait for him to stand up, to say that I disgust him, and to walk out.

His eyes widen a little. He fingers one of the tags. I can't even remember what item in my closet it was once attached to.

"I wondered how you were affording so many new clothes," he says, "but you didn't seem too concerned about it, so I figured. . . ."

We're silent for a moment. Our conversations are now full of these tiptoe moments.

"So you don't hate me for it?" I ask softly.

"No. Just surprised."

A small part of me wants to make a snarky remark about how I'm the better thief, but I already know he would tell me not to be crass. There is no triumph here, just fumbling for words that don't hurt. We can't find very many. He leaves and I flatten out on my bed, stunned. It didn't matter. All that anxiety, and it didn't matter. The tears return.

When I tell my therapist that I shoplift, I wait for some analogy about my lack of impulse control, some link to my terrible childhood and daddy issues—all that shit we hash through every session. I wait for the reprimand.

Instead, she laughs. I'm startled. But her laughter allows me to laugh as well, and to confess to liking the part of me that gets away with it.

She continues laughing, surprisingly hard. "That doesn't surprise me," she says. "You're smart, and you can be charming."

I sit quietly for a second. I've just told her the most horrid thing about me—not just that I steal, but that I *enjoy* it—and she isn't repulsed.

"Perhaps you should try channeling that deviant behavior into something else," she says, still smiling. "Something that won't get you arrested."

I'm not going to claim an overnight reformation. The shoebox is still in my closet. But now when I get the urge to add to my stash of tags, I remind myself that being a good thief is not a talent that needs to be regularly sharpened; I can still know how much I'm capable of, even if I'm not actively doing it.

And there is a different thrill in opening the shoebox these days. Every time I share this story with someone, the power of that box of secrets deflates a little. In its place is the realization that, when I share the dark, ugly parts of myself with another person, it frees us both to be human. This still astounds me. My best friend trusts me, my therapist laughs with me, my ex has never condemned me, and I continue to be surprised and a little giddy when someone discovers my imperfections and likes me anyway. I was wrong about secrets; the safety I bought with them came at the steep price of authentic connection. Being honest feels vulnerable, but I also know that a thousand shoeboxes couldn't save me from getting hurt.

WELCOME, VALUED CUSTOMER

Emily Chenoweth

t's 9 AM on a rainy Monday, and I'm not intending to buy anything except a very large cup of coffee. But the blouse catches my eye as I'm walking toward the Fred Meyer Starbucks, through the familiar second-floor gauntlet of cheap flip-flops, sensible dresses, and vivid rayon scarves.

It's probably clear to anyone with more than a crumb of fashion sense that one should not buy one's clothes at a grocery store. Grocery stores, after all, are for *groceries*: It's right there in the name. They're where you get apples and sandwich bread and toilet paper—and maybe, in a pinch, a sweatshirt, if the day turns suddenly and unseasonably cold.

But this blouse doesn't look like a grocery store blouse. Or at least I don't think it does. It's a beautiful bright turquoise, with subtle gathering at the shoulders and what looks to be a flattering neckline. The fabric is silky and cool to the touch. I squint at it, then hold it up to my body. It would look nice with leggings, wouldn't it? Leggings and flats? And maybe a chunky statement bracelet, whatever that is?

The truth is I have no idea if it would or not. I try to imagine what my fashionable friend Rachel would say if she saw it. (Rachel shops at fancy boutiques, for her clothes *and* her groceries.) Or my friend Cynthia: What would Cynthia think of it? Once, a long time ago, she said she liked buying clothes at Fred Meyer, and she's pretty punk for a forty-something mom of a seven-month-old baby—imagine David Bowie in kindergarten-teacher drag. Would *she* wear this blouse?

But my attempts to outsource my fashion sense fail, because I can't tell if either of them would like it. It *is* 60 percent off, though, and I don't remember the last time I bought an item of clothing for myself. Maybe the turquoise would bring out my eyes.

Impulsively—and uncharacteristically—I grab it from the rack. I don't even try it on; I just pay for it at the Starbucks counter, right alongside my venti Pike Place. I'm sort of hoping the barista will say, "Nice shirt," but she rings it up without comment. The blouse plus the coffee is $19. I swipe my Fred Meyer card, the one that earns me reward points. The one that makes the computer say, "Welcome, valued customer."

I know what I paid for almost everything I own. Furniture, shoes, *bags of dried beans*. In general, my memory is terrible, yet I can tell you that the orange chair in the living room that I bought eight years ago was $125, and that last week the kale salad I love was on sale for $5.99 a pound, which is two dollars less than normal.

My theory is that this embarrassing fiscal recall is a holdover—an adaptive strategy, if you will—from the years I spent being poor in a rich city. I lived in Manhattan on a graduate student's stipend first, and later on the fruits of unlucrative editorial jobs. I tried to feed myself on five dollars a day, which meant eating nutrition bars and dehydrated Nile Spice soups, which, when reconstituted, taste like salty, brothy sawdust. I used to pace back and forth outside the deli on Broadway and 115th, trying to decide whether or not to buy myself a cup of their terrible coffee. "It's a dollar, which is *nothing*," I'd think, walking one direction. Then I'd turn around. "It's a dollar, which is a whole *dollar!*"

Nine times out of ten, I didn't buy the coffee, and the dollar in my pocket felt like reassurance. Safety. Proof of my thrift and wisdom.

Or of my penury and self-loathing; it depended on my mood.

Now that I'm fifteen years older and capable of buying myself a coffee, I have a different ritual of shopping self-denial. I go, alone, to the basket aisle of Fred Meyer. (Yes, there's an entire aisle of wire, wicker, and wooden hold-alls; it's distinct from the plastic storage-container aisle, or the fabric storage-container aisle, or the laundry basket/hamper/sundries aisle. "Bounty" is Fred Meyer's middle name.) It's late in the evening. My kids are asleep, and I've remembered that I needed half-and-half for my coffee in the morning, or bread for toast.

Or that's the excuse, anyway.

I inspect a rattan basket, and I think about how if I bought this basket, it could hold the mess of shoes by the front door. Sure, the basket is kind of ugly, but so is a pile of muddy shoes. And the previous container for them—a cardboard diaper box—got recycled. So maybe I *need* a rattan basket.

I walk ever so slowly up and down the aisles. Some baskets are 25 percent off; others 50 percent. Some are white; others are gilded. How ugly is too ugly? How cheap is cheap enough? Would one be enough to hold all the shoes, or do I need two?

In the end, though, it's just window-shopping: I never buy the basket.

I have this idea that everyone else window-shops aspirationally, which seems like the sensible way to do it. It's pleasing to feel luxurious fabrics; to try on boots of thick, supple leather; to drink the free Perrier that Mona, the saleslady, brings. The lighting in the dressing room is flattering; so is Mona ("What are you, a size two?"). For a moment, it's possible to inhabit the fantasy: I will be the woman in the $600 T-shirt.

It sounds nice enough, but it's not the kind of fun I'm after. For me, the act of shopping, both window and otherwise, is less about desire and acquisition than it is about denial. The pleasure—which is a complicated one, and sometimes less enjoyable than I might hope—is in *not* buying. Since I'd never actually buy something at a fancy boutique, trying things on and deciding not to purchase them doesn't spark the faintly masochistic sense of deprivation and superiority I so enjoy.

It's much better to go to places I can afford—and *then* I don't buy. Hence the late-night visits to my neighborhood Fred Meyer. There's something thrilling about being able to have any- and *every*thing before me: the decorative pillows, the pink and violet duvets, the gauzy curtains, the votive candleholders, the eight-quart slow cooker, the sun-tea container shaped, inexplicably, like a rooster.

Fred Meyer is the domestic mother ship: It speaks to the secret 1950s house-wife in me. It's also the only store open when I have the time and energy to shop, which is 9 PM.

And so here, on the second floor, not too far from the Starbucks (still open!), is a cardigan sweater. It's black, cotton, and a nice summer weight. I sort of need a black cardigan; it's supposed to be one of those wardrobe staples, and yet I don't have one. I take it off the rack and carry it around for a while, thinking how nice it'll be to throw it over my shoulders after the sun goes down at a July barbecue. How it'll keep me warm when the wind starts blowing at the beach.

But we left our barbecue grill behind when we moved. And how many times am I going to go to the beach?

Later, after I've fetched the half-and-half, I put the sweater back.

As I walk away from the rack, I tell myself that maybe I have money at this point in my life precisely because I *didn't* buy the coffee and the baskets and the sweaters all those years. As Montaigne wrote, "*Divitiarum fructus est in copia: copiam declarat satietas*" (The fruit of riches consists in abundance: abundance is shown by having enough).

In other words, you have a sweater. You have *fifty* sweaters. What do you want with another?

It's a fine question, and it leads to another: Why oh why did you buy the blouse, which is now crumpled on the floor in the corner of your home office because you still can't decide if it's ugly or not?

I really have no idea. Whenever I look at it, I cringe.

Last year, on Buy Nothing Day (the day after Thanksgiving, "your special day to unshop, unspend, and unwind"), my friend Christy decided to go window-shopping. An ancient clerk at a fancy boutique began putting sale items in a dressing room for her, saying how the "pieces" were excellent, and a bargain to boot. One such "piece" was a navy-blue item with bright silver snaps, part vest, part smock.

As she drank the free Perrier she'd been given, Christy began to believe that this smock would be the sort of odd but perfect piece of clothing that could become a trademark look. Something she could wear over just about anything, that would make her seem effortlessly stylish. So she bought it.

An hour later, she ran into some friends and proudly modeled the smock. "Wow," said her friend Jo. "That is . . ."

Jo's husband tried to help. "That's something, all right," he said. "That is . . . *Huh*. Yeah."

Jo was honestly grasping for something positive to say, but what came out was, "It's kind of cool how you can pick things so *unlike* what other people pick."

Christy's heart sank, but she laughed it off like the sport she was. She put the "piece" back into its fancy bag. In a flash, the odd but perfect vest had become the Smock of Shame.

My turquoise blouse has become a Smock of Shame, too, and I haven't even shown it to anyone yet. It tells me that I'm cheap, that I very possibly have no taste, that I've all but given up on being an attractive, reasonably well-dressed person. By this time next year I'm going to be in kitten sweatshirts. You know, the pastel ones with glitter detailing—the ones my young daughters will think are beautiful.

But maybe the blouse would look good with designer jeans. (The leggings I originally had in mind now have a bleach stain.) I have several pairs, all but one hand-me-downs from my friend Holly. The only pair I purchased is over a decade old, impulse-bought after September 11, because I thought I was going to die in an act of bioterrorism and thus would not have to pay my Visa bill.

There's nothing to do but put together the outfit and see what comments, if any, it elicits. We're having people over for dinner, and maybe *they* have some sort of on-trend blouse sensibility. When they arrive, I greet them and then vanish. I pluck the blouse from the floor of my office and, steeling myself for possible humiliation, slip it over my head.

I slink into the kitchen where my partner, Jon, is making the salad. Maybe no one will even notice.

"Where'd you get that?" he asks immediately. But he sounds curious as opposed to disgusted.

"Fred Meyer," I say, in a rush of both pride and shame. "It was 60 percent off at least."

This causes a certain reevaluation on his part. "Fred Meyer, huh?"

"I like it," says his sister. "That's a pretty color."

"Cynthia said she likes to get her clothes there," I blurt out.

Jon nods. He knows how good Cynthia looks.

I finger the tags. Of course I've left them on. "Should I keep it?"

Everyone nods. Not enthusiastically, but they do. *Sure, why not?* is the general sense I'm getting.

I wear it for the rest of the night, but I still can't tell how I feel about it. Before I go to bed, I throw it in the corner of my office again. The cat promptly curls up on top of it.

Three weeks later, the blouse is still there. I still don't know what I'm going to do with it, because I still can't decide if it's ugly or not, or if it's worth the hassle to take it back for the approximately $17 I spent on it.

If I return the blouse, I'll probably have to wait in the customer service line behind someone who wants to pay for cigarettes with a bag full of pennies, or who needs to send a fax, *right now*, to a number she has transcribed incorrectly.

If I don't return the blouse, will I ever wear it again? Or will I leave the tags on forever, and let it become the cat's newest and silkiest bed?

So many questions swirling around one absurd piece of clothing. Seventeen dollars: am I worth it? Am I, really, a valued customer?

Five more weeks pass, and the shirt's still here. It's not even an article of clothing anymore; it's a symbol: of everything from my general indecisiveness to my penny ante laziness. But realizing that makes me sort of like it.

I bought this shirt when I didn't buy hundreds—no, thousands—of others. That must mean *something*. I pick the blouse up off the floor. The cat didn't shed too badly on it, and the color really is pretty.

Maybe I should keep it. Maybe I'll buy a bracelet to match.

On the other hand, the shoes are piling up by the door again, spreading into the living room even, and I could really use a nice basket. Or a kitten sweatshirt. In either case, the exchange would probably be even.

WORTH IT

Ru Freeman

L'Oréal may have a $2.3 billion advertising budget, but it stole its slogan from my mother. Long before I arrived in America all the way from Sri Lanka to attend college with nothing less than her belief in my potential and my two suitcases stuffed with puff-sleeved dresses, toothbrushes, toothpaste, gardenia talc, and ballpoint pens—things she didn't believe America could provide for me—my mother had engraved an aphorism into my brain: *buy pretty things for yourself because you are worth it*. Or, the unplugged version: always buy beautiful things, and buy them for yourself *first*. Before you buy anything for your husband, your friends, or even—and this last was inconceivable to contemplate in a culture such as ours—before you buy anything for your children.

Her life was testament—she often demonstrated and I dutifully observed—to the fact that doing otherwise had been the biggest mistake of her life. Bigger even than falling in love with a radical communist whose notion of a good time was reading Karl Marx and leading an uprising against the Official Languages Act of Sri Lanka (passed, 95 to 5), bigger than becoming pregnant before her marriage to her thwarted revolutionary, bigger than letting her shame distance her from her high-caste relatives, bigger than being too afraid to let her own oldest son apply to American colleges in the mid-1980s though she had already been sidelining as a guidance counselor for a decade, one whose legion of students she managed to place in the finest colleges across America, earning a special award from Harvard University for her work. Nothing could compare to, though it certainly explained, the setbacks in her life better than the fact that she did not buy herself a new sari and a pair of shoes with every paycheck. It was advice that her own mother had imparted to her: my Buddhist grandmother, who had, herself, given up school to marry at the age of nineteen, who expended her intellect in serving on the board of the Catholic convent she had attended and in running the estate she brought with her as dowry.

In an effort to inculcate in me a love of—some may call it an addiction to—beautiful things with which to clothe myself, my mother spent money not on herself but on me. As a schoolteacher, she earned two hundred and fifty rupees a month for most of her life, a sum that had increased to nine hundred and sixty by the time she retired, after twenty-five years of service. Except for the years of austerity the country went through during the reign of the world's first female head of state, Mrs. Sirimavo Bandaranaike, when there was nothing pretty to be seen in the shop windows, let alone purchased, my mother made it her business to locate and buy lengths of fabric that she kept in a suitcase on top of her *almirah*. She participated in a system referred to as a *seettu*, a forced-saving program that her fellow teachers dreamed up, whereby they all contributed a hundred rupees each month to a fund that then went to one or the other of them. When it was her turn to collect, she bought finery for me, even though, by the prevailing standards at the time, I was utterly devoid of any redeeming feminine charms: I was extremely thin, flat-chested, dark-skinned, short-haired, quick-tempered, opinionated, and, in general, a boy without the boy package.

And yet. There I was, encouraged to look at the fabric and design my own clothes, almost all of which she approved of and which she then turned into wearable creations by hiring the best tailors she could find. The dresses I designed—for my skinny boy body—veered between strapless, tight-fitting numbers that she once exclaimed made me look like *a spaghetti wrapped around a noodle*, and flowing fairy-tale dresses I modeled on the gowns worn by Princess Diana. Yes, I dreamed big. I was going to stand prettily and at ease in the center between road-tart and royalty.

It was also my conservative mother, who never wore so much as a swipe of lipstick, who placed a giant check mark next to my spending the entire salary I earned at my first job after high school (seven hundred and fifty rupees, and a little extra borrowed from her) on a designer party dress in yellow silk for New Year's Eve. I cringe a little, recalling my appearance at the dance where my beau at the time—I realize only in retrospect—was not knocked off his feet by my beauty but, rather, was reeling at the glare of my canary-in-a-coal-mine presentation or, rather, the coal-mine-decked-in-canary-feather presentation.

What I was learning along the way was that there was nothing wrong in wanting to possess something I considered beautiful no matter what was considered fashionable; I loved the feel and shine of that yellow silk. And when my father had the opportunity to go to Italy in the course of his work for the government and he asked me, the only girl in the family, what I might like, I replied "patent leather pumps with four-inch heels." He wore out his own sandals walking the length and breadth of Rome, being told by one scornful shopkeeper after another that four-inch patent leather pumps were no longer in style, until he was able to find the last pair in existence and bring it home for me. They did not fit me and so I sold those shoes and, once more, borrowed a little extra from my mother to buy a different pair, one that matched, exactly, the color of a dress that I had designed and sewn out of a length of fabric that she had bought for me at Harvard Square where, once more, she thought nothing of spending most of the money she had brought from Sri Lanka when she arrived to attend my brother's graduation, on a $69 (five thousand, four hundred, and fifty-one rupees at the rate of exchange at the time) extravagance for me. I wore that dress and those shoes to my own boyfriend's—now husband's—graduation from the college we both attended.

That boyfriend tried to temper the message my mother engraved on my heart. In America, perhaps this is necessary for, after all, unlike in Sri Lanka where money is a fluid commodity, borrowed and shared and going where it is needed, here I am reminded daily that money is finite and "more" comes with steep interest from banks. When I was dazzled by the tchotchkes at K-Mart as we were checking out one day, early in our romance, he asked me "to just consider how many hours you have to work in the library at $4.25 an hour in order to buy that." It was a grim reality that I had to face. I had a full scholarship to college, but everything "extra" I had to earn with the three jobs I held on campus throughout my time there—one at the library, one at the gym, and one at the science building where I had to feed and water (though I also picked up and caressed, holding each against my chest in commiseration, my Buddhist upbringing so at conflict with the entire business) hamsters shipped in for experiment and eventual slaughter.

I took stock and I adapted. I discovered Goodwill. Each fortnight when I collected my check, I gathered my best friend, Josh Kennedy (son of the poet X. J. Kennedy), and had him accompany me to the local store where I shopped for clothes. At the annual dance I sallied forth in a lace-trimmed ankle-length creation that cost $5. The boyfriend-now-husband, oh he who was not on scholarship, said, with some amazement, "You look nicer than all the girls in their fancy dresses." And that comment served to ice the cake of my fantasy, the fantasy in which I would manage glamor by hook or by crook.

I have a closet in which I can still see some of the dresses I once designed, the cut-lawn top, the Gipio lace–edged blouse that I wore to my thesis defense with the factory-reject deep-green paisley skirt, the outfit I would wear each time I met one of my future in-laws, *the good girl suit*, as my then fiancé, now husband called it. I still have those green shoes my mother found to match my green dress. And I have hundreds, yes, hundreds, of other items, the shoes, dresses, skirts, pants, jackets, scarfs, and jewelry, that remind me of what sits at the core of my anticonsumerist left-wing activist self: the knowledge that beauty is 99 percent belief, 1 percent standard; the proof that there is no funk, no setback, no ridicule that can erase the bliss of knowing that I can put myself together faster than most people can relieve a full bladder. And that at the end of it I can look pretty damned good.

I don't have a lot of discretionary income. By the rules of sanity I have none. I do not have six months of savings "in case of," I do not have cash diligently socked away for a retirement I may never live to enjoy, I will not be able to pay for college for my three daughters, I cannot afford to shop at Anthropologie or Free People or even Macy's, and most of what people go to buy as bargains at T.J. Maxx are out of the reach of my unique purse. What I do have is eBay and consignment stores and a keen eye for knowing that how I carry myself makes my fashion current. What I do have is a daily boost of happiness as I walk past my beautiful possessions on my way to the shower or on my way to bed. What I do have is the incredible joy of watching my daughters come shopping among my purchases (and the double joy of knowing that every purchase I make will be happily worn by one or the other of them). What I do have is the uplifting thrill of knowing that each one of my girls is slowly absorbing that old message passed down from my grandmother to my mother, neither of whom were able to live the truth, that we earn money not to save for the future but to live today, that all money is mad money: It is just a matter of where you choose to indulge your madness.

I did not grow up to be the high-profile policymaker fighting for justice at the United Nations. I did not grow up to be the high-profile human rights lawyer I always wanted to be. I do not live in an artsy community in Park Slope or Soho, inhabiting a loft and being called by NPR for my opinion on this and that. There are half a dozen talents that I know lie dormant in my unfulfilled other life, the one that author Cheryl Strayed described in one of her Dear Sugar columns as *the ship that did not carry us*, and on more than one occasion I have described myself as a MacBook Pro operating at 2 percent capacity. But for everything that I have not done, for every disappointment that I have ever faced, for every loss that I have endured, including and more devastating than any other, the death of my mother, I have a life in which I feed my soul with the artifice of adornment.

Somewhere out there my mother is delighted each time she hears me shut my eyes and quote her as I make a purchase that has nothing to do with anybody but myself: the clothes, the shoes, the bangles, the lotion, the better shampoo, the fancy haircut. Somewhere out there she is whispering in my ear the priceless gift she gave me: You are worth it.

PLAYING HOUSE

Rachel Sontag

a s a kid I roamed around furniture shops, lying down on their master beds in their model bedroom with my shoes off so I could feel what it was like to be an adult. My parents didn't do adulthood the way that others seemed to. Despite my dad being a successful doctor, our house was a collection of furnishings from the Salvation Army and things my folks had salvaged from the dump. There was nothing matching in our bedrooms. No flowered linens, no fitted pillows, no duvets or box springs or bed frames, just simple mattresses, each with a flannel sleeping bag for warmth.

When a boyfriend took me to Macy's to buy me a down comforter for my twenty-fifth birthday, I was struck by what an ordeal it was to buy bedding. "Well, what do I do when I move?" I asked, my arms filled with the light feathery weight of something I didn't know how to own. He looked at me, confused. "Seriously. What do I do with all this shit then?" We got in line and waited for the cashier. "Just think about now. It'll feel good," he said. "Much better than your sleeping bag. And it looks nice, you know? Better than that brown and orange flannel monstrosity." Under his arm was a pack of matching off-white sheets and pillowcases he'd selected for me as I wandered around in awe. "You know how much of our lives we spend in bed?" he asked. I'd never thought about it. "You know how nice it is to lie in a bed you don't want to leave?" I shook my head. He took my hand and briskly led me out of Macy's in what felt like a race to get home and show me just how good this life in bed could be. I was taken by his generosity and how he held my hand as we walked through the Macy's parking lot. Later he stuffed my cocoon of a sleeping bag into my closet and we ripped open the sheets and he showed me how to make a bed. He was right about the comforter and the loveliness of being warm but not trapped. It was spring and we opened the windows and let in the cool air and stayed under the fluffy white blanket. I remember thinking this was the beginning of a certain kind of love, a love I wanted more of.

Five years later I found myself in New York City, no longer with the boyfriend or the bedding. I was back in the sleeping bag on the floor of an unfurnished room in Brooklyn I shared with strangers from Craigslist. I was broke and lonely and dating online for dinner and distraction, which was how I came to meet Brad, a salesman from Denver, Colorado, who traveled to NYC for business. We made plans to meet in the lobby of the Waldorf Astoria, where he was staying, and have sushi at the restaurant across the street. He was chivalrous and friendly and not my type at all. I filled myself with fish and sake as Brad told me about a certain Russian hairstylist who'd broken his heart. A beautiful and spoiled gold digger, he said. He'd broken off the affair after his back surgery, which was how he learned of her true nature. "As I lay paralyzed, she went shopping. As I recovered, she disappeared. When I needed her help doing little things I couldn't do for myself, she rolled her eyes like I was an invalid."

"A blessing in disguise" was what he called "her betrayal," or else he would have spent his life with a woman who cared more about money than she did about him.

"But girls like you," he said, "who make their own way in this world, they deserve to be spoiled."

I began to dread going home. The hour-long commute, the cold, the sleeping bag bed. I was quick to accept Brad's offer to stay the night. "There are two beds!" he said, as if he had to sell me on it. Brad took a Valium for his back and propped himself up with pillows. He turned on the TV. "Oh, Rachel, I'm really in bad pain. I'm gonna crash." I was warm and comfortable and I trusted this man, not because of his character but because of his helplessness. He snored softly. I felt safe.

I woke up the next morning to the smell of coffee brewing in the bathroom. The ironing board was out and several white button-downs had been placed on the chair beside the bed. I watched him move around the room. Then I turned on my side and tried to imagine how it would have felt to be in love with this man. After all his shirts were ironed and hanging on hangers Brad tried each one on, holding up a set of cufflinks for each shirt. Then there was the matter of his jacket. Was it better to go formal or casual for this particular meeting, to show more or less of himself? He asked me to button his cufflinks, and, when he noticed I'd never buttoned cufflinks before, he told me what to do. He asked that I take the lint remover and brush off the back of his jacket. Then he tended to the business of packing.

I played a lot of house growing up. I spent a lot of time air kissing my husband before he left for work. I had five children who required much attention. I conducted tantalizing, illicit affairs with the gardener. I pantomimed sweeping and cooking and walking the dog, watching soap operas and making sandwiches for the children. But what I most remember from these games of house was the sheer relief in knowing it was just a charade. I had a whole lot of living to do before I became an adult.

I got out of bed and walked Brad to the door. I wished him luck with his meeting and waited for him to wish me luck in life, because we both knew this was the last we'd see of each other. "Thanks baby. I'm gonna nail this one." He told me to get back in bed, order breakfast and a pay-per-view movie, to stay as long as I liked. "But please," he said very seriously, "call downstairs and have them fix the room before you go." I got back into bed and stayed there for six hours, drinking coffee, watching movies. I wrote a postcard to my sister. "Greetings from NY!" I imagined Brad returning. I imagined myself being dressed and seated at the desk. I imagined he'd make himself a scotch and soda from the minibar before we window-shopped and dined and went to see the Broadway play with tickets from his client. I imagined waking up and going to sleep in a bed I shared with a man I loved in that lasting sort of way. I imagined a lot of things those days that had nothing to do with the life I was living. I loved the life I was living, in all its uncertainty. It was exactly where I wanted to be, but I always thought the life I was supposed to be living was just around the corner, having a mug of tea, waiting for me to grow up and choose it.

"You're making it very hard for yourself to meet a man," said Cheryl, the sharply dressed, middle-aged, feng shui consultant a friend had sent me as a birthday gift. For many years I'd been living solo in a brightly painted, charming, fifth-floor walk-up apartment in Chelsea and, despite the water leaks and rodent problems, it was the first place that felt like home. Cheryl walked around the room and scribbled notes on a pad of paper.

"Can I ask you a question?" she asked.

"Sure," I said.

"Are you single?"

"Yes."

She let out a sigh and ran a tape measure across the length of my bedroom wall.

"There's a reason for that," she said. "This is no place for seduction." She examined the sparse contents of my bedroom. "You're making love to your books, you know." I nodded.

"I love my books," I said.

"I can tell. You've built a shrine around them. They're gobbling up the energy you should be putting into attracting a man."

I scanned the titles, thought about how many times I'd arranged and rearranged them so the most impressive titles were at bed level, how many interesting, lively, morning-after-sex conversations were inspired by them.

"This room has no passion, no fire. You're depriving yourself of prana! What you need are some throw pillows and a bed skirt. You're definitely going to want a nice piece of fabric to cover up those stains on the side. It looks like a bed." *It is a bed*, I thought. "You want it to look like a palace. You are a lioness! Big bold fiery shades, like red and orange and gold. You need candles and better lighting." She was right about the lighting, but I was pretty sure I'd lost no great future love to the problem of my bed.

She looked at the bed as if it were a dirty article of clothing left in the men's locker room and then she made her way into the living room and sat down on the couch, like a doctor about to deliver some bad news. "Okay," she said, looking through her notes. "For starters, you're going to want some better material, soft silks or satins, something sensual." Apparently my odds of getting laid would increase if I dropped a couple thousand to revamp my bedding.

"You'll want to decorate your walls," she said. "You need posters of people in love."

"Posters?" I said. "That's so collegiate."

"Posters of couples, kissing and hugging. If you want babies, you'll want to display some pictures of babies. Nieces? Nephews?"

I could feel myself shutting down, irritated. She looked at her watch. "It's a good thing Paul got you the full hour and a half session. You've got a lot of work to do to get yourself ready for love."

At 35 years old on a sunny Saturday afternoon I walked into PJ's Mattress Shop on Hawthorne Street. I was dating a guy named Geoff who not only accompanied me on the daylong shopping expedition but also listened patiently as I rattled off a chronological history of various mattresses in various cities for the sake of painting the significance of this purchase. I was thirty-five and had still never paid a penny for a mattress. Like cigarette lighters, they were things I acquired, always free but stained with the histories of others. The frequency with which I dragged them up and down stairwells, on and off trucks, and in and out of storage was a constant reminder of the nomadic state I was trying to overcome. Inside the store, we sprawled ourselves across beds asking intricate questions about memory foam and organic cotton, springs and frames. "My god," PJ blurted to Geoff. "I've never seen such confusion. Usually the ladies know what they want." Geoff went for lunch and I pondered, revisited the beds on my stomach and my back and my side, probed deeper. When he returned we made a list of pros and cons until I'd narrowed it down to three. Then we got in the car and drove around town so I could clear my head and make the right choice.

"If it feels right for you, it's right," said PJ as he wrapped my mattress in plastic. "I'll tell you what. You take it home, decide it's not for you, you bring it back and return it, okay?" I took out my credit card. "It's cool," I said. "I'm buying this bed. I'm not gonna return it." I was not only buying a bed; I was investing in my newfound adulthood. I'd just moved from New York to Portland, Oregon, and I had every intention of putting down roots.

In my twenties I watched my friends take their wedding vows, happy they'd found love and relieved I didn't have to do the things they were excited to do. There was still time for adventure, travel, love, and more love. For fifteen years I'd moved through cities, careers, and relationships. Then one spring I found myself house-sitting for a friend in Portland. He lived in a quaint, family-oriented neighborhood where people gardened and drove slowly and left their doors unlocked. I made coffee in the mornings and drank it on the porch. I played with the dogs. I went to the farmers market and cooked myself dinner. I pulled weeds. I watched parents with their children and it looked quite nice and satisfying. Suddenly everything I'd boxed away and shoved into some distant future seemed attainable, like a husband and kids and a house. I felt so inspired I called my sister and proudly announced I was leaving New York and moving to Portland.

And so it came as a surprise to me when I failed to settle down in the easiest, most manageable place I've ever lived. I'd planted the seeds, signed my very first lease, enrolled in graduate school, and bought myself a 100 percent organic cotton mattress. Three years later I sold the mattress to buy a plane ticket to India. I was convinced that Portland had not lived up to my expectations, that had the right man come along I would be planting tomatoes in the backyard of our three-bedroom craftsman house and having his babies.

When I returned from India, with nowhere to stay, I took a cat-sitting job just two blocks away from my friend's house where I'd fallen in love with Portland, or rather the idea of myself in Portland. It was the same season and the sun shined brightly and all the kids rode their bikes down the streets as their parents mowed the lawn. I drank coffee on the porch and played with the cats. I shopped at the farmers market and cooked dinner for myself. I took baths in their fancy claw-foot tub and slept beautifully in their bed, and I realized that it was not so much the tub or the bed that I wanted, but simply the knowledge that this life of comfort and stability, which I held at a safe distance, was obtainable if I wanted it.

I imagine myself in the park reading the paper while my future husband tosses our laughing future four-year-old over his shoulder. Still I long for the freedom to fly to India at the drop of a hat. Some days I want the mattress; some days I don't. I may never have the adult life I expected as a child, though I've learned to appreciate the uncertainty of the life I live. It allows for just the right amount of longing.

THE BOOK MONEY

Aryn Kyle

I was twenty-seven the year my first novel sold for half a million dollars. During the three years I spent writing the book, I'd gotten by on next to nothing, eating ramen noodles for dinner and living in a rented apartment in Colorado over what may or may not have been a meth lab. I had $10,000 in credit card debt and $30,000 in student loans, and the most I'd ever earned in a single year was $15,000. Half a million dollars, I remember thinking, was more money than I could spend in a lifetime.

I'd never had money before, and, now that I did, I had no idea what I was supposed to do with it. I met with bankers and accountants, strangers in suits who helped me divvy my new money into the kinds of accounts I hadn't known existed, for purposes I hadn't ever thought about: a CD for the significant chunk I would owe in taxes, a health savings account (HSA) to cover the deductible on the medical insurance policy I could finally afford, an IRA to protect a portion of the money for the unimaginable day when I would need it to live on. Afterward, they would shake my hand and congratulate me on my success: I was making such good choices with my money!

In other matters, my choices were less admirable. While working on the book, I'd become involved with a man to whom I was now hopelessly and desperately committed. He was smart, talented, and unwaveringly confident in my ability to succeed as a writer. He was also my former professor, twice my age and married with two children.

He lived in Montana, and, though our relationship had developed almost entirely over email, it was my most shameful secret, more isolating and terrifying even than my poverty. Again and again, I told myself I had to stop, but again and again, I found myself writing to him, waiting for him, wanting from him. Then, a few months before the sale of my book, he separated from his wife. A few months after, we moved in together.

For a brief time, I existed in a kind of dream state. It was as if every wish I'd ever made had suddenly been granted. After years of doubt and loneliness, of suppressed guilt and profound longing, of jolting from sleep in a panic about how I would pay my rent, there I was: Author! Girlfriend! Half-a-millionaire!

As soon as I arrived in Montana, I began to awaken to the reality of the situation. My boyfriend had joint custody of his two children and had rented an apartment a few blocks from the house he'd shared with his wife, but he'd brought almost nothing with him except for a table and chairs. During our first dinner together, the children stopped me before I could sit down. That, they said, pointing at my chair, was where their mother sat. Not in this empty apartment, of course, but in the house where they all used to live together. The children were skittish and brusque in my presence, their grief and confusion still raw on their faces. I was a total stranger. No space existed for me at that table, yet there I was, glass of wine in one hand, fork in the other: there wasn't much else for me to do but stay and eat. And so we stood for a moment, all of us, and then shuffled places.

In the weeks that followed, we passed many awkward meals together. Someone often yelled and someone often cried and someone, sometimes, got up and stormed out. From his friends and family my boyfriend received calls and emails and visits: What was he thinking? Had he lost his mind? I began to envision his life as a giant set of scales: On one side were his marriage, family, friends, and reputation; on the other side was me. Despite the obvious imbalance, he had chosen me. I could say I hadn't known the suffering I would cause simply by showing up, but the truth is that I hadn't wanted to know. Once I was there, though, the knowledge was unavoidable. Sitting at the dinner table night after night, I found myself face-to-face with the reality of what had been broken, of how many things had been lost.

And because I could not undo what had been done, because I could fix nothing, I tried instead to replace it. I was nobody's mother, nobody's wife, but I began to imagine I could be a kind of fairy godmother, armed with the power of my newly earned money, granting wishes with a magical wave of my credit card.

I started with what had been left behind at the other house: gas grill ($1,000), electric guitar ($1,200), PlayStation ($250). I bought rugs ($3,000), high-thread-count sheets ($350) and matching duvet ($400), a black leather sofa ($2,000).

The more I bought, the less I seemed to have. Though we had been involved for years, my boyfriend and I were in many ways strangers. We had opposing patterns and practices. We fought over everything: when to clean, what to eat, who said what to whom in which tone of voice. Mostly, though, we fought over money.

"I'm paying for everything!" I cried.

"So stop!" he said.

But I couldn't stop. Paying made me feel useful, important, in control. It made me feel absolved. Well, it made me feel as though I might someday be absolved. After I'd paid for all the things I thought we needed, I kept on paying for things we didn't. When the children argued over what they wanted for dinner, I paid the check at a restaurant where we each could order what we liked. When tension began to rise or blame began to fall, I paid for plane tickets and shopping sprees. But all the while, I felt an awareness growing: My money wasn't solving any of our problems; it was just making it easier for us to avoid facing them. All I was buying was time.

For a bit, that was enough. I would pay for a trip or a party or a new set of clothes, and the whole family would, for a few brief moments, seem to have everything they wanted. I longed to lock those moments down, to own them, to get a receipt. Which is how, a year after I moved to Montana, I found myself writing a check for $125,000 to make the down payment on a house.

There are plenty of reasons that buying this house would turn out to be a Big Mistake, the most obvious being that (1) I could not afford it—the house cost $500,000, the same amount I'd gotten for my book, only before the cut that went to my agent, and the cut that went to the government, and the cut that went to all that crap I'd bought; (2) only a fool would believe that an empty house could be enough to make people happy; and (3) the day I signed the check, I already knew that nothing was going to be enough to make us happy. Once again, I found myself jolting from sleep at night, panicked not about rent or groceries but about the man sleeping beside me and about the distance between us, which, every day, widened a little more. The more time I tried to buy, the more quickly it seemed to pass.

Two years after I bought the house, my boyfriend and I called it quits. I put the house up for sale and fled to New York, a city where no one looks too closely at anyone else's humiliation, where people let you be alone with your shame.

This was in 2009, and the house was worth 25 percent less than it was when I bought it. For the year it sat on the market, I paid the monthly mortgage ($2,500) along with rent on my sixth-floor walk-up ($1,500). Because the house was empty, the monthly cost of insurance doubled ($1,000). In the fall, the basement flooded ($500). In winter, the sidewalks had to be shoveled ($300). In spring, the front yard sprouted weeds ($600).

That's the thing about the big mistakes: You don't just pay; you pay, and pay, and pay, and pay.

I spent a lot of time on the phone with strangers that year, pleading for deferments, or reductions, or loans. Every time I opened my email, another bill was due.

I told the real estate agent in Montana to drop the asking price, but he said that if he dropped it any lower, I wouldn't get any of my down payment back. That didn't matter, I told him; just make it disappear.

When I called the accountant about withdrawing money from my IRA, he said this was the worst time to take out money. I'd lost more than half of it in the crash. If I withdrew the money now, I would suffer a substantial loss. There was $45,000 left in the account; it was the last of my book money. But I could not imagine a loss more substantial than the one I had already suffered.

Before we hung up, he told me I should know I wasn't the only person this had happened to. I was still young, he said. There was time to recover.

But recovery is incremental. You can't simply make a declaration to live more consciously or choose more carefully or consume more responsibly. The work is delicate and deliberate and difficult, and it happens so gradually that, without your even noticing, the events from which you're recovering begin to seem fragmented, dreamlike, and very far away: that time I blew through half a million dollars and ended up with a black leather sofa; that time we went to Amsterdam; that time we made a wrong turn and saw a house we thought we could not live without.

I recently sold my third book, but I no longer indulge a fantasy of money as a magical power or cure-all. It's a tool, nothing more, something that, with care and caution, will buy me only enough time to write the next one. And that's enough. Real power, it turns out, comes not from what you are able to give but from what you are willing to share. There is magic in healing, and it has nothing to do with gifts or trinkets. It comes, instead, from straightforwardness, from sincerity, from vulnerability, from the capacity to stand, empty-handed, before the people you love and admit, I made a mistake, and from the willingness to say, free of agenda or expectation, I'm sorry.

THE KIDS ARE ALL RIGHT. THEY'RE JUST A LITTLE GAY: A MALL HATER'S TALE

Traci Foust

the day I turned eight my mother took me to see a psychic for my birthday. Initially I was supposed to see Eric Estrada, who was appearing with his teeth and signing autographs at Shakey's Pizza, but then my older brother—doing everything first and better—came back from the place Eric wasn't and happily announced it was "just the other guy."

So no Eric. No Eric's teeth. The psychic would have to do.

In a room filled with cigarette smoke, a RuPaul-ish woman held my hands and revealed the prophecy of my future. "You will grow up to be a writer," she said. "I think I see Austria as the place where you'll settle to raise a lot of children. A whole bunch of children. Six or seven boys."

She said she saw a lot of testosterone around me.

I wasn't sure what testosterone was or how close Austria was to my school, but the idea of getting paid to make stuff up took away the disappointment of not becoming a Solid Gold dancer and marrying Scott Baio. The whole-bunch-of-children part was okay as long as she was sure about them being all boys. I liked boys. I liked boyish things. Even when I played Neonatal ICU, I gave all my dolls tragically masculine names like Edward and Montague. Names that looked sickly yet regal on pretend death certificates.

I was the only girl in my fourth-grade class to have the Joey Stivic doll (named after Archie Bunker's grandson), the first anatomically correct poly-cotton-filled infant. His little pee-pee fascinated me. I spent hours forcing him to drink from his precious blue bottle, and then I'd hold him over the toilet, press his chubby tummy, and watch with love and jealousy as he tinkled away his insides.

Me and all boys. I could totally see that.

As it turns out, the psychic was right on the career choice (writer coming twenty years after Confused Orange Julius Cash Register Girl and Napping Office Assistant). The Austria move never happened, and, unless she was counting ex-husbands, she was only half right on the boys.

"Isn't this exciting?" my mother asked that day as we pulled away from the psychic's office in her gold Monte Carlo. Full of tricks and nicotine, my mother had another birthday surprise up her sleeve. She turned on the AC and lit a cigarette. "We've got the whole rest of the day," she said. "Just you, me, and the mall."

The psychic mentioned nothing about me leaping from a moving vehicle into oncoming traffic.

Few things cause me more anxiety than shopping. Both then and now. Not even a pop quiz on multiplying fractions made my stomach as knotty as when I heard my mother announce how much fun we were going to have looking at pants.

It was her use of the word *looking* instead of *buying* that was always the tip-off. Looking meant hours of sifting through discount bins, lengthy belt/shoe/purse assessments, blouse and skirt decisions based on seasonal colors. "Pink's still okay in October, right? Maybe fuchsia? Would this fall under fuchsia or red? Why is the light so poor in here? We should bring this jacket down to hardware, it's brighter there. You know why it's always easier to see in hardware? It's men. They won't buy if they can't see things in clear light. That's called market strategy. But now I'm thinking this is more purple than pink. Okay, so that's a no. Here's red. Or would you call this cherry?"

Sure, things would begin well enough. We'd get up at the crack of dawn, all Egg McMuffins and sale ads, but come midafternoon the fun would begin to unravel. This usually started with me announcing I was hungry; I was hot; I was itchy. By my third unheeded demand for a wheelchair rental, I could be found red-faced and crying through a seizurelike meltdown in the Sears garden section.

But *buying*—now that was a safe word. The get-it-done-yesterday word. A word with purpose, lists, organization. All the things a nervous shopper can use as an anchor to keep from hyperventilating on the escalator. Buying meant a sensible amount of time picking out one shirt, possibly sunglasses, no dressing rooms, and then a speedy delivery back home where I would be safe once more with a bag of Frito's and *General Hospital*.

Growing up with obsessive-compulsive disorder, and then a later diagnosis of Asperger's syndrome, I was assured that shopping would always be nothing more than a giant sensory overload for me. Other, less distressing activities come to mind when compared to those nonstop aisles of ADD-infused decisions: looking out the safety-glass window in the suspicious persons holding room at Chicago O'Hare International Airport, for instance. Jogging around Hong Kong's metro district in the middle of July without a face mask sounds as if it might not be as bad as a stroll beneath the Drakkar Noir pollutants and unbearable house music of Abercrombie and Fitch.

OCD can turn even the smallest shopping errand into a Lewis Carroll whirl of terror. Obsessive-compulsives feel calm and protected in order, more so if they are the ones responsible for making that order. Not being able to understand why a display rack of men's bathrobes would be placed next to camping gear was enough to set my mind reeling. Maybe outdoorsy types enjoy comfy sleepwear after a day of hiking and fishing?

As I grew older, so did the inability to get my thoughts together for any shopping trip that required more than twenty minutes of browsing. Even with the help of a therapist, it was nearly impossible for my mother to understand the craziness all that stimuli inflicted. I had to make detailed lists of everything I needed the night before, arranging each item according to their shelf coordinates in the store. How well I handled picking out a suitcase in T.J. Maxx depended on knowing exactly how long I would be there—that I could leave in a hot-mess hurry if the power went out or someone coughed too close to where I was standing.

Along the way of my neurosis there were a couple of things that would help ease the panic and terror that is me and the stores. One, by the time I hit puberty, my mother—older, wiser, and completely exhausted from having to explain to onlookers that a preteen girl crying in the customer service lounge of Mervyn's was simply tired from dance class—decided it was best for everyone involved if my clothing needs were handled via mail order. Or by my dad. Also, I never forgot the psychic's prediction of being blessed with rearing the sex that hates looking at pants as much as I do. Visions of handsome young men who shared my love of books and vacuuming would take the frightening place of the exchange line at Ross (though many years would have to pass before I understood that if your child is the kind of boy who gets excited over cleaning out your makeup drawer, chances are pretty high he's going to be a shopper).

The word *metrosexual* had not yet been invented when the psychic told me about my sons.

Flash forward twenty years and I am sitting nervously on the dressing room sofa in Macy's while a smart-mouthed seventeen-year-old boy tries on jeans. I have been appointed Personal Wardrobe Technician.

"These are black. I asked you to bring me the gray ones."

"What's with the pockets on this pair?"

"Not Wranglers, Mom. I'm not Charles Ingalls."

If my teenage version of Jean Paul Gaultier would calm down enough to see how upsetting the whole ordeal of shopping is to me, maybe he could sympathize about the panic I feel under the restraint of these lights, these smells, this fucking Coldplay Muzak. Maybe if I had forced him to read my memoir on growing up with OCD, he could better understand that the Xanax I took in the car hasn't kicked in enough to make me give a rat's ass about straight leg versus boot cut, and he would suggest I stay outside near the planters and the nice security guard. I could smoke my cigarettes and read my copy of *Clouds of Secrecy: The Army's Germ Warfare Tests over Populated Areas*. Maybe if he read anything at all, he would also know that Charles Ingalls wore Levi's.

But it isn't just Black Friday or the buy-one-get-one rack at Kohl's that can make all four of my boys go from zero to slightly homosexual in less than ten. I truly believe their retail tool tendencies may boil down to something that makes me rethink everything I learned in tenth-grade biology. Aside from the fact that teenagers have about as much compassion for anything that doesn't affect them directly as, say, a garden snake, my boys are very much into their looks. And all of them are very good-looking.

Of course, I know every mother thinks her kids are pageant-worthy—mine would never stop crying long enough to actually do any pageants—but as much as I think their beautiful full lips, flawless skin, and big eyes are the stuff of a Dante Gabriel Rossetti painting, the problem lies in the way *they* see themselves, which is exactly the way I see them. Also, my boys are half Sicilian, and where my lower Mediterranean blood proves useful for important Italian things like knowing how to peel an artichoke and stealing, something must have happened in utero to turn my Regular Joes into the cast of *Jersey Shore*.

People say boys don't come with as many accessories as girls. People are wrong.

My oldest, Ricardo, is obsessed with hair and skin care items that he usually acquires by asking me to send him my Ulta coupons and any leftover product I feel isn't working for me. Last Christmas he called me from what sounded like a drunken slumber party and asked me to guess where he was. Of course, the first thing that came to mind was his hairdresser hosting a Yuletide makeover celebration, which actually occurred a few Christmases back. "Nope," he said and then lifted his phone into the cackles of middle-aged women and Mariah Carey's "Never Too Far" blaring in the background. "I'm at a Botox party!" he shouted. "Can you believe it?!"

Yes, I could.

At an age at which he should be attending keggers and tailgate parties, my first baby boy had been captured, cougared, and forced to sip chardonnay to the *Glitter* soundtrack.

They were getting ready to stick needles into his little face.

My two middle boys, Jordan and Julian, are the clothes shoppers. They know the definition—and importance—of the phrase "to the nines" and are disturbingly versed in the difference between a retro Izod shirt and one that's "trying to perpetrate a flashback."

Last summer they pooled their money to buy their own iron because mine was "crusted up with old lady." They have separate accessory caddies in their closets. One for ties. One for belts. Lint rollers are purchased every week and kept at an arm's reach lest a cat hair make its way to a new tank top.

My youngest, Rocco, is the cook and crafter of the bunch. Model airplanes, birdhouses, potholders to match the colors of his Easy Bake oven. He designs his own T-shirts and has recently taken his Martha Stewart up a notch to duvet covers. "Better than IKEA," he says whenever he finishes one of the only two square patterns he knows. Once he actually said, "bric-a-brac" in front of a bunch of people at JoAnn Fabric's.

Who *are* these children? And even more perplexing, how did a shopping/craft/hair product hater manage to pop out four of them? When the psychic said she had seen a lot of testosterone around me, I am now certain she meant *just* me. The only glimpse of reassurance I have that mama has done something right is the fact that each of my boys, with the exception of my eleven-year-old, would rather spend an afternoon taking their girlfriends to get pedicures than sitting around watching ESPN.

The only person I have ever been able to spend some quality J.C. Penney time with is my father, who is old and mean and sits in his truck picking his ears with his car keys while my stepmother makes all the important open toe/strapless sandal decisions.

Shopping is one of the few activities my father and I can do together without the day ending in a vow of never speaking to each other again. We have been known to negotiate entire outfits, shoes included, at Nordstrom's Rack in just under fifteen minutes. We are the Special Forces of the retail industry. Get in, identify, seize, and then get the hell out.

Isn't that how it's supposed to be with boys? My friends who have sons complain about soccer carpools and violent video games. Although those things certainly have places in our lives, it's hard to share my frustration when I have to leave a coffee date early because my youngest has sent me twelve texts reminding me that today is Michael's BOGO on embroidery thread.

No parent wants to hate the things her children love.

Almost every other weekend I run into my next-door neighbor and her teenage daughter at Starbuck's. I watch with envy as she and her daughter giggle in line, whisper, and playfully nudge each other. "Another Saturday looking at homecoming dresses," my neighbor says to me. "And school hasn't even started yet!" She puts her arm around her daughter's shoulder and gives her a giant *can you believe this girl* squeeze. Loving every second of the things I can't even force myself to like.

I want that, too. I mean, I think I want that.

Two years ago I came up with what I was sure to be a fail-free bonding idea to start me and my boys on the path to girly togetherness. The epiphany came from that show on the Learning Channel. You know, the one in which the women save five million dollars a year by scanning the Internet for bargains and purchasing vats of medicated lip balm they will never use but will happily give away to friends who have a tendency to break out in mouth sores.

I'm talking about coupons. Good, old-fashioned buy-ten-cans-of-tuna-and-get-fifty-cents-off-your-next-purchase-of-fiber-laxatives coupons.

I can do coupons.

If women who don't even bother to wear support bras on national television can stock up on sliced beets and save enough money to take their families to Busch Gardens, then what the hell is stopping me? My boobs aren't that big. I can force myself to love beets.

Like a New Year's resolution dieter who must convince herself of how much she's going to enjoy those rice cakes, I first had to declare my intention. I gathered up my brood from their clouds of Axe cologne and announced we were starting a new project. "You know that couponing show you guys are totally addicted to?" I said. "Well, that's going to be us!"

After reassuring them they would be spared the humiliation of appearing on television with their mom, and that no one would have to do anything involving putting together a shelf, it was time to prepare for my mission. Armed with a week's worth of grocery money and a new, though somewhat forced, optimism, I went to Staples and went a little crazy. I bought markers and paperclips, a top-of-the-line pink Velcro Trapper Keeper, plastic baseball card inserts, four packs of printer paper, more baseball card inserts, four pairs of scissors, stickers of shooting stars and ladybugs, lined paper in purple and orange, neon and pastel Post-It notes, a scientific calculator, and a leather accordion index card folder that cost as much as my best pair of shoes. I spent three days signing up for every deal-buster website I could find. I bought triple subscriptions to three newspapers (a cost totaling, almost to the penny, the down payment on my youngest son's braces), and printed out the coupon policies for the stores I planned to bitch slap with my giant folder of savings. Then late at night, my eyes burning from instant messaging about *Downton Abbey* instead of coupons on the Krazy Saver Facebook page, my fingers bent and numb from arranging those hateful baseball card holders, I watched and studied each recorded episode of what the kids and I were now simply referring to as "our coupon show."

I may not be able to walk through Tilly's without a shot of vodka in my Crystal Light, but, by God, now I was ready to shop the fuck out of my local Ralph's. With my children.

Couple of things you should know about extreme couponing. First, you have to be very good at math. I don't mean I-passed-eighth-grade-algebra-with-flying-colors-because-I-let-the-teacher's-aide-feel-me-up good, I mean Pythagoras-meets-*Good-Will-Hunting* good. A constant eye for sum versus difference is a couponing *must*, so you pretty much have to turn yourself into North Korea the minute you step inside the grocery store. Although basic addition and subtraction come easy for lots of folks who aren't newborns or Muppets, in my case, having OCD makes dealing with numbers, odd ones in particular, extremely stressful. I do okay with 50 percent off because half of something is easy, but throw me into the middle of a two-hour sale in which 75 percent is the number of the day and my mind turns into a blathering swirl of gobbledygook. A million little Courtney Loves and Rush Limbaughs competing for air time in my frontal lobe.

Yes, you can bust out your calculator along with the other Extreme Couponers, but you still have to know what the hell you're doing on said calculator. Especially the kind I shelled out fifty dollars for.

I was in the checkout line, right after my first massive purchase adventure, when I discovered my savings estimation on Epsom salts and Rice-A-Roni was off by two hundred and seventeen dollars. Red patches of panic swelled through my neck while I frantically pushed buttons on a machine that was clearly designed to be used by astronauts. It was my youngest son, only nine at the time, who grabbed the calculator out of my hand and asked why I was trying to work out exponents.

Ever the professional obsessor, I would not give up so easily. By my third shopping trip, I was kind of—sort of—getting the hang of it. I clipped and sorted, rearranged, and self-medicated. I involved the kids in the preshopping activities by assigning them their own scissors and delegating a Math Emergency Person should another aspirin and dish soap FAIL find me forcing the boys into McDonald's while I sat outside in my car crying.

Luckily, it never came to that again.

In our little storage-challenged house I stocked every shelf and cabinet with stacks of toilet paper and instant mashed potatoes. Eyedrops and bandages lined the walls of what used to be our linen closet. Did you know you can fit twenty containers of Tic Tacs in a Crock-Pot?

My boyfriend Max, who pays the majority of our household expenses, had entrusted me to use our joint account for what I was now calling "My home business."

"Three hundred dollars is a lot to spend on just three different items," he said one night, a squiggly green vein plumping against his forehead as he peered into my bags of toothpaste, gravy mixes, and feminine douches. "We don't even use Crest."

"So what," I said. "I needed to get the extra credit points on my saver card."

And what did he know about big business anyway? Max is a PhD who works in a tiny office building where they make robotic arms and microscopes. He stands around in a lab coat all day taking stock photos of latexed fingers holding test tubes. Every entrepreneur knows you have to spend money to make money. And from all the things I'd been learning about how the credits on sale items worked, it can take up to three years before you attain the type of savings status where you get your twenty-ounce cans of tomato sauce for free. And if you're doing it right, you shouldn't really see that much of a difference in your usual grocery budget.

I told Max not to worry. Sure, we were completely out of our regular staples like milk, bread, vegetables, butter, meat, cheese, fruit, and eggs, but I tried to explain all the macaroni salad we were eating was still within the range of what we usually spent.

Yet as the weeks went by, my checkbook began to tell a very different story.

Turns out, to get these super-savings points—a "check" of sorts that comes in the mail from the store where you're saving all this money—you have to spend a certain amount within a certain time frame. To simplify: If we were going to reap the benefits of a prime rib dinner for less than a dollar, I would have to find a tasty way to incorporate panty liners and shaving cream into my casserole. And fast.

Just before the start of a new school year, my youngest said his sewing machine needed some repairs. He'd been hand-stitching colored squares onto more colored squares and showed me where the thimble raised two big blisters on his little hand. "I don't know," I told him. "That sounds expensive. Why don't you make something nice out of your puffy fabric paints? Draw a peace sign or a dragon."

He told me his puffy paints were all dried up. "The only one I have left is hot pink. I'm kind of over that style now." He grumbled on about how much he missed going to the fabric store, then went back to eating his instant mashed potatoes with rice.

That night I sat down at my computer and started printing out more coupons for more of the same crap that now seemed to be ruining our lives. My family was eating poorly. My sons needed new clothes. My printer blinked to let me know its ink level was low.

As I watched my instant message box pop up from the Krazy Saver Facebook page—someone in Atlanta just scored an entire year's worth of Vitamin C pills for two dollars—I imagined my little fashion designer and his broken sewing machine, my sweet blue-eyed *feme*, starting the fourth grade in a crummy old T-shirt with a Wimpy Kid sad face above peeling letters that read:

my mom went to the grocery store and all I got was this stupid t-shirt because she spent all our money on mouthwash

I slumped into my chair and thought about what to do next.

Do they let you sell toothpaste on eBay?

Something that is stressed in OCD therapy is to know your limits. Sure, going outside your comfort zone to conquer phobias like hyperventilating during a job interview or touching doorknobs is pretty important because those things are required if you want to have any kind of a life outside of Meals on Wheels and cats. But I kept thinking about the limits part. "Accepting them," a counselor once told me, "is very different than avoiding them."

I looked at the stacks of newspapers on my desk, the piles of coupons that still needed to be sorted, the sheets of ladybug stickers that now seemed the stuff of a grown woman losing her mind. And her money.

A mother's defeat is a wretched thing, but, despite all the time and energy I had put into the intention of spending more time and energy with my children, I was beginning to feel as if my effort was just me trying to close that long-ago rift of failing to make my own mother happy. All the shopping anxiety I experienced as a child was still there, in every checkout stand, in all the numbers I couldn't figure correctly. "Don't crap on others when you're working out your crap," someone once said. But that's exactly what I was doing. Instead of accepting my anxiety about shopping, I was avoiding it by trying to turn it into something else.

Shit shined up, and so on.

I poured myself a drink and wrote this on the grocery list I had started for my next coupon trip: *In this world there are the spenders and the savers. I am neither. I am not sure what I am.* Yes, it's cheesy and reeks of people in folding chairs introducing themselves by first name only, but an honest to goodness list maker makes lists of everything. Even her lies. The truth gets truer when you write it down. I folded up the paper and stuck it in the act now! section of my leather accordion file.

And that was that. I had made the decision to release myself and my family from the perforated hell of pretending to be someone I wasn't.

When I laid my head on my pillow that night, it was the first time in six months I didn't see the cereal aisle in monochrome swirls behind my eyes.

It wouldn't happen in a day. The transformation from Super Shopping Mom back to Super Stay-at-Home Mom—with a huge emphasis on the stay-at-home part—would have to be a slow adjustment, one that began with lies and excuses, and then small sprinkles of truth to be added later as my children warmed up to the idea of doing the mall without their mother.

Sometimes, that's the way it is with anxiety disorders. People don't always understand right away when you tell them the reason you seemed unsociable at the cocktail party was that you had an overwhelming urge to Windex the bathroom mirrors (which you did, and then felt bad for rummaging under the bathroom sink of someone you hardly knew looking for cleaning products). It's easier for others to accept that your son fractured his shin during soccer practice and that's why you had to leave the baby shower early, rather than telling someone her house was so damn hot it gave you heart palpitations and you were afraid you might have a panic attack in the middle of "Guess What's in the Diaper."

Even if you've never had troubles with OCD or anxiety, it stands to reason that the truth of what is *really* going on inside your head should only be revealed when you trust someone enough, when you're certain someone likes you enough not to press harassment charges because you have to touch the tip of their nose every time you see them or something awful will happen.

It took many years of excuses for my girlfriends to finally realize I was not the person to call during a sundress emergency at Anthropologie.

My kids would have to learn this as well. And I would have to hold onto the fact that they would not stop loving me because of it.

Last week my son Julian handed me his iPhone and said, "Here is my wish list for prom." Then he asked if I could go with him to price tuxedo rentals.

I told him I could not. I reminded him of our last dressing room adventure that ended with me driving away, him taking the bus home, and, for some reason, a heated argument over Sylvester Stallone. "Believe me," I said, "this is a big deal for you, and I think we both know everything will work out for the best if I'm not a part of that." I suggested he go with Max or his best friend, Devin. "Make a man-date out of it," I said. "Pizza afterwards, maybe a trip to Game Stop."

It didn't take long for him to agree, which made me feel weird. Relieved and sad.

"They're starting not to need me anymore," I told Max as I watched my son and his friend drive away from the house.

"That's not true," Max answered. "They're starting to let you breathe."

I often joke to my sons that one of them had better give me a granddaughter for all my years of boy trouble. Though I'm only in my forties, I can already see her little face in my dreams. Tiny and smart and perfect. I will read to her from all of my Laura Ingalls Wilder books. I'll paint her little nails and do up her hair. We'll put makeup on each other and have tea parties with all the stuffed animal characters from Angelina Ballerina. Of course, I realize a granddaughter will up the chances of me having to once more endure the horrors of the mall. But who knows. Maybe she'll hate shopping as much as I do. Maybe she will be gay, but gay in the right way. Totally butch, caring only about sales if it's a buy-one-get-one on neck tattoos. Perhaps she will share my love of cleaning, opting to organize the closets rather than buying the stuff to fill them. I'll give her a little pink cleaning caddy and her own DustBuster. We'll spend entire afternoons together scrubbing and labeling while her father and uncles loiter around Foot Locker. We'll put stickers on our Swiffers and stay in the house, where it is properly cleaned and temperature controlled.

"Just you and me," I'll tell her, as I pass her the bleach spray that she will happily accept with her flowered rubber gloves. We'll make everything sparkle and smell like lemon. We'll make sandwiches for the men when they come home from doing the things they love to do. If she asks me why I never take her shopping, I'll say, "It's more fun in the house." Because it is. "And Grandma is a better person in here than out there." I know she won't understand at first. That's all right. When you love a child you'll say anything to make them happy, to protect them from the absurdities and confusion of people and their problems. Sometimes you'll have to lie just to get them off your ass. And that's all right, too.

THE MALLS OF MY YOUTH

Abby Mims

i was standing in the middle of the blandly named Beaverton Pharmacy—
which should, in the spirit of truth in advertising, be called the "Little Shop
of Horrors"—surrounded by every kind of aid/tool/gadget one can imagine to help with gout, varicose veins, inconvenient swelling of body parts, or the
inability to get in and out of the shower. I was there shopping for a sling for my
mother because her useless arm (Clem, as we named it early on, as in "Clem
the Claw" for its propensity to catch on everything: my mother's clothes, other
people's clothes, chairs, the commode, etc.) was giving her fits, and she'd gone
through several slings in the course of her illness. They were all slightly wrong in
some way, so she pulled at them, constantly readjusting, always just a bit uncomfortable. The tumor in her brain sat on her motor strip, which left her paralyzed
on the right side almost immediately. Since her diagnosis, she has lost much of
her short-term memory, nearly all of her speech, and, most recently, her ability to
read. In terms of the sling, most of the time her shoulder hurt, or her limp hand
ended up flopping out the end of it and banging into things. Her fingers there
were one giant bruise.

Walking up and down the aisles, I was reminded of something David Rakoff
wrote at a time when he was faced with the possibility of losing his arm. When
he considered having to wear a prosthetic, it was "the depressing neutral almond
color of all aids designed to help the ill and infirm" that really got to him, and
I couldn't agree more. The almond-colored everything at the Beaverton Pharmacy personified all of my fears about getting old, death and dying, brought to

life as they were via compression socks, shower handles, and walkers. I will just go ahead and say it: It all gave me the fucking creeps. I was there as obsessed caretaker, propelled by my feelings of utter helplessness as I watched my mother actively dying. This particular helplessness frequently resulted in a laserlike focus on small, tangible tasks that involved some form of shopping. Often, this led me back to predictable comforts—the shiny bright aisles of Target, Bed Bath and Beyond, or T.J. Maxx—in my search for cheery pajamas, lavender lotions, and fuzzy socks. These trips made me feel better, imagining as I did the pleasure my mother would take in feeling these small luxuries against her skin. In the Beaverton Pharmacy, however, all I could do was keep breathing through my mouth so as not to take in the smell of impending death that seemed to be everywhere, a mix of cling peaches and old cottage cheese. No amount of scented candles could mask it. I stood amid the almond-colored everything and willfully resisted the urge to sprint out the door. What kept me from running was the fact that I was powerless to stop the clock that continued on, closer and closer to her death. With that knowledge, I was determined to fix some other tiny corner of her life, and in a way mine, by buying her something. That day, it was the sling.

Except for a brief period of time before she was diagnosed with terminal brain cancer, my mother has never liked to shop, particularly in malls. In fact, she loathed it, avoided it at all costs. Trying on clothes was torture for her, not to mention the noise and the rampant American consumerism she has always hated. All of it overwhelmed her nearly on contact, and she would only indulge my sister and me in a trip once a year to the local mall, Washington Square, to buy us $200 each of back-to-school clothes. We wouldn't be there more than an hour before my mother would be wincing at the soundtrack of the Brass Plum or J. Jacobs, before she was saying, "I have the phobs! I have to get out of this store. Let me know if you want to buy anything; I'll be outside." My mother's "phobs" came upon her frequently in my childhood, as it was both short for claustrophobia and for her general, somewhat constant state of being overwhelmed as a single mother. Upon hearing this, my sister and I would roll our eyes and go right on shopping.

Beyond her general aversion to consumer culture, my mother made a purposeful decision early in her life to develop her inner self rather than focus on her outer shell, and to raise her daughters the same way. As a result, she read voraciously, Anais Nin, Carl Jung, Christopher Isherwood, J. Krishnamurti, and Elisabeth Kübler-Ross, to name a few. She started doing yoga and meditating in the early 1970s, embarking on a deep study of Eastern religions, landing on Hinduism as her chosen philosophy. Later, she got a master's degree in social work and spent her career working in geriatrics and hospice care. Much of this internal exploration was propelled by the emphasis on outer-beauty-as-everything that she grew up with in the 1940s and 1950s, when little girls were seen and not heard, controlled by their parents and the societal norms of the time. Her parents may have been more obsessed than most in this arena, as her and her sister's hair, makeup, clothes, and weight were closely monitored throughout their childhoods and beyond. The many photos of the two of them all the way through high school dressed identically in dresses, pinafores, and various camp outfits, hair combed just so and held back by large ribbons, are both hilarious and heartbreaking. So focused was my grandfather on my mother's appearance, that during the last conversation they had, the day before he died of a massive heart attack, he asked her how much she weighed.

"One hundred and thirty-five, Dad," she said and hung up the phone. She was thirty-six years old.

In direct opposition to this, she raised my sister and me based entirely on the premise that we were beautiful, valuable, and perfect just the way were, inside and out. I have only recently begun to absorb this gift she gave us, because no matter her efforts, for much of my life I remained consumed by all things external, which naturally led to endless amounts of shopping. For me, before there were boys, there were malls. Solid, shiny things, full of flash and order, well-lit grace. What they contained was the promise of another life and another girl better than me—one with two parents living in the same house, a house they owned, complete with a lawn the color of AstroTurf, a father grilling on Sunday nights in the backyard, and a mother in the kitchen, smiling, wearing pressed khakis and a string of pearls. And the daughter? She had a room with a comforter set from Meier & Frank, a trundle bed, a bathroom counter full of department store makeup, Clinique, perfection bottled in a collection of sea-green containers. And oh, the clothes. More sweaters than she could count, ditto jeans, skirts, shoes, purses, earrings. Everything matched; everything coordinated to a season; everything was name-brand: ESPRIT, Izod, Generra, Guess? Laurel Burch, L.J. Simone, Nike.

This girl of a different life lived and breathed in the malls of my youth. Every weekend in junior high it was the same: the mall, the mall, roaming with a small pack of girls who also didn't have access to their parents' credit cards. Slurping Orange Julius, eating Auntie Ann's pretzels, buying very little else, unless there was a two-for-one sale on sweaters at Forenza. I couldn't have been happier splitting the cost of those sweaters with another friend and getting the matching socks for free. The fact that I'd be dressed the following week like everyone else who'd gotten in on the two-for-one was lost on me for a few minutes, at least in the soft lights of the dressing room. I remember one black-and-white flecked sweater that fell nearly to my knees, hiding all the things I hated about my body: my too-big tits, my lumpy stomach, and those awful thighs. From the right angle I was entirely hidden, even to myself. I was almost that other, different girl.

I was so obsessed by the mall at thirteen that my mom, on her tiny salary, somehow managed to scrape up twenty-five dollars a month to give me as a clothing allowance. I was not as grateful as I should have been, explaining to her that it would pay for maybe a fourth of a skirt at Nordstrom's.

"So, save," she said, leaving the room with a swish of her secondhand skirt and Birkenstocks, the only shoe she'd ever spent more than $10 on in her adult life. I glowered and howled, and proclaimed I was so deprived it made me sick.

High school did nothing to relieve my fixation, as girls were unofficially ranked by other girls based on clothes, purses, and shoes. We all fell victim, and I got a job at Häagen-Dazs at fourteen to save for a car *and* a Dooney & Bourke purse, while two girls I knew were fired from their jobs at a dry cleaner's when they were caught wearing the clothes of various customers sometime between drop-off and pickup. At school, my friends and I would track the outfits the rich girls wore, how long it took them to wear a sweater, blouse, or skirt again. Sometimes, it took months. The poorer among us traded clothes and tried to wear them weeks apart so that no one would catch on; it was also verboten to wear the same outfit twice in a week. In the interim, I spent my time trying on outfits my mother could never afford, which led to the obvious: stealing a blouse from Nordstrom's once. It had a slightly silky feel and was covered with pink and blue and green flowers. I was surprised at how easy it was, slipping it into my purse in the dressing room, but I was terrified at the core and never tried it again. However, this did not stop me or my friends from exploiting their generous return policy. Years ago, you could buy any item of clothing, wear it for as long as you wanted, and then return it with no receipt, no questions, and a smiling saleswoman handing you cash. When my mother found out I had done it with a red sweater covered in miniature snowflakes that I'd grown tired of after a few months, she explained to me that this was not ethical, not acceptable, and that I would be grounded severely the next time she caught me. I sulked and pouted, protested about the general grossness of how much money Nordstrom's made every day, but her words stayed with me, and I didn't do it again.

If that weren't enough, along with tracking what other girls wore and longing for my own expensive outfits to better blend in, I constantly lamented the state of my mother's wardrobe. That was my particular suburban dream, to look perfect and to have a perfect-looking mother. She did not wear the neat, suitable garb of the stay-at-home mothers I knew (no matter that she was a single, working mother): neatly pressed pants, loafers, polo sweaters and Izod shirts, Land's End monogrammed bags. Instead, it was those Birkenstocks or black Chinese slippers, along with terrible, terrible shapeless hippie dresses. Nearly everything she wore was secondhand, and seeing the way she dressed caused me endless amounts of angst. In one particularly dramatic fight, I yelled, "Don't you want to look better? It would be nice to have a mom who wore good clothes, you know!"

Shocked, she said, "Don't you think I'd like to? I can't afford it. That money is going to you and your sister, for your wardrobes."

I was shamed into silence, briefly.

Things did not improve much as I got older, going as I did from suburbia in my teens to the plastic of Southern California and Los Angeles in my twenties. Here, the malls were the churches, the churches often inside the malls, and there was nothing else to worship but the skinny, the tan, the stylish, and the rich. I ran on this hamster wheel of impossibility for nearly a decade, on Melrose Avenue, Hollywood Boulevard, and the mall at its core, the Beverly Center. (Never Rodeo Drive, never, as the humiliation of all I couldn't buy would have been far too great.) When I look back on my years there, much of what I recall are endless days of shopping with my friends, looking for what exactly, I have no idea. Well, actually I do—we were looking for that blouse or pair of jeans or shoes or eye shadow that would effectively change our lives, that would make us appealing to the right men, and barring that, appealing to ourselves, always the harshest critics.

I was often reduced to my junior high self on those boulevards and in that mall, as much was the same. We were never thin or beautiful enough, and we could afford little of what we saw because we were waitresses, barely making our bills and rent. So we did what my girlfriends and I did back then—ate pretzels, drank Jamba Juice in place of Orange Julius, and tried on clothes that we couldn't afford or that didn't make us look quite the way we wanted, and always, always, no matter what we bought or didn't buy, left each store feeling progressively more unsatisfied and depressed. And then we did it again, the next free afternoon the next weekend, the next week. I was so exhausted by Los Angeles after six years, that in 2004, at the ripe old age of thirty-two, I embarked on a sabbatical from life. I moved home to my mother, to Portland, Oregon, straight back into the bedroom I grew up in. Many things fueled this decision, from the hopelessness of dating in L.A. to graduate school PTSD, but I came home in part because I knew I needed to shed this intense and endless need, this decades-long search for another, entirely superficial skin.

My transformation didn't happen overnight, and in many ways is still happening nearly nine years later. My sister would get cancer first at twenty-eight, and

I moved again from Portland a few months after I'd relocated from Los Angeles to Bainbridge Island, across Puget Sound from Seattle, to help her through treatment. To cope, in between chemo, radiation, and surgery, well, we shopped. We shopped nearly incessantly that year, the two of us, in part because the mall was nearly the only place to go on that island unless you counted the wilderness, and my sister and I didn't. She had just barely survived two years on twenty acres with no water or electricity, and she wanted civilization and, moreover, all its artifice. It was also a salve to what was happening to her—when she lost her hair, we shopped for stylish hats; when she dropped so much weight she barely looked like herself, she bought her first pair of ridiculously expensive 7 For All Mankind jeans. I bought myself a new wardrobe, too, during that time, trying to pin down the person I was going to be now, a chic northwestern career woman, buying cashmere sweaters and hip, if sensible, shoes, wool wrap-skirts, heavy tights. The mall we frequented was an old one, run down and retro in a bad way, a forgotten warehouse full of chain stores that no longer existed in more updated malls in bigger cities. It had what we needed, no matter the scuffed linoleum and fading paint.

Oddly, it was in this mall, maybe a year before my sister's diagnosis, that my mother began to discover the pleasures this type of shopping can bring. She was attending her fortieth high school reunion that summer and had decided to make herself over. It started with new, refined glasses, finally getting rid of the ones with lenses the size of espresso saucers. Then came the shedding of her hairdresser of two decades who had faithfully permed my mother's hair for the better part of that time, and a chic new haircut that made her sixty-year-old face look fifty, if that. When we were all together for spring break, we dragged her to that old mall, to the Gap first where nothing was quite her style and then to the ladies' section at Macy's. There, she discovered the glory of Ralph Lauren, Jones New York, and Eileen Fisher, buying jeans that fit her right and were comfortable for the first time in her life, silk shirts, and long, elegant skirts and jackets that hugged her in the right places and hung elegantly over the hips she tried to hide. She was a size six but always bought eights, tens, twelves, or fourteens, still dressing for the thirty pounds she'd put on while pregnant with my sister, although she had lost them decades ago. When she went back to work the following week, all her coworkers asked how she'd lost so much weight so quickly, and strangers stopped her in stores to compliment her outfits or tell her how fabulous she looked. I know she was overwhelmed by the attention at first, but I think she relaxed into it after a few months and began to enjoy this newfound aspect of herself. She had worked so diligently for decades to develop her intellect, compassion, and spirituality that it was refreshing to see her allow herself this less meaningful indulgence, perhaps even revel in it in ways she hadn't known were possible.

By the time she and my stepfather traveled to India in the fall of 2008, six months before her diagnosis, my mother looked and felt better than perhaps ever in her life, and was nearly as gorgeous as she was in her twenties. She saved for months to be able to buy herself what she wanted on that trip: rugs, paintings, bedspreads, scarves, and half a dozen everyday saris in hot pink, brick red, ivy green, indigo blue. In her bedroom, there was an electronic picture frame that flips through a selection of photos, many from this trip. When I could take it, I stared at those photos and marveled. She is a flat-out beauty in those shots, one that I can only now see fully. Her skin is rich and olive colored, her black hair glossy, the lines on her face minimal. In these pictures she simply glows. Almost four years later, she resembled more closely a decades-old photo of my ninety-year-old great-grandmother that sat on the bookshelf downstairs. Her face was full, with rosy balls for cheeks and a puffy layer of skin between her chin and the rest of her neck that never before existed. She was an aged, soft-angled version of her former self, sixty or seventy pounds heavier, her fingers, legs, face—everything—all puffed out from immobility and steroids. Going on them long-term was one of her greatest fears. Given her experiences in hospice care, she knew how the drugs would ravage her body, and death aside, she didn't want to look exactly the way she does now. She was so adamant about this that she informed the neurosurgeon, politely, that she wouldn't be taking the steroids—it simply wasn't an option. He smiled and nodded, and then informed her evenly that, actually, *not* taking them wasn't an option, as they were one of the only things that would buy her time and stave off the swelling in her brain. It wasn't about vanity, really; it was about completely losing control. You are dying, the doctors told her, and you will look like hell for the duration.

None of those beautiful clothes she bought over the last few years fit; they hung on racks in the spare bedroom or were shoved into a closet in the basement. She was a miraculously good sport about this, but I know it bothered her. One day as my sister and I were caretaking, as I was getting her from the bed to the commode and back, my mother said, "Don't look at my butt!" My sister was sitting directly behind her and had a full view.

"Okay, I won't," she said, and I watched her half-cover her eyes in mock horror.

I got my mother's pants back up and positioned her back in bed, and we were all quiet for a moment, and then my sister started laughing, saying, "I couldn't not look at it. I mean, if you say that, that's what everyone is going to look at, right?"

My mother laughed and sighed, holding her head in her one good hand, cheeks going completely red. "I accidentally caught a glimpse of it in the bathroom mirror the other day," she said. "Let's just say I never, ever want to do that again."

A few months later, she seemed less interested in food than usual, and it alarmed me, as hospice had told us it was one of the biggest signs that someone was starting to go, really beginning to die. When I brought up the fact she was eating less, she denied it and then said that three meals were too much. A day or so later, she told me not to worry, that it "wasn't as bad as I thought."

"Okay," I said. "Whatever that means. It's all pretty bad, you know?"

"I know," she said. "But it's not that bad."

The next day, when we were alone, I asked her what she wanted for lunch, since it was nearly three and she hadn't eaten since breakfast. She shook her head and sighed. "Here's the thing," she said. "I don't want to get any fatter. That's what the eating thing is about."

"What?" I was shocked.

"Yep," she said.

"Oh my God, Ma. That's what this is about?"

She looked at me knowingly.

"Well," I said, "I do understand." I had recently subscribed to Jillian Michaels's website and purchased several of her DVDs. I was attempting to get shredded for summer while my mother sat, dying. I'd approached my workouts lately with a near-religious fervor.

"I knew you would," she said. "I knew you would."

And it was our secret, at least to the rest of the family. We didn't think they would get it. I teased her about it, however, when they weren't around.

"There will definitely be whispers," I told her. "Did you hear about that poor Bobbie Mims? She's gotten so, well, fat. I mean, huge. And then there's that brain tumor. Poor thing."

Ironically, when she was first put on steroids in those early months, we had to talk her down from buying everything in sight. She went completely manic for six weeks or so and ordered cookbooks written by the naturopath at her cancer center for nearly every family member, silver lotus bracelets for all the women close to her heart, Guatemalan beaded ones for the men, baseball caps with the Hindu word "ram" (which means God) on them in every color for the "God Squad," as she coined it—everyone who circled around her with love and prayed she would heal. She sent us on myriad trips to Target for the things she was sure she needed: basket upon basket to store her sympathy cards and reply notes; scotch tape, which she used on everything she could, affixing whatever she could get her hands on to the walls and bookshelves that surrounded her chair in the living room; paper plates and napkins for all the people who came to visit, so that we could offer them snacks and not have to do dishes, and on and on. Thankfully, she adjusted to the steroids after a few months and this phase ended, but, during that time as she shopped manically (or sent us to do it for her), I was so exhausted by it and the general prospect of knowing my mother was going to die, I began to lose my taste for shopping altogether, at least in the ways I used to do it. As her illness went on and I moved in to help my stepfather with her twenty-four-hour care, I was consumed enough by what was happening that there was simply no time to worry about that new shirt, sweater, pair of jeans—anything, honestly— in the face of losing her.

I lost track of myself enough a year or so into her illness that for a friend's upscale out-of-town wedding, I didn't even think about buying something new. Instead, I wore a fuchsia dress I hadn't put on in years, five maybe, from a time when I was notably tanner and thinner. I squeezed into it with the help of some Spanx, and, as I modeled it for myself in the hotel room, I realized it wasn't as flattering as I remembered, and the color did not illuminate my skin, now northwest-winter pale. I was screwed, with nothing else to wear. Worse, at the wedding, I realized the dress was very much out of date (having completely lost track of current trends) and nothing like all the fashionable, off-the-shoulder, slinky miniskirt numbers most of the other women there were wearing. One, a former model with an eight-week-old baby at home, was dressed in a red silk version of said dress, looking as if she could have easily done a bikini photo shoot later in the day if pressed.

Normally in this kind of situation, I would have felt fat and awkward, insecure that I had worn the wrong thing, and horrified that everyone would notice. Miraculously, after a few moments of self-consciousness, I found myself simply not giving a shit, realizing that no one cared what I was wearing or what I weighed, most surprisingly, me. My mother still dying, so what did any of it matter? This attitude has stuck with me for the last three years as she continues to defy the odds and live. This internal shift wasn't a fully conscious one; it's just what was, and now is, and the freedom is quite something. This process of shifting to deeper concerns in life, of putting someone else's needs before my own started with my sister's illness, but with her, there was hope of recovery and a future, whereas my mother wasn't supposed to live longer than eighteen months. It was this devastating understanding of how little time we had and my mother's immediate level of need that caused this shift in me, too, as suddenly, leisure trips to the mall became irrelevant. From then on, my shopping trips, along with my life, became about necessity and her comfort, and more often than I liked, confronting the things I most feared.

A few weeks after we first learned of our mother's tumor, my sister and I made a trip to the main mall of my youth, Washington Square. This was a time suspended in hope, as the mass hadn't yet been biopsied and we could still believe things were going to be okay. We were there to buy several boxes of

See's suckers, which our mother loved and also wanted to pass out at her various doctor's visits to the staff and fellow patients and their families. She wanted to be able to give *prasad*, she said, which literally means "gracious gift" in Hindi, and is often the bit of food or sweet treats that are placed on altars in India as offerings to the gods, blessed by them and then eaten by the devotees. This was yet another part of her steroid-fueled missive, but my sister and I went along.

The mall had recently been fully remodeled, and it was all too much really, between the Pottery Barn Kid's and the Sephora and the slick black-and-white marble floors that led to the twenty-foot-tall doors of the ubiquitous Cheesecake Factory. It was gaudy now, transparently fake. Little was as I remembered, and nothing was in the same place except the See's Candies store, on the same corner it had always been, and I found this incredibly comforting. We bought our suckers, got our free samples, and were headed out when we came across a kiosk full of swirling wind ornaments, silly things to hang on a patio that no one actually needs. My sister and I were inexplicably mesmerized as we watched them twirl. They were in the form of everything from lotus flowers and island scenes to rainbows and University of Oregon logos. Much of it was tacky crap, but a brown-eyed boy came up to help us before we could walk away. He was very good at his job and sold us entirely on one in less than five minutes, in part by holding up a copper-orange sun against the black exterior tiles of the Ben Bridge Jewelers a few feet away, showing us how you could see it at night. The sun he demoed had a coiled silver tail attached to it, with a ball inside that moved up or down according to what direction the wind was blowing.

My sister liked the lotus, but I insisted on the copper sun, and she eventually agreed. "But no tail," I said. "I don't like the tail."

"Okay," he said but put another offer on the table while ringing us up. He had first quoted the tail at an extra thirty-five dollars, but now he said, "For you, how about five dollars for the tail?"

"No," I said with far too much emotion, "no tail. I don't like the tail."

"Geez," he said, "you scared me. Anyone else would say, sure, five bucks, I'll take the tail."

It was then I started crying. "Our mom has a brain tumor," I choked out, "and see, we want it to stay round, if it grows tentacles or tails or whatever—" When I looked up again, I saw tears in his eyes.

"Oh, no, not your mother. If anything happened to my mother, I don't know. I'm Israeli and the oldest, the closest to her. Oh, I am almost crying. I just hope your mother is okay."

My sister was nodding along with the two of us, for that wish to be true. "I think we should have a group hug," she said, and so we did. When we separated, she held his hand and said, "We love you."

"Oh, I love you, too," he said. And we smiled and bought the copper orange sun without the tail and opened up the box of See's suckers and gave him one. I tried to explain it, calling it *prassat* instead of *prasad*, and my sister corrected me, and he looked confused but happy. We waved to him all the way to the door, all the way back out into the day.

We hung the sun from the roof's eave, just outside the sliding glass doors that lead to the backyard. She could see it from her chair in the living room, and watching it twirl, she said, "Oh, wow. It's just what I've always wanted."

I stopped buying my mother new clothes a few months ago, as it overwhelmed my stepfather, who is already faced with the huge surplus he will have to get rid of when she dies. I only see her once a month now, as I moved to California last December to be with my long-term boyfriend. My mother insisted I do this from the earliest months of her illness and eventually wouldn't take no for an answer. When I finally left, she told me that I had cared for her for two years. She said I had done enough and needed to move forward with my life. So I left, but it wasn't easy, and because I am no longer with her every day, I find myself buying her more than a few things every time I come home, usually the reliable lotions or socks or soft T-shirts. Overall, I've bought her more clothes than she needs, clinging to this last vestige of her outer vessel.

When I was home recently, we were going through her normal morning routine of brushing her hair and teeth, when I offered to shave her mustache. She looked surprised at the suggestion, although she has asked me to do this since she got sick. (We share this genetic blight, although I had mine lasered off years ago.) She shrugged and said okay. In the beginning, this shaving was always part of our bathing routine, along with her reminders to wash her back and the inadvertent moans of pleasure she let escape, small sounds inherent in the act of getting clean. My mother loved nothing more than being clean or soaking in the bath. I christened her in a different way, on a shower bench, her paralyzed right side dragging along behind her. It was a sitting shower really, not a bath, but it doesn't matter now, I realized, as we were done with all that, as close to the end as we are. We were done with the feeling of water running over her head and down her body. We were done with her leaving the house, the room, the bed. She was done wanting pajamas or lotions or worrying about the hair on her upper lip; she was done with vanity.

When she shrugged, I sensed the nearly complete liberation in where she was, no longer worried about anything but the current moment.

"Thank you," she managed to get out when I finished.

I nodded and reached for her, knowing there was nothing left for me to buy, that there was only this to do: the act of sitting here and holding her hand.

I looked at her and felt her baby-soft skin, remembering the day I found the saris in the hope chest at the foot of her bed. She had completely forgotten they were there, but when I pulled them out she marveled, touching the hems, telling me she'd had all of them altered in India to fit.

"Do you want to wear them?" I said.

"Yes," she said, excitedly. "Yes!"

I started dressing her in them on Sundays, for the meditation group she and my stepfather hosted every week. I let the seams out as far as I could and wrapped her in the matching scarves, light as spider webs around her neck. When she wore them, she sat taller in her wheelchair and I could see she felt beautiful. And she was, incredibly so, and for a few moments, we were both transported back to that time before, when she was well.

GLASSES

Elizabeth Scarboro

n my wallet, I have a receipt for a pair of eyeglasses. It's an old-fashioned receipt: unwieldy and rectangular, with an imprint of my credit card—the kind of receipt I wrestled with when I was fifteen, working at Fred's Restaurant, ringing people up incorrectly. The receipt is my ticket to claim my glasses when they come in, which is probably something that wouldn't make most people feel triumphant. It probably shouldn't make me feel triumphant; it's the kind of thing I should be good at by now. These transactions should be effortless and weekly—I need glasses; I get glasses.

I lost my last pair in a river in Alaska. I was in a raft, attempting to paddle, spacing out. It was the summer after my first husband died; keys and glasses and days slipped through my fingers. It was 1999, fourteen years ago. In those years I have managed to grieve more and then less, teach, quit teaching and start again, fall in love, study Spanish in Mexico, have two children. I have not managed to get myself in the door of the glasses store.

My reluctance isn't about trying not to consume, or feeling the errand isn't worth the time. It could be that I am terrible at pausing during the day, at planning ahead so I have time to pause. It could be that I've never been good at taking care of things that are useful but not necessary. I wear contact lenses, so technically I don't *need* my glasses. But how many times in the last fourteen years have I lost one contact and walked through the world with a headache, everything skewed? Or gotten up in the middle of the night hungry, and mistaken the sour cream for yogurt? I can see about a foot in front of me before it all goes blurry, and you would think this alone would get me into the store.

I'm not sure what my reluctance is about, except that I dread the part where the saleswoman will start picking things out, and I will have to put them on, and none of them will be great, and she'll love the especially ugly and expensive ones, and then I'll have to choose. Do I sound like I am still fifteen? How could I have not learned this skill?

The problem is, I've treated shopping the way I've treated playing the guitar or meditating—it's one of those things that I intend to learn to do but never get around to, something I'd like to be good at, theoretically, except I never manage to put in the time. I waited until three weeks before my first wedding to start looking for my dress. During those three weeks, I drove around Denver, causing panic in saleswomen throughout the city. My friend Forest came to my aid and took me to her favorite store, which held the kinds of dresses she could see herself getting married in someday. "You already have ideas for your dress?" I asked. She nodded. So did many of our friends, it turned out, but since I was getting married young, I was the only one with an upcoming wedding. I felt hurt that I'd never been a part of these conversations. "How come I've never heard about this dress planning?" I asked. Forest shrugged. "We know that stuff doesn't interest you," she said. I tried to act more interested as we undertook our search. Eventually we found a nice dress, after which we had two hours to find shoes. I grabbed some so-so sandals, figuring no one would really see them under the dress anyway. I wasn't bothered; Forest felt terrible, as if she'd failed at her appointed duty to make sure I got this right. All through the reception, she kept glancing at my feet and shaking her head.

I don't want to give the impression I'm a slob. Although I tended toward jeans and oversized sweatshirts when I was seventeen, I understood at some point that I needed to move on. But in a way I still stick to a uniform. I probably should have been a guy, because I can't help the fact that when I find jeans that fit perfectly, I buy two pairs and wear them until they get holes in the knees. They are comfortable, they look good, and that's where I stop because then I don't have to go to the store. I have my dress-up uniform, too—a look acquired with the help of my friend Daniel, who is always happy to see me expand my wardrobe. (We have a plan to trade skill-sets—he's supposed to help me learn to enjoy shopping, and I'm supposed to help him learn to enjoy saving money.)

What's hard for Daniel to understand is that I am store-avoidant. I can't quite explain it myself. I don't avoid many things in life—I'm fine with hard conversations, tough times, jumping into the freezing ocean at midnight. But it takes me an inordinately long time to get around to replacing shoelaces or buying a sunhat. I don't even like the grocery store. I try to like it each time I make the large weekly trip for my family, and, though I don't look forward to it, I always get it done. But if I could, say, trade someone my trip to the grocery story for their weekly visit to a sick relative in the hospital, I probably would.

Stores that hold things I will be wearing conjure up the most dread. Nothing seems to ever come out quite right. I've realized, as I've gotten older, that it might have all started when I was fifteen. After years of devoting myself to ballet, I gave it up. I'd been dancing three times a week for two hours at a time, and I hadn't realized this had affected my body much, until I went from being flat-chested to wearing an underwire bra in the span of a month. I stared at the mirror, horrified to see a Dolly Partonish figure, but with Michael Jackson hips. Thus, the large sweatshirts paired with Levi's. I've gotten used to the body, but I can still end up feeling humiliated when I try to find swimsuits and dresses to fit it. Plus, because I am five-foot-one, the clothes that work for my frame don't quite work for the rest of me. My personality feels suited for loose, casual things, and yet if you put those things on me I am barely visible under the fabric. So the typical visit to the store involves the saleswomen pleading with me to try on whatever I've chosen in a smaller size. It doesn't seem to matter what size I choose, they want me to go one smaller. I do, and then after trying the clothes on at home and finding them tight and uncomfortable, I bring them back. Daniel once complained that Americans, unlike Europeans, dress as if they need to be able to hop up and play baseball at any moment. "Exactly!" I told him. If I can't move around, I feel restricted, and what's the point of that? The point is looking good, he told me, and I guess he's right, but is it worth it? I'm the one inside the clothes, not looking at them, and the person inside the clothes probably benefits most from getting to move around.

But I need to change my attitude toward shopping. Not only do I need clothes from time to time, but I'm concerned that I'm rubbing off on my daughter. She's only five and she's already saying things like "I hate outfits." To most mothers this might sound like a good thing, but it makes me nervous. My friend Lorraine laughed when I told her this. She said she works hard not to let her daughter see her fuss over her appearance; she thinks it's great that my daughter sees me throw on my jeans uniform or my dress-up uniform and walk out the door. I may be the only mother out there saying she wants to encourage her daughter to shop. I don't want her to shop excessively; I just want her to learn how to do it well, so she's got the skill when she needs it. I want her to think, *I need a new shirt*, and then proceed to go get one, rather than having a month (or in the case of my glasses, fourteen years) lapse between the thought and the deed.

So I'm trying to get on track, to take care of purchases when they occur to me, the way I take care of other obligations in my life. Which is why I'm very happy to be heading to pick up my glasses. I wish I could say that I'd purchased them on my own, but it actually took Lorraine saying, "Why don't we do it now? There's a place down the street." That's the kind of thing she knows, a place down the street. And there I was, staring in the mirror under the saleswoman's scrutiny, and I couldn't tell which frames looked good and which didn't, honestly, but I trusted Lorraine, and none of them were perfect anyway. If I can remember this—that none will be perfect, that it's not about something perfect but something good enough—I may be able to change my ways.

MOVE OVER AND LET
THE BIG DOGS EAT

Stacy Pershall

S he has a raven for a pet, a great black bird in a great black cage with a great sweeping view of the Financial District. Human beings pay an extra thousand bucks a month to get this raven's view, and the bird shows its gratitude by squawking constantly and dropping bits of dried corn on top of my head. There's nowhere else to crochet besides the red velvet fainting couch just below the birdcage. The rest of the room is taken up with an imposing black desk, a spinning wheel, mummified animals, a coffin, and a hundred cones of yarn (mostly single-ply merino, dishcloth cotton, and novelty yarn that looks like spiderwebs).

The bird is trying to out-yell the lady I met on Craigslist, the one whose ad I answered when I applied for a piecework knitting job, the one whose apartment this is. It's 2006, just before the recession, and people in the Financial District are still living as if they don't know it's going to happen. The Craigslist lady goes by S.M., or Shaman Marinelli, to which she has changed her first and middle names—partly, I suspect, so she can have the initials *S.M.* She's an Italian girl from Jersey who, fifteen years ago, took the train to a Goth club in the City and met a Wall Street guy with a fetish for large women in tight leather corsets. He used his wallet to sweep her off her feet, and now they live in this apartment with the raven and the coffin and their kid named Salomé and the inventory for her soon-to-open knitting and crochet boutique, "I'm a Flowerpot."

S.M. is now in her midforties and still wears black lipstick, black nail polish, black eyeliner, Stevie Nicks dresses, and Madonna bracelets, the black stacked rubber kind, with diamond tennis bracelets mixed in. At five-foot-seven, I'm taller than most women I meet, but she hulks over me; she'd be at least six feet even without the Demonia platform boots. She holds her crochet hook like a pen, which I've never learned to do; I hold mine like a knitting needle. She *tsks* at this, but however you learn is what gets into your muscle memory.

"So I tell ya," she says, "I couldn't believe it when Felicity offered me the money."

It's the third time in three days, at least, that she's told me the story of how she got the cash to open the boutique, for which we are making the inventory. It was not, as I first suspected, from the Wall Street Husband. In fact, Wall Street Husband's having a little trouble paying the bills, what with the kid's Bilingual Montessori school and all, but the kid "needs the Bilingual Montessori because she's gotta learn to speak Chinese. Salomé was about to have to drop out of school until Felicity paid the tuition, but it's just for a little while, just until the store takes off. Felicity says it's an investment. Thank gawd she realized Salomé was a genius."

Felicity's ringtone on S.M.'s phone is "Hips Don't Lie" by Shakira. When the phone rings and the song plays, S.M. acts like a teenager, wiggling her shoulders and squealing. When she's not talking to Felicity, she's telling me stories about how great Felicity is. They are, apparently, soul mates.

They met at an open house at their daughters' school, where S.M. clung to the sleeve of the husband who wasn't very good at Wall Streeting while Felicity clung to the sleeve of one who was. It becomes fairly obvious fairly quickly that the situation S.M. views as a fateful meeting of the minds is, in fact, a case of a rich woman using a striving woman for her amusement, but I, of course, do not say this. Instead I say, "Can I sit somewhere else besides underneath the raven?"

"It's a *craven*," she says.

I sit on the floor.

Whenever Felicity calls—which she does, often—S.M. pauses midconversation to relate to me what she just said. "Listen to this!" she'll crow. "Felicity went to an auction for the Bilingual Montessori and outbid this otha mutha who really wanted this lamp. Do you know what Felicity said to huh? She said she crossed out the woman's number on the silent auction sheet and said, 'Move over and let the big dogs eat!'"

She cackles, which makes the (c)raven squawk.

I'm writing my first book and supporting myself with piecework. One of the things that helps pay the bills is knitting and crocheting samples for knitwear designers. S.M. is paying me better than anyone ever has, and, although I dislike her behavior, I love her designs. I relate to her beat-up Victorian aesthetic, and her pieces are challenging to make. I try to focus on the fact that I'm learning a lot and ignore the class distinction gnawing at my soul, which I think may be transference gnawing for the soul S.M. doesn't have.

The first day we worked together, she told me about her sex life, in the way one does when one wants to establish boundaries: How far can I push you? How much will you submit to my will? What does it take to embarrass you, to make you uncomfortable? The second day my boyfriend Gideon gave me a ride to work in his van; I sat sandwiched between the instruments as he and his band headed out of town for a gig. When S.M. came barreling out the front door of her luxury building, barefoot, her phone in her hand, shouting, "Felicity, hang on a minute! The girl I told ya about is heah!" Gideon physically recoiled and drew his elbows into his jacket, the guitar player scooted closer to me, and the guy who played the washboard said, "Your boss is Elvira."

Now it's the third day, and I've been here for eight hours already, after working twelve yesterday. Just as S.M.'s husband wooed her with tales of his money, she woos me with tales of Felicity's. The boutique is in Alphabet City, on the corner of Sixth and A, right in my neighborhood, and it's opening as soon as we can construct the inventory. S.M. got some buzz in *Marie Claire* when a contestant on *Project Runway* cited her as a favorite designer, and she's "seizing the moment, baby! Ya gotta seize the moment!"

It's the kind of success story that can turn a hole-in-the-wall into a phenom-
enon, and the phone's ringing with pre-orders. While S.M. photographs pieces
and puts them on the website, I knit an enormous lace tube made of ripped silk
and dream the ridiculous dreams of every artist who's ever been flattered.

"You're good at what you do," she tells me, "and you're fast. Stick with me,
kid,"—she actually says *Stick with me, kid*—and we'll make some money off
these rich bitches." This is a segue to telling me how rich the bitches are. After a
few minutes of this, I want to offer her a drool cup.

I don't like her, but I want her to like me, so I find myself telling her my life
story. By the end of the third day, she knows what Gideon is like in bed.

Every night that week I curl up in that bed, the one that still smells like going-
on-tour sex, and I wrap my face in the sheets and try to breathe in Gideon's
realness. Being in S.M.'s world all day makes me feel dirty, overstimulated, and
synthetic, and I become more and more psychically indebted to her. It astounds
me how quickly it happens, how quickly I begin to dream of her money just like
she's dreaming of Felicity's. I know she doesn't really have any money, but she
acts like she does, so I link arms with her, casting away on this dream of making
it in New York, New York, stumbling upon set-for-life like lottery winners and
people whose cupcakes get discovered by Oprah. As her hand-spun yarn flows
through my hands, I feel as if we're becoming blood sisters, pricking our thumbs
on the playground and swearing to love each other more than boys. The problem
is, she's already sworn that oath with Felicity, and I've forgotten the rules of
recess, so I don't see it.

In the evenings we take what we've knitted to the store and hang it up, display
it on mannequins, assessing how much more we need to make to fill the space.
We crank it out stitch by stitch, her hands flying, mine struggling to keep up.
She teaches me to purl left-handed and to make a magic adjustable circle in the
middle of a crochet flower. I learn the difference between *Fair Isle* and *intar-
sia*. Every day, more and snootier decorations come in. First there are velvet
chaise longues the color of vapor, then a plush handwoven rug, then vintage

blue-willow wallpaper. When the chandelier arrives, it is so enormous I have to duck underneath it, but she swears that's how they do it in Paris.

I defer.

Her phone rings with the Shakira song.

S.M. squeals like a schoolgirl and shoots across the room, swipes her phone off the desk, silences Shakira with her thumb. "Hello, Flowerpot," she says, pointedly using their pet name, the origin of which she will not tell me, not that I'll ask. S.M. chooses certain moments to stop oversharing and get all personal-boundaries. It's calculated, the skill of those who want to maintain power, those who need to say "I'm the alpha." She has a tattoo of a phrase in Italian that takes up her entire forearm, and she won't tell me what it means. "It's a secret," she says, smiling smugly, tight-lipped.

"I just got the chandeleah," she squeals into the phone. "I love it, Flowerpot! It's so . . . like the time in Rhinebeck." She giggles, pauses, blushes, puts her fingertips over her mouth. "I know," she stage-whispers. "Me, toooo."

After more giggling and blushing—if you could will yourself to blush, as some actors can will themselves to cry, she's doing it, which is impressive through the white makeup—she titters goodbye, hangs up, and clutches the phone to her chest, against her heart.

"So," I say, because I find myself strangely wanting to know, and because I am expected to ask, "you and Felicity?"

She nods. She's too close to bursting to be private. "Oh, god, don't tell my husband. I mean, he knows, but he doesn't. Not officially."

"Does Felicity's husband know?" I knit one, purl one.

She shakes her head. "He can't know. This is his money."

One more link in the chain, one more step removed. I am depending on a woman who dresses like She'll Be Your Gypsy to give me a comfortable financial future, at least for a few precious months. She's depending on her illicit girlfriend, who's depending on her husband. The boutique is precarious, built on sand, but it could pay off. S.M. is determined it will. She quotes Felicity frequently: "Move over and let the big dogs eat," she says, and cackles, and marks up the price of something already overpriced. "Hey, do you think I should sell my voodoo dolls here? They're not just for entertainment purposes, so they'd have to be priced accordingly, but our customers could afford them."

Everything in the store gets more expensive every time we go to the boutique. By day, I sit beneath the corn-dropping craven and work on a full-length drop-stitch gown, if "gown" and "spiderweb" are synonymous. By night, I watch serial killers on *Cold Case Files*, have my own steamy conversations with Gideon, and crochet flower barrettes. S.M. would like to display as many hair accessories as possible in the glass case on opening day. She's told me she'll pay twenty-five dollars each, which means three will pay my electric bill, which means the chain is Mr. Felicity, Felicity, S.M., me, ConEd.

She keeps Felicity from me like a deep dark secret, like a box of contraband kittens. As a child, I had a friend named Katie whose mother never let her play with her Barbie dolls, forcing her to keep them high on a shelf in their boxes because they'd be worth something someday. Because of this, nobody ever wanted to spend the night at her house, but Katie parlayed her jealousy toward those of us who got to play with our toys into tall tales about all the other things she had that we couldn't see. The magic wand in her mom's closet, she said, would turn us into real-life Barbies. She couldn't take it out of the package, but we'd be sorry one day when she was a Barbie and we weren't. I wonder briefly if Felicity is S.M.'s version of a magic Barbie wand, if she really exists at all, but S.M. keeps handing me twenty-dollar bills for Twizzler runs and telling me to keep the change. I don't really care where the money comes from as long as it's buying my groceries, so I don't argue.

I do, however, feel like I need to take a bath in Sea Breeze every time I leave the shop. One afternoon, biking home to my Tupperware-sized fourth-floor walk-up studio apartment, I actually find myself humming the song: *Beautiful skin can be a breeze with Seeeeaa Breeeeze.*

My stash of crocheted flowers is growing, taking over my bed, because that and my desk are the only pieces of furniture that fit in my apartment. I'm so tired I push them aside and pass out, but my cat wakes me up an hour later batting me in the face with one that's stuck to his claw. I flip on the light to free him and squint at the tangle of yarn my apartment has become and realize this has gone way too far. She's taken over my days, and now she's taken over my nights, but more than that, she's taken over my very bed, the side Gideon sleeps on when he's not on tour. Instinctively, I wrap the blanket around me, because I don't want her to see me in my underwear.

I know I have to quit; I just can't quit yet. Not until I finish the flowers.

This is what living in New York City will do to you. It will make you sell your soul to pay the next month's rent. When I walk down Fifth Avenue, which I try not to do very often, I grit my teeth at the women coming out of Fendi or Gucci or Armani or some other store that ends in *i* with a small, crisp bag, the contents of which could keep a roof over my head for a year. I don't want to be one of those women, but I do want to open my eyes in the morning and look at the cable box to see what time it is without fearing I'm going to see *your account has been suspended, please call Time Warner* scrolling across its face instead. I want to know what it's like for your clocks to always tell the time instead of occasionally scolding you for being poor. I want to know what it's like to go shopping for something you don't really need.

I'll make a year's supply of flowers, I tell myself, and then I'll hand them over and she'll pay me and I'll say "Have a nice life" and go pay my bills. It is worth it not to get *Project Runway*–famous if I never again have to hear about the big dogs eating, if I never again have to hear Shakira, who is even worse, as a ringtone.

I go to the shop the next afternoon bleary-eyed but determined. I made twenty flowers last night because I couldn't go back to sleep. I don't bring them in yet, because I still have to block them, which means washing them and pinning them flat to dry. I toss my bag on the floor, take my seat beside it since I'm not allowed to sit on the furniture, and pull out a darning needle to sew up the lace camisole I've been knitting all week. S.M. perches on the edge of the chaise and breathlessly says, "Guess what?" She is practically bouncing up and down.

"Felicity something," I say.

She punches me in the arm, just a little too hard to be playful. "Felicity's on her way ova heah! Right now! Look sharp!"

I am not sure how to look sharp, given that it's ninety degrees out, I'm wearing a beat-up Laurie Anderson T-shirt from 1986, and I'm still sweaty from the bike ride over, but I smooth my hair a little bit. S.M. *tsks* at me and says, "We have to get you some betta clothes before customahs start coming in next week." I know that by *we*, she means I need to summon money I don't have to buy a wardrobe I don't want, so I just nod. *Quitting*, I tell myself. *You're quitting. You don't even have to survive this for seven more days.*

I am visualizing handing over the flowers, taking the money, and running away so hard my lungs burst when Felicity throws open the door, filling the air-conditioned room with oven-hot air. She has perfect blond highlights, a perfect spray tan, and a French manicure on her toenails. She's wearing a coral-colored linen dress without a single wrinkle, as if she got dressed in the morning and stood up all day. I check my watch. It's 2:30, so I calculate she's been standing for roughly five and a half hours.

"Flowerpot!" S.M. squeals, practically crushing her in a bear hug, her Herman Munster boots coming within centimeters of Felicity's pedicure.

Felicity endures the hug and air-kisses S.M. on both cheeks. S.M. forgets Felicity's going to do the other side, European-style, and their noses bump. I imagine both their faces wrapped in bandages and S.M. being happy because everyone at the Bilingual Montessori will think they had nose jobs together.

I place my palm on the Ikea click-lock hardwood floor to press myself up to standing, knowing the thing to do is to shake this woman's hand before she can air-kiss me. But Felicity steps squarely in the middle of my bag, and I hear my sunglasses crack.

"Time to move," she says, not looking at me, brushing me aside by flicking her diamond-covered hand twice in my direction. She heads for the racks and starts flipping through the clothes.

The room goes red, literally red; first it's a tunnel and then it's just crimson. My eyeballs are hot blood. I yank my bag out from underneath her foot, throw it over my shoulder, and run out the door before I punch her. I'm halfway home on my hot-pink bike before my vision returns to normal. I give thanks I'm wearing a helmet.

At home, I pull my broken sunglasses out of my bag. Then I turn the shower on full blast, ice cold, and I strip naked and stand under the water and scream.

Late that night I get the email.

Stacy,

Your behavior in the shop today was unacceptable . . . Felicity was very offended by the way you acted . . . it is obvious you have a problem with wealth, and due to the fact that we will be dealing with wealthy people in the shop . . . I am no longer willing to work with you . . . good luck in all your future endeavors . . .

Sincerely,

Shaman Marinelli Zagnoni
Necromancer

I start to write back, but I have nothing to say. This is, after all, someone who uses ellipses instead of periods, and who thinks necromancers are real. It's not the freedom I wanted, but it's freedom. I won't get paid for the flowers. I won't be able to pay my bills. But I'm free. It's just that I'm also, for some reason, crying.

One thing I know for sure is that I can't have these goddamn crochet flowers in my line of vision for one more second. I pack them, crumpled, lumpy, into a plastic Petco bag and ride back to the shop.

The gate is closed.

I ask myself, briefly, what I'm doing. Am I being a martyr? Is giving her my work for free exactly what she wanted all along? Am I brave or craven; am I submissive? Am I rolling over and showing my belly to the big dog?

It doesn't matter. Nothing matters but that I am uncaged and free to go. I shove the bag through the mail slot, pull a bottle of hand sanitizer from my purse, *splap* some on my palms, and rub my hands together furiously. And then, in the light of the dive bars and the shadows of hipsters, I walk my bike down the block.

You can't text your landlord to tell him your rent will be late when you're riding.

SHOPPING WITH CLOWNS

Gigi Little

One of the reasons I left my ex-husband, the circus clown, was all the shopping. You'd think once you married a circus clown, you wouldn't have to do that anymore. Shopping. Tromping up and down the mall, trying on dresses in those little fluorescent horse stalls, attempting to be pretty so some guy will like you. First, you were married now, so some guy did like you, so you could relax. Second, that guy made his own sequined hats and his mother sewed all his polka-dotted overalls and ruffled collars, so why the hell was he ever going to want to shop?

Circus memorabilia, that's what. Books and programs and newspaper clippings. A three-hundred-dollar poster of a grinning Victorian clown with enough teeth to eat your face off. An old, frayed photograph of a man in a handlebar mustache posing next to an elephant in tights.

No, the man in the handlebar mustache was the one in the tights, and they bagged at the knees, and the picture was cracked like a spiderweb and faded almost to nothing, and it cost twenty-seven-and-a-half bucks, and finding it took an hour and forty-five minutes of John wandering the aisles of the antique mall, flipping through baskets of old pictures. Not talking to me as I followed along.

Now he looked up from the basket, flashed the photo at me, and smiled. I smiled back.

"Great." I tried to make it sound sincere. "Can we go now?"

"Just a few more minutes."

John's face pointed back down into the basket of old pictures, and I moved off, wandering past display cases of Star Wars action figures in their original boxes, pulp fiction paperbacks, jewel-red carnival glass goblets. I wished there were something I wanted so I could enjoy shopping, too. Antique shops smelled like dust and must and made me lonely. Made me want, but not for things. Made me want the kind of husband who would want something—anything—other than things. At the end of an aisle was a headless mannequin wearing a 1950s dress with Joan Crawford shoulder pads and rhinestone buttons. I would have liked to wear that dress, but I didn't want to take the time to try it on. In the corner of the room, by the door marked *bathroom*, was a corkboard papered with flyers: garage band looking for a bassist. quiet cat-lover seeking roommate. rebuilt harley for sale, frame slightly warped. A badly photocopied cartoon of a worm looped into the shape of a heart with the caption *true love*. Everyone wants something.

I met him the summer after my second year in college. I was nineteen; he was thirty-one. He was six-foot-two, with dyed auburn hair and John Lennon glasses. When he told me what he did for a living, he opened his briefcase and brought out pictures of himself in white-face clown makeup with a red-glittered nose and jeweled feathers on his sequined hat. The clown makeup made his face look feminine. Not completely feminine, but some blend of feminine and masculine that looked beautiful. That Halloween, he dressed up in drag. Regular drag, not clown drag, with lipstick, with foundation over his perpetual five o'clock shadow, with nylon stockings. A long blond wig draped in loose coils down over his wide man's shoulders. Sitting there in the restaurant booth, I couldn't stop staring. He looked so different. So enticing, and I wasn't sure why.

He batted his mascara-black lashes and made an exaggerated limp-wrist gesture at me, his voice a sing-song: "Well, my dear, you have *got* to see my new gown; it's simply divine!"

In a way, he was mocking my sex, but I didn't care. He was a six-foot-two man who looked like a woman and I wanted to kiss him.

Kissing John in his lipstick wasn't as exciting as I thought it would be. As I brought my face up close to his, breathed in the sweet smell of perfumed powder, the illusion fell away, and he was just him. Underneath the woman's makeup, or the clown makeup, or the charming smiles of his everyday face, he was a little boring. When I thought about how he wanted to marry me and take me on the road and teach me the ancient art of clowning, I tried to forget that he wasn't really into anything except going to the circus and shopping for memorabilia. And that I wasn't sure I wanted to spend the rest of my life with a man who rarely thought of asking me what I'd like to do.

But I wanted to fall in love and none of the guys I knew gave me the kind of zing I got tonight just looking at him, a funny, hot shame that lit up the underside of my ribcage like the kick-up of flame from a barbecue.

That was what it felt like—shame. I didn't understand it. And I didn't understand why I liked it. But I liked it.

And just look at him: sitting there with his legs crossed, the coils of hair pressed under his nylons, the way the gauzy blue drape of the dress fell across the dark scrabble of hair on his chest. I could imagine him out shopping for that dress. Slipping secretly into the men's changing room to try it on.

In seventh grade, my best friend Kristin said real girls loved shopping and feathering their hair and Duran Duran and horseback riding, but shopping was boring and horses smelled like poop. Still, I didn't like disappointing people.

Kristin was the tallest girl in class. I was the smallest. She had broad shoulders and a big nose and looked like the seventh-grade girl version of Boy George but with a bit less makeup. When she didn't like what I was wearing, which was often, she made her priss face, squeezing her lips into a sour little strawberry and pointing them at my old jeans and T-shirt.

"Can't you do better than that?"

I kind of hated her, but I liked having a best friend. It's an invaluable thing to have when you don't know how to talk to the kids in your class and are mortified anytime someone notices you're by yourself. Trips to the mall to follow behind Kristin as she tried on denim skirts and plastic sunglasses were a small price to pay for not appearing friendless.

Kristin was the one who told me Tom, a boy in our class, was gay.

"How do you know?" I asked.

She rolled her eyes at me. "Oh, come on. Just listen to his voice."

Tom did have a voice that sounded different. Something thick and almost cloying about it, a gob of honey at the back of his throat. And there was the way his eyes looked, that odd mix of boy and girl in his eyes. Exotic. A weird sort of beautiful. As I looked across the classroom at Tom, I felt a tiny hint of warmth stirring just under my ribcage.

Kristin made her priss face at Tom. Her voice was low and flat and full of distaste. "He's a total fag."

That stirring again, hotter this time. Like pleasure could be shame or shame could be pleasure.

Kristin turned to me. "So, let's go to the mall this weekend!"

Always the mall or horseback riding. It bugged me that she never asked me what I wanted to do, and the last thing I wanted to do was go shopping with Kristin. Trying on outfits while she stood by giving my choices the same priss face she'd just been giving Tom. But at least the mall didn't smell like horse poop.

I did want to love shopping. My best friend Kristin loved shopping. My mom loved shopping. Mom and me out at Mervyn's department store, Mom grinning as we clinked through hangers draped with silver-studded jeans and neon pink tank tops. Mom telling me, "Ooh, now this would look sharp!" She always used words like *sharp*. And *slacks*. Kristin would never say *slacks*. Still: Mom's big grin, the way her eyes arced into pretty crescents when she was having fun and she thought I was, too. There was no one I wanted to enjoy shopping with more than Mom.

I tried, but I just couldn't do it. I hated every kind of shopping. Clothes, books, CDs, jewelry. Faded photos of acrobats on giraffe-neck unicycles. The circus is certainly an exotic subject, and John got so thrilled when he found something new for his collection, but, once you've seen one antique iron-jaw mouthpiece with the tooth prints still intact, you've seen them all.

If only John didn't so enjoy having me there wandering around the antique stores with him. During every jump we made from one town to the next, following the route of the circus, there were antique shops we'd never been to before. I supposed I didn't have to go along with him. I could stay in the van in the hot sun and read a book. Or take a walk and see what I could find. The thing is, all I could find were shops. That's all people wanted to do, shop. And usually we were pulled off on the side of the highway at some antique mall the size of an airplane hangar and there was nothing around for miles but weeds and road.

Of course, this was all an excuse. So I wouldn't have to speak up. One of these days I would speak up. I'd say, "You know what? I hate shopping. There it is: I hate shopping. And today you're going to take me to a museum instead. Or hiking. Or to a movie. And it's going to be a movie that has nothing whatsoever to do with shopping."

Yes, one of these days, I was going to do that.

Having an affair with a gay man made the shopping easier. John and I had been married for fourteen years by this time, and, now when he went wandering up and down the aisles looking for *cartes de visite* of women straddling tigers, I at least had something to think about.

A fabulous artist who painted himself in dresses. The exhibit, which I'd seen on a trip to Portland, Oregon, visiting family, was called "Mythos." Greek mythology all done up in 1930s Hollywood gowns. It was magnificent. A portrait of the artist as Medusa, a chic art deco ingénue with carefully coiffed snake hair, a man's body wrapped up in the slink of cream-colored satin and tulle. Man hands with red nails and diamond bracelets. The elegant cut of a masculine jawline under a mouth soft with red lipstick.

This was nothing like the half-convincing drag John had done on Halloween years ago. The Medusa in the self-portrait was the perfect mix of woman and man, and it was the sexiest thing I'd ever seen.

By affair I mean that the artist and I had a secret online relationship. And by secret I mean not secret. I did tell John about it. Some of it.

"Remember how I told you I saw that art show out in Portland?" I said.

It was the off-season at the circus, and we were sitting around the living room. By living room I mean circus room, one of the many circus rooms in the house, with framed circus posters on the walls and shelves of books and circus movies. John sat sprawled on the couch with piles of circus programs all around and a pad and pen for taking notes. For me to take notes. By now I'd been emailing back and forth with the artist for nearly two months. Offering to help catalog John's collection made me feel slightly less guilty.

"Yeah," I tried again, "that art show? Remember? How I told you?"

John's eyes pointed down at the circus program in his hands. He leafed through pages slowly, gently.

"So, I loved that art show so much," I said, "I wrote the artist a fan email."

John said, "*Mm.*"

"He was so nice," I said, "that he wrote back."

John said, "*Mm.*"

My heart rolled in my chest. Already the thread of my emails with Stephen— wasn't that a nice name, Stephen?—spooled out and out. All the things I was learning about this man, how his grandmother taught him to notice the way objects absorb and reflect light, how he'd been fat as a kid and had never really felt attractive. Personal things, opinions, the kind of talk I rarely got out of John. How luxurious to have someone to really talk to.

But I was keeping it secret. Why was I keeping it secret?

"So, yeah, guess what? We've been emailing back and forth," I said. "A little."

John said, "*Mm.*"

"We talk about art and life and," I said, "art."

John said, "Corner missing on page nineteen," and I wrote it down.

"He lives in Portland, Oregon, and works at some famous bookstore," I said.

John looked up from his stacks of programs, his eyebrows high on his forehead. "Powell's Books?" he said. "That place is amazing! It's three stories high!"

He started telling me about some circus books he'd bought there once, and I let the rest of the conversation go.

Eight months of emails with this man I'd never met, never seen except in paintings of himself in a dress. Eight months but it wasn't a secret, not really, because periodically I mentioned his name to John in passing in order for it not to be a secret. And Stephen and I lived in different states and we were just talking and Stephen was gay, so it's not as if you could really call it an affair, could you; it's not as if he were going to fall in love with me or anything.

I suppose you could say I might fall in love with him. But that love thing—I just wanted to feel it, not necessarily do anything about it. I just wanted to have it.

Eight months, and the things I told him. How inadequate I felt all the time. How I hated shopping and didn't understand fashion and beauty and wished I had someone who could just tell me how to look good. How I wasn't in love with my husband.

Took me the whole eight months to get around to admitting that. It was July again, a full fifteen years since I'd met John, and we were home in Wisconsin while the circus was on a summer break. I was alone in the computer room. By computer room I mean circus room—another of the circus rooms—and I sat surrounded by stand alone shelving units full of antique circus shoes and big papier-mâché costume heads from old circus parades: a clown head, a bird, the three little pigs.

Even now, knowing what I wanted to say, I couldn't say it outright:

> You know how when you're a kid, Christmas has that feel of magical happiness? I remember when I grew up and realized that the feeling wasn't the same anymore. It took me a long time to be okay with that. That's kind of how my marriage is. It took me a long time to come to terms with the fact that the feeling is gone. I've tried to find it again, but I think it's like the magic of Christmas. Once it's gone, it's gone.

A tingle went out to my fingertips as I wrote that word, *gone.*

I knew right then, sitting there under the watchful gaze of papier-mâché pig heads, that I was making the decision to leave.

For fifteen years, this had been unthinkable. To leave. The dread of confrontation, the shame of divorce, the fear of setting out on my own. But here, now, with the word *gone* under my fingers, with racks of clown shoes all around, some fashioned to look like feet, with big white toes and corns painted red, I felt a lightness inside. If I left him—*when* I left him—I'd never again have to set foot inside an antique store. Wouldn't it be lovely if I could just live the rest of my life in cyberspace, in the place where I'd met and gotten to know Stephen? No body to clothe, no home to furnish, no reason to ever go shopping again.

After I left John and moved back to California where I grew up, my mom and I went out shopping. I was ecstatic.

I was thirty-five years old and a free woman with a new life ahead of me. I wanted to look good. I wanted to reinvent myself, as Stephen did in his paintings of himself in women's clothes. Mom said, "Wouldn't it be great to do a little shopping? We have all day; the sky's the limit."

This was going to be fun.

Maybe.

Unfortunately, the stores were as overwhelming as they ever had been, racks and racks of stuff I didn't know what to do with. The jeans were boot cut and straight leg and low rise and high rise and curvy cut and I didn't care, and I didn't know what size I was since I'd spent the last fifteen years wearing mostly leggings I'd had since high school and old T-shirts that used to belong to my brother. When I wasn't wearing plaid clown pants and bow ties. Clown costumes look fine when you've got no shape and you've got no boobs and you aren't trying to impress anyone with your great sense of style and good looks.

Mom made happy crescents of her eyes as I stood in front of the full-length mirror by the changing room, modeling a blazer in bright orange paisley. She grinned at me and I grinned at her, but I had no idea if I liked the blazer or not. No matter what I tried on, it looked the same. A bunch of fabric doing what fabric does to bodies. Hanging there. How the hell was I supposed to know what looked good?

Mom held up a black blouse that looked as if it was made out of the spandex version of burlap. "Try this next! I think this is going to look sharp!"

She kept talking as if we were buying fun new clothes for my trip to visit my aunt and cousin in Portland, but we both knew the one I wanted to look good for was Stephen. Back in the alternate universe of my old life, two months ago, admitting that I didn't love John had led to my admitting that I wanted to leave, which had led to Stephen saying sweet and supportive things, which had led to me admitting I had a little crush on Stephen, which had led to Stephen admitting, amazingly, that he had a little crush on me, and now I was on the verge of flying up to Portland to meet him in the flesh for the first time.

It was ludicrous. Impossible.

Standing in front of the full-length mirror in the black blouse made out of the spandex version of burlap, I struck a model pose, hip out, three-quarter turn. The skirt Mom had picked out was blue and straight to the floor, with buttons running all the way down. I wondered if it made me any less of a new woman, having my mom pick out my clothes, but I just couldn't figure it out on my own. What did it matter? I was a new woman. This was a nice outfit. I did a twirl. I looked slinky. I looked good. This wasn't ludicrous.

How many illusions can you hold on to at once?

I stepped back into the little changing stall to take it all off.

Off through the spitting rain, umbrella up, new shoes quick along the leaf-plastered sidewalk. Off in my new outfit—the blouse made out of the spandex version of burlap and the blue skirt with the buttons running all the way down—off to meet Stephen in person for the first time.

Portland was rust-orange trees and skies as gray and heavy as wet newspaper. I was late. My body was a corked-up bottle of champagne, all sparkle and pressure inside. You could say that pressure was the thrill of what was surely going to be a fantastic encounter with the man I very well might spend the rest of my life with, but you'd probably be laughed off the stage. I was scared he wouldn't be there. Scared he would. Scared I wouldn't recognize him and would stand at the doorway to the coffee shop like a dolled-up doofus.

Lately Stephen and I had graduated to talking on the phone, and, just the other night, I'd remarked casually, again, that I didn't know beans about fashion and beauty, that I just wished I had someone who could tell me what to wear to look good. This was, of course, a preemptive strike. Because what if we met and he was disappointed? I was pretty sure I wouldn't be disappointed. I'd put too much hope into this thing to be disappointed. But Stephen was an artist. With a critical artist's eye. I was not at all certain that my mom's sense of fashion was any better than mine. I was also completely and utterly a girl. What if he didn't like what he saw?

At the doorway to the coffee shop, five minutes late, seven at the most, I stopped. I tried to do that thing where you take a deep breath and center yourself, but my center was a frantic fizz of champagne trying to bust its way through the cork. The cork was in my throat. What if I throw up? That's it. I'll walk in, in my nice new clothes, and throw up on the doormat. Stop. Calm down. It's important to make a good first impression.

I took another breath. I grabbed the knob. The door opened with a jingle bell.

Quick pan through the crowded coffee shop, left to right, then left again, and, yes, there he was, across the room at a table with one empty chair. Looking so weirdly real in his regular jeans and man's button-down shirt. After all my gazing at his face in his paintings, here he was in the flesh, Stephen, six-foot-four, with dark hair, a little mustache, and a soul patch.

I took another deep breath. I was ready. I looked good. I exuded confidence. By which I mean I practically ran down the ramp, across the room, and threw myself at him, grabbed his hand, pumped it up and down, dropped it, then flopped into the empty chair, and leaned in way too close. Stephen stood immediately, as if he might flee the scene.

He said, "Would you like some coffee?"

I didn't need any more energy coursing through my bloodstream.

"Iced mocha," I said. "One shot."

After my energetic entrance at the coffee shop, we'd actually relaxed with our mochas and had a nice, if odd, afternoon. What do you do when you've been sharing the depth of your soul with an artist who paints himself in dresses? You go to the gallery. Where, after all this time, the painting of Medusa looks so small. You look at his art, you look at other artists' art, and you talk about art, a comfortable topic that doesn't get too close to the freak-out that's going on inside both of you.

But later, as we sat having dinner at a table for two, without the illusions of Medusa and Venus and Eros between us, things felt weird. Stephen made rivulets through his pile of Pad Thai with his chopsticks, looking at the noodles, then looking at me. He was too quiet. So of course I was filling that quiet up with anything I could think of.

"Pad Thai," I said. "I guess maybe that just translates to 'Thai noodles.' That seems strange, that there would be a food named after an entire country."

"American cheese," Stephen said.

He smiled, but it was a pained smile, his lips stretched flat across his face.

I tried to be casual. "Whatcha thinking?"

He just flashed more of that smile, and then went back to playing close encounters with his pile of noodles.

"American cheese, that's right," I said. "Although that term was invented by the French. *Fromage Americaine*. It was actually originally called 'Home Plate Cheddar.'"

I was making this up. I didn't know what else to say. The champagne inside me was gone. In its place was Portland sky, that heavy gray, like a slab of wet newspaper.

Stephen looked at me, looked at his noodles.

"Alright," I said. "What?"

A little surprise, that tiny take-charge popping out of my mouth.

He looked up again. "If," he said.

I was starting to get impatient.

"Okay," he said, "it's just that you could look so much better."

Our first date. Me all dolled up in my new outfit. And Stephen was saying, *you could look so much better*.

It was the rudest thing anyone had ever said to me.

I was so relieved.

Stephen's body went all sheepish, and his shoulders tried to swallow up his neck. "Well," he said, "you told me you wished you had someone to tell you what looked good," he said, "and, well, you're so pretty, but you could use just a little," he said.

"What are you trying to say?" I said.

"What would you think," he said, "if I took you shopping?"

My arch nemesis.

Shopping.

But if that was all.

I could handle it.

LET'S SEE HOW FAST
THIS BABY WILL GO

Gloria Harrison

i wake up before 7:00 on the morning of Tuesday, June 4, 1996, and know three things instantly: I'm in labor, I have to return the car to that awful man, and I have to go buy another car. If I don't, I won't have any way to get myself to the hospital. I am twenty years old.

The pain in my belly and lower back is intense and I flop over onto my knees and bounce up and down, which wakes up my roommate Tim, who sort of doubles as my boyfriend.

"I'm in labor," I tell him.

"Are you sure?" he asks, having just spent the last week listening to me declare the same concern regularly. Tim's on standby, as is my sister, Kim, who has a flight arranged from Kansas City. The moment she hears word that I'm at the hospital, delivering, she will grab her packed luggage and the diaper bag she's had waiting, probably since the moment I agreed to let her, and her new husband, adopt my child.

"Yes, I'm sure," I tell Tim. "I'm going to go buy a car."

He considers me through half-open eyes for a moment, says, "Okay," and then rolls back over and goes back to sleep.

The first order of business is to return the used car that I picked up the day before.

My contractions are about ten minutes apart.

I discovered that I'd contracted an acute case of pregnancy within two weeks of moving to Albuquerque from Dallas, where I'd lived for the last five months. I made the decision to place the baby up for adoption not long after, having found myself homeless and broke and with no one to turn to. I told my family that I wouldn't be keeping him and, within a week, my sister Kim called and asked if she and her husband could adopt him. She was twenty-two and had been married for three weeks. "Of course," I said, relieved.

Seven months later, I am no longer broke or homeless. On Christmas day, I walked into a fast food restaurant and told them I needed a job. They hired me on the spot. I met Tim there and he and I found an apartment together soon after. Neither of us had a car.

A week ago, I received a large portion of a $50,000 insurance settlement in the mail, my in-pocket amount from a lawsuit that has been going on since I was seventeen. I had to sue multiple insurance companies—including the one belonging to the drunk with the .28 blood alcohol level who had crashed into my foster family's van nearly three years before. Three people died in the accident, which mangled the rest of us.

I've also had to sue my foster dad, who had collected an upfront check for $25,000, which was supposed to go toward my medical care. He kicked me out a week later, despite the fact that I was on a walker and had nowhere to go. We settled and he had to pay back $15,000 of the money he'd taken. The money came out of his personal account. When his check eventually arrived, the memo read, *gloria's blood money.*

I received my money a week ago and still haven't bought a car. All of the grownups in my life have an opinion about what kind of car I should drive and I'm scared and unsure of my ability to make a decision. And I actually really don't care; I just want mobility. Last night, at the behest of Tim's stepdad, I went to a car lot that sells used rental cars. The slimy salesman delivered his spiel to Tim, not me, even though I made it clear that I was the one with the money. Still, he barely looked at me and, instead, locked eyes with Tim while he explained the great benefits of buying this great car with low miles at this unbelievable price.

I was not interested in this car, and I told the salesman that.

"Tell you what," he said derisively, finally looking at me, "you just drive it home tonight—free of charge—and think about it."

Now I have this burdensome car to deal with before I can buy my Nissan, which is what I have wanted from the start. Tim's stepdad was pushy and insistent about not buying a car new off the lot. And though I'm normally incapable of standing up for myself against aggressive men, I'm now currently in labor and I feel a strength and self-composure I've never felt before. I don't want this fucking rental car and I don't care who knows it.

I drive the car over to the lot, which is conveniently located on the same boulevard as most of the car lots in town. I walk into the office, find the swaggering salesman, hand him the keys, and tell him I changed my mind. His mouth drops open and, incredulous, he frantically begins negotiating with me all over again. He stands too close and speaks too loudly. The contractions are coming more frequently now—perhaps seven minutes apart—and the urgency to take care of the business at hand fills me with confidence. I tell him I have to go—I'm going down the street to the Nissan dealership to buy the car I wanted in the first place.

I begin walking off the lot and he shouts after me, "That car will lose $5,000 in value the second you drive it off the lot!" My back is to him and I can't see his face, but I swear he spits on the ground when he's done shouting.

By 9:00, I'm walking the two blocks to Melloy Nissan, telling myself that walking is good for labor. I enter the building and look around. I see a customer service window, walk up to it, and ask the representative, "Do you have a female salesperson?"

A few minutes later, Carolyn walks up. I can tell right away that she's a nice lady. She makes eye contact with me, shakes my hand, and introduces herself. "Looks like you're due pretty soon, huh?" she says, gesturing toward my massive midsection.

"Yes, today, actually," I tell her, stretching the truth by a few weeks. "I'm in labor."

Next thing I know, Carolyn is showing me my options. I know that I want a Sentra and I don't want any bells and whistles, just the basic package. This makes the decision easy. There are only two cars that meet my desires, and I just have to decide between teal and black. I'm leaning toward black, but Carolyn explains that black cars are harder to keep clean, since dirt shows up on them so easily. While we have this discussion, I'm pacing in circles, holding my lower back and choo-chooing every few minutes.

"Can I test drive it?" I ask.

Carolyn looks at me, startled and uneasy. "Sure," she says, and within three minutes she has the keys and we're on our way in the teal car.

We don't drive far and, to be honest, I'm not even sure why I want to test drive the car, other than, as always, I'm preemptively explaining myself to the overlords in my head. Test driving is something I understand as a necessary step in the car-buying process. I know I'm buying this car and I know that I would buy it even if Carolyn had said no to taking it for a spin. Carolyn tries to chat me up while we're driving, asking me about my pregnancy and the father.

"I'm putting it up for adoption," I tell her. Carolyn talks to me about this for the duration of the drive and, when I answer, my voice rises an octave each time I have a contraction.

Next thing I know, Carolyn and I are in her office, and there is paperwork in front of me. I have a checkbook to an account that holds nearly enough money to buy the car outright, but Carolyn is trying to finance the whole amount. She explains that if they take a personal check, they have to hold it for a week until it clears and I won't get my car today. My contractions are now about six minutes apart and I know I have to get to the hospital.

Banks are called; documents are faxed. A man comes in and tries to discuss floor mat options with me. I am highly agitated and I stand up every few minutes to pace and pant. The frenzy of activity around me is intense—suddenly all the sales associates are in the room, each trying desperately to help the pregnant girl get the car bought before a head emerges from her vagina in the middle of the showroom floor.

Finally, my brain kicks into action and I announce how it's going to be. I don't want to finance the whole amount. Even in my less-than-right mind, I know that 22 percent interest is a lot and I just want to pay for as much as I can right there. I tell them all that I know it's against their policy to take a personal check, but I need to get to the hospital. And if the check bounces, which it won't, they know where to find me. If they can't agree to this, then I'm just going to call a cab and come back another time. I tell the floor mat guy that I don't give a rip about my options, I'll just take whichever mats come stock with the car—and if I change my mind, I'll come back and upgrade later.

Within twenty minutes, Carolyn has her manager's approval to take my check and my car is waiting in the front lot.

Carolyn hands me my keys and tells me this is the quickest she's ever seen the car-buying process happen in all of her time in sales.

"One last thing," she says. "You have to go get insurance. I've already called a local agent, whose office is located two blocks away. She is waiting for you and has your paperwork ready to sign."

I thank Carolyn and she wishes me good luck and I'm off.

I drive to the insurance agent's office, only vaguely aware that I am driving my first new car ever. My manic obsession to buy a car—to buy *this* car—is now overtaken by my manic obsession to get to the hospital. I'm not aware of it, but I need something tangible in place after I've had this baby that is fighting his way out of my body. I'm not yet aware that, after he leaves, I'll transfer all my maternal love onto this car. That this car will literally help me run away from all the shit I've been through and am going through. I don't know it yet, but the freedom this car will bring me will help put 130,000 miles of distance between the me that I've been and the me that I will become.

I don't know it yet, but tomorrow the nurse will bring newborn Dillon into my hospital room right after Kim calls to announce that her flight has landed and she is on her way to the hospital. Dillon will come in and I will look down at him and I will cry. I will tell him I'm so very sorry that I couldn't keep him, but that I'm positive that I've found a surrogate who's just right and that I know he'll be loved. I will tell him that I love him, that I will always love him. I also don't know yet that I will stare at him so long that my nipples will start tingling. I will have an almost crippling need to pick him up and place him to my breast and let him nurse. "Just for a second," I will tell myself. But the moment I start to reach out, the exact moment, my sister will come walking in and instead of picking Dillon up to breastfeed him, I will pick him up and hand him to his mom.

And then, then I will begin driving.

FOR YOUR AGE

Susan Senator

'm what you'd call a young fifty—I pass easily for forty-five, sometimes even a few years younger—but for a long time this hadn't helped me much. My mental age was catching up with me and with it, my beauty style was changing. The old familiar ways of dressing no longer worked that well for me. I no longer knew what to look like. I didn't know which clothing type I was anymore. In my world, not knowing your look is tantamount to not knowing what your persona is. And indeed, it was almost as if I didn't know who I was anymore.

This may seem like an overstatement, and a first world problem, and I suppose it was. But it was a pretty painful problem for me. I would get out of bed each morning and feel paralyzed by not knowing what I was supposed to wear. Yes, I knew who I was to the degree that a normal garden-variety neurotic white upper-middle-class overeducated Jewish woman can. I was in good shape, I had a reasonable BMI, I have always been basically a size 6-8-10 depending on the store. It was not about thinness. Well, sort of. The slimness entered into it when I realized there were clothes in my closet that I simply could not wear anymore—because *they* didn't fit. They didn't fit and they probably would never fit again. Some of these had been favorites for about six or seven years—the black satin cocktail dress with the ruffly hem, for instance, which had a neckline that was meant for a much smaller, controlled bustline. Back then I could strategically fasten a fabric flower there; now I would need an entire bouquet for coverage. I loved that dress, as much as I loved the tiny black top with the hot pink sash and the size 4 skirt I wore with it. But now there were a few inches here and especially there that prevented my clothing from closing. My zippers bared their teeth at each other across my wide back, and nothing could get them to make peace with each other. Even though I exercised regularly and ate sensibly enough, there was just something that had shifted on me, physically, and, no matter what I did, those inches and five to ten extra pounds were there. It was nothing anyone else could really see, or so they told me.

There was just something different about me from ten years ago, when I felt Fabulous at forty and could wear anything I wanted. This may be because Fabulous at forty really meant I could pass for someone in my thirties, and they *really* can wear anything they want. Of course, the alliterative possibilities are still there for fifty, but it just doesn't sound right. And that's because it doesn't feel right. Sure, I felt kind of fabulous some of the time, but what happened then was I would get the *qualified* fabulous. I would tell people I'm fifty, they would usually say something like, "Wow, you look great for your age!" Why did they have to add that last bit? And so, it was the "For Your Age" Fifty, and that did not feel that fabulous.

Back in my forties I discovered Anthropologie, and, with it, a kind of fashion identity. I remember first walking into that store, with its stage-set decor, festoons of floor-to-ceiling filmy fabric, dazzling castlelike stacks of glassware in their home section, and artfully scuffed country French sofas strategically placed for tired husbands and boyfriends. And the clothes—! It was like playing dress-up, only I didn't have to return the clothing to grandma's closet at the end of the day. I had always been a romantic, a girly girl, and so the racks and racks of lacy tops, velvet brocade bustiers, and bejeweled angora sweaters filled my heart with excitement. And yet the stuff was not simply romantic; there was also a funky, urban edge to most things, such as blouses purposefully askew and cashmere with gigantic, mismatched buttons. It was Scarlett O'Hara meets Carrie Bradshaw. Here was a store that understood me.

And so I pretty much bought all my clothing at Anthropologie. I didn't have to worry about looking fat or old, because I was also a young forty and so I felt I could wear anything. A-lines, pencils, I probably could have even worn dirndls, for God's sake. In this particular Anthropologie, the sales items were not crammed into a little seven-by-seven room, as is the practice in most stores; they actually took up the back quarter of the store. I could brush aside hanger after hanger of shirts or skirts, ingeniously arranged by color. I was in fashion heaven and I knew it.

Every now and then, I'd have to cheat on Anthropologie because I was a bit of a clothing slut, and so I'd dip into J. Crew. Why judge me? You can't always be frilly-hip. Sometimes you need just a plain cardigan. The Jackie cardigan at J. Crew was fifty-nine dollars back then and now it is sixty-eight dollars, sort of reasonable, because you can wear them forever and they go with anything. J. Crew's was a classic look, a cold refreshing glass of water after the sticky pink milk shake at Anthro. Even though I was slimmer than I ever had been, I was still not meant to be with J. Crew in the long run because the chest button on every top of theirs barely stayed buttoned. In my heart I knew I was not meant to run with the preppy sailing crowd that grinned lanky and untucked from their delicious catalog.

Still, I had found my look, and, in my early forties, I also found my voice. I published my first book, appeared on the *Today Show* with it. I felt like the sky was the limit. I got invited to a dinner at the White House. I broke with tradition and shopped for that at Marshall's, finding the perfect pale pink gown almost immediately. I felt like Cinderella.

The clock eventually struck twelve—in this case, fifty. With three books under my belt and two of my sons leaving the nest, I knew I was on the brink of a change. And indeed, something had changed; I was not the person I'd been at forty. My body was different, almost overnight. My weight had shifted more to my middle, and my old form of dieting no longer worked. I realized that I really was not the person I was at forty. I was now fifty. And so far it only felt like the end of things. I started feeling a little bit scared, because I did not know what I wanted to do, now that my kids were—now that I was—grown-up.

I slipped into a pretty bad depression. I spent a lot of time indoors, on my computer, and, of course, surfing the net. I often went to the Anthropologie page. Maybe it was depression, or maybe because of the static two-dimensional mode of lap-shopping, but for some reason this online shopping gave me no pleasure. The home page of the store was always beautiful, always enticing. A leggy brunette leaning, eyes closed, against an aqua-tiled wall in Morocco. Her layered cottons were just right, strewn across her body in faux mismatch. Her four-inch platform sandals wrapped around her tanned ankles so delicately, so right; they truly did seem like the perfect walking shoes for touring Marrakesh. I'd take my cyber walk to the back of the store—the menu item marked "sale"—and click through dress after dress. Ugly, weird, strange. Then sweaters, then tops. Sometimes shoes. There were the brunette's Moroccan platforms: $238, but, without her feet inside them, they looked like garishly colored gaping-mouth fish. I'd end up buying nothing, telling myself I should go to the store and try them on there. My virtual shopping cart always had at least two things in it, and when I'd go online later I would wonder what I saw in them.

I'd close the tab and get Anthropologie off my desktop, but I was not done yet. I needed something. My empty feeling inside wanted filling, and I just kept hoping I'd find it in a clothing store. I'd go to the actual store and gather armloads of flowy tops, blouses, and casual dresses, just like in the old days. But the cuts were wrong somehow; they were strange. The colors were all a bit retro, in that college-girl thrift-store way: tarnished yellows, 1950s Studebaker blues, rusty reds. The off-center plackets or the empire waists sometimes fit, but they looked awful on me. "Does this make me look pregnant?" I'd ask a shopping buddy, who would look at me with something like pity and say, "No! Not at all!" Sometimes I actually wanted them to say "Yes!" because that would mean that I still looked young enough to be pregnant.

Around this time I started riding my bike nearly every day. I had always been a faithful exerciser, but it was at a gym, and it was not for fun; it was for fitness. But bike riding was different. It was the only time when I felt good, because I found I couldn't think while on my bike. I'd start a thought like, "Okay, so what am I going to do about—" and suddenly I'd lose track and hear the tires. In the late summer I biked off-road; in the winter I rode in the ice and snow. I sought out hills. The bigger the challenge, the better. The joy of the fresh air rushing at me, the bursting relief in my lungs as I finally topped a hill, the high after five miles—this became everything to me. The ride was so important to me; nothing must spoil it. And this meant that I had to dress right for it. Leggings that wicked moisture. Layers that could be easily removed. Puffy, ugly, but oh-so-warm fleece. I'd go out looking like a fat round beetle with all my layers, my helmet, and big sunglasses—and I found I didn't care, because it was all about staying outside as long as possible. I knew I did not look feminine, and sometimes I even looked fat, but for the first time in my life, I was happy anyway.

I started going to a bike store near a local university to get repairs, which I needed more and more frequently. It was so different from walking into Anthropologie or J. Crew. In those stores I knew what I wanted. I could tell the salespeople, "No, I don't need any help," but "sure, start me a fitting room." But in the bike store, run and operated by guys, I was shy and unsure of myself. I felt in the beginning that I almost wasn't supposed to be there. It was like a club, with people walking around looking like spindly insects in their tight spandex bike clothes with mud on their calves. These guys could pop off a wheel, disembowel the intestinal tire with the grace of a Samurai, and flip in a new tube in minutes. They talked about crankshafts and toe clips and twenty-nine-inchers. They were confident, subtly macho, beautifully fit young men. I skulked around the edges, asking why my bike made that jingly noise, wishing I could be like them.

Gradually, as I visited there more and more, they got to know me by my first name. They even knew the name of my old bike: Mr. Yamamoto, because of the Sumo wrestler horn on the handlebars. Chris, the guy in repairs, showed me how to change a tire. Mark taught me how to wear bike shoes. And Travis introduced me to the world of specialized mountain bikes. Just before I turned fifty, I bought a top-of-the-line mountain bike, bright red, with huge knobby tires that could crush anything in their way. I named her Scarlett, after that tough Southern beauty.

There was nothing like riding with Scarlett. It wasn't just the speed. It was the feeling of strength. Mountain biking is the sport of young men, after all, guys who go hotdogging off boulders and skidding through forests. Suddenly, that was me—or what I wanted to be. And biking was *not* exercise: It was play. It was everything. It was—fun. I realized that, at fifty, biking was helping me become a kid again.

I still went clothes shopping, but I really had a hard time buying things. My body was different—not thinner, because biking did not help me lose weight. I ate more and I couldn't help it. I could not put my finger on what was different, except for more muscular thighs and that fifty-year ring around my waistline. But the stores like Anthropologie were definitely not for me anymore. Not only the slip-of-a-girl fit of the clothes, but the whole hipster romantic ethos made me feel like an impostor. And J. Crew? Fuggedaboutit. Those clothes, with their neon brights and conservative cuts, felt like Pat Nixon in Miami Beach. I felt ridiculous in there.

Eventually my clothes shopping became mostly about bike gear, and how to improve my ride with the right accessories. What were the warmest fabrics? Did charcoal hand warmers work in the toes of my sneakers, or were the neoprene shoe-wrappers better? How could I keep my eyes from tearing in the wind? These were the questions that occupied my thoughts, rather than how to wear a one-shoulder top with a 34DD granny bra.

I'd like to say that ever since I bought Scarlett, I'm a new woman, that trying to look like a thirty-something no longer matters to me. But it's not that simple. I still look in Anthropologie, in the sales area, searching for something, that perfect something. I guess I'm still nostalgic for my slip-of-a-girl days. A part of me still wishes I could look like fortyish me, and that there will be an outfit at Anthro that will prove I "still got it." Once I find it, I will see that I'm not old yet. But I just haven't yet. And it's not getting any easier, for I *am* getting older—old—and that is a hard fact to grasp in a country where people strive to be a size zero. I go into the stores, and I go out, usually empty-handed. But no longer empty inside. Because as long as I can suit up, beetle-style, and puff up some hills, I am okay. I am more than okay: I am whole, and happy. I never thought I'd be the outdoorsy type; I never thought I would exult in being strong and daring. A badass. And so, what's my look now? I guess you could call me Biker Babe.

Janet Clare

O ne of my earliest memories of shopping was going up the escalator of a local department store with my mother gently poking me in the back to make me stand up straight. I'm not sure how old I was, maybe ten or eleven, old enough to be embarrassed and none too happy about it.

My mother wasn't mean, although perhaps a bit insensitive, but she's ninety-six now, so I've pretty much left that particular incident in the dust. I think. However, I recall most shopping trips with her as a kind of endurance test. She was fond of weaving in and out of the aisles looking at everything while I trudged behind, uninterested and bored, wanting nothing more than to go. Please, can't we just go?

No doubt, this early experience with my mother is at least partly responsible for my general lack of interest in shopping to this day. Certainly I lack the enthusiasm for what I call hard-core shopping—schlepping from store to store, rack to rack, searching through every item . . . for hours. I have friends with great wardrobes who do this on a regular basis.

I don't have a great wardrobe. Still, I manage to get dressed every day. Because I do like to buy things; I just don't like to shop for them. I like to walk down a street and happen upon a store and happen to go in and happen to find something I can afford that fits. I especially like shoes because you don't have to take off your clothes to try them on, which is particularly wonderful when traveling or in really cold weather. Also, I'm happy enough to go into a tried and true store, spend maybe twenty minutes checking out the merchandise, find a couple of things, and dash. Having gone through times of plenty and times of scarcity, I know how to look in store windows and keep on walking, and, at this point in my life, I rarely covet anything. More important, I'm old enough to know that whatever we have is transitory and merely on loan. Pass it on, hand it down, hopefully to a welcoming recipient.

This became even more obvious to me a couple of years ago when I helped my mother move from her home of forty years to a small apartment in an assisted living facility. She went from a closet the size of a small chalet to a closet the size of a closet. She was a trooper, ruthless even, and together we sifted through tons of clothes, handbags, shoes, belts, hosiery, hats, scarves, and jewelry collected for years, meticulously hung and boxed. Nevertheless, after the move there was still too much. My niece, a professional organizer, stood in front of her grandmother and held up her choices. "Here are six pink shirts, you get three." And my mother would choose, seeming relieved of the whole process.

Her closet is full once again, but she still needs things, she says, and so I take her shopping. Her eyes wander over the store, checking it all out. But she tires easily now and moves slowly with her walker. I fetch her things from the racks in seconds. She knows what she likes and she buys what she wants and we leave. It's a much faster trip these days and I'm more than happy to do it. Always independent, perhaps to a fault, my mother needs me more, and, in fact, I think she likes me more. She tells me she loves me, something I don't recall hearing as a child, and she misses me if I'm gone for a few days. How different from her own years of travel. Well, I love her, too, and it seems we've somehow met in the middle. So, yes, I shop for her and with her and do whatever I can, aware that I'm also doing it for myself. This time, after all, is finite. And now, of course, I'm the one in the driver's seat.

THE ONE THAT GOT AWAY

Jennifer Finney Boylan

When I go fishing, I go with my son Luke. We leave early in the morning, when the mist still rises off the lake. Luke will have his rod and reel, a sandwich, a carton of worms. In his tackle box is a Hula Popper, a spoon, a tiny-trout Rapala, and a fake mouse. We get in the boat and start up the engine, and I ask him where he wants to go, and he points out across the still water.

When I go shopping with Grace, we, too, leave in the morning, heading down the highway south. In her purse Grace will have a cell phone, her credit cards, a tube of ChapStick. We'll pull over at the Quick Stop to get a couple of bottles of water, and maybe, if it's early enough, more coffee. Then we'll get back in the car and drive to Freeport, Maine.

By midmorning, if I'm fishing, Luke and I are in a groove. I'll cut the engine about twenty feet from the shore, and, with the right breeze, we'll just drift along for a while. We don't talk a lot, Luke and I, not when we're in the boat. Mostly we look at the water, or at the pine trees on the shore. Now and again we look at each other, and he smiles with all the bright wattage of his ten-year-old self, and I smile back.

I like to start out with a plastic jelly-slug. This ties right on the end of my line, and there's a weight inside it so I can get a little momentum on my cast. Then I sit in a tall chair, in the back of the boat near the outboard, and I cast the jelly-slug out so it lands about five feet from the shore. I reel it back in slowly, and, as I do, I jig the end of the rod so the jelly-slug hops along the bottom of the lake. Ideally,

I'll draw it across a bass nest, and a mamma bass will rush forward, mistaking it for a predator, and grab it with her mouth.

Grace likes to start out at the L.L. Bean outlet store. I try to pull the Hyundai into the big lot right near the warehouse, but sometimes I have to park down the street behind the Patagonia. As we walk toward the outlet, we'll look in the windows on our way there and see what's going on in the other stores, maybe even detour into the Dansk outlet and look at the patterns on the pasta bowls, at water glasses and espresso machines and sherbet cups.

Grace and I talk while we're shopping, sometimes about things of no particular consequence: the weather, the Atkins diet, our workouts. Sometimes the talk will be serious, too—about our children, about my mother. Less frequently, we talk about our own inscrutable relationship, perhaps because it's a question that doesn't have any particular answer.

That question—namely, what are you two?—is one that continues to bewilder and occasionally amuse us, as it no doubt amuses others. Born James, I came out as transgender in 2000; after a long transition, my wife and I decided to stay together, even though she still identifies as straight. We know what we're not: we're not lesbians; we're not man and wife; sometimes we call ourselves "quasbians." And yet we are a family, we are best friends, and we are, in our own way, lovers. For the most part we have accepted the unsettled, ambiguous nature of our relationship, and, though it is hard to have something this unresolved right in the center of our lives, we also know that what we have kept is more important than what we have lost. Quite frankly, we know a lot of couples who are more intimate than Grace and I are who like each other a whole lot less.

The people who love us occasionally ask us, not unreasonably, when we'll start to see other people, when we'll "move on." We know that behind this question is a well-intended concern for our own futures, but it is hard, sometimes, not to feel as well the weight of normative culture behind it. The suggestion is clear: you two aren't ever going to be happy until you each find a man. Even though one of you used to be one.

The fact that we are content with each other, and with our little family, at least for now, is hard for many people to accept. A dear friend pulled Grace aside at one point and said, meaning to be kind, "What you need to do is get a divorce and move on with your life."

To which Grace had replied, "You don't understand. This is my life."

We were at first bemused, and then frustrated, by the urgency with which other people wanted us to get a divorce. But in time what became clear was that it wasn't our world that they wanted to restore to some equilibrium; it was their own. After all, if two straight women could be legally married and in love with each other and raise their children, then all sorts of other things might be possible. And these were the kinds of possibilities that, to some people, destabilized the world. It seemed odd to us that a simple family—defined by the same issues of parenthood, work, and love as most other families—could be responsible for the unraveling of reality. We didn't think of ourselves as unravelers, and we didn't think of things like fishing, or shopping, as radical. But maybe this wasn't a revolution we fought. Maybe, instead, it was a revolution we lived.

By midmorning, if I'm fishing, things have gotten serious, especially if we haven't had a strike. Luke will have snapped one lure and then another onto his swivel, and the longer we go without a bite, the more silent it gets. We'll feel the sun beating down on us, and I'll ask him if he remembered to put on sunscreen, and he'll look at me and reply with an annoyance well out of proportion to the situation, "Yes, Maddy."

Then I'll suggest we start up the motor and try somewhere else, and Luke will just sigh and say something like, "It doesn't matter. We'll never catch anything, ever again."

If Grace and I have gone for a couple of hours without finding anything, we, too, will have fallen silent, a faint air of crabbiness beginning to cast a pall upon our adventure. Grace will depart for L. L. Bean's fitting room with an armful of things, only to return fifteen minutes later empty-handed. "These sizes are running small," she'll say, with a faint air of disgust, and, if I suggest that she go for the next size up, she'll just give me a look. Then I'll suggest we go somewhere else—maybe Ralph Lauren or the Jones New York outlet, and she'll just sigh. "Whatever, Jenny," she says. "There are no clothes for me."

Then it happens: the first strike. Luke's line bends like a willow branch, and his line goes out like kite string. "Maddy," he'll say, breathlessly, and a little scared. "I got one!" I'll put my rod down and go over and stand next to him. "Let him play with it for a while first," I say. "Don't pull him in too soon."

"What do you think it is?" I say. "I hope it's a pike!" Luke has been wanting to catch a pike all summer.

"I think it's a bass, from the way he's running with it."

Suddenly, about twenty feet from the boat, we see an enormous fish, jumping into the air, the white underbelly flashing in the sun, Luke's line flying through the air, his Hula Popper in the fish's mouth. "Maddy!" he shouts, so excited he almost drops his rod. "It's a largemouth!"

The fish goes down again, and Luke's rod is alive, bending and twisting like a small tree in a hurricane.

Then, all at once, things are silent, and the rod goes dead. "What happened?" says Luke. "What happened?"

But we both know what's happened. By the time Luke has reeled his line back in, the fish is long gone. So, too, is Luke's lure. The end of the line, snapped by the enormous fish, blows loosely in the summer breeze.

We're in Jones New York now. Grace is wearing a lime-green pastel jacket and looking at herself in the three-way mirror. "Jenny," she says, "does this look okay?"

"It looks fantastic on you," I say, and it does.

She takes it up to the front counter. "Can I leave this here?" she says, and a somewhat disinterested clerk nods, sure, okay. Then she's back into the store to see what else she can find. Now that we know there are bargains to be found, we're working the room. There was a matching skirt, Grace says, that she figures is probably also on sale. Suddenly the morning is bright with prospects, and the two of us are thinking, *It's a great day for retail.*

But we don't find that skirt, and, when Grace returns to the front counter ten minutes later, travesty ensues. Another customer, observing Grace's good fortune, picked up the jacket she'd set aside, took it to another register, and made off with it. Now Grace's jacket, a jacket clearly designed with her in mind, bringing out her pretty green eyes, is somewhere out in Freeport, maybe already in the back of someone else's car. Grace is devastated. "But that was my jacket," she laments.

"I'm sorry, ma'am," says the clerk, but we both think, *Not sorry enough.*

After Luke's tremendous strike, we get serious, convinced by our own eyes of the nearness of fish. I switch over to a Hula Popper, nearly identical to the one Luke was using, and he clips a similar backup lure onto his swivel. We aren't talking at all now; we are just casting out lures and reeling them in. Surely, we think, if it worked once, it will work a second time.

But the minutes pass, and there are no more strikes.

Grace and I move on to Ralph Lauren, aware now that there are bargains out there and that someone is getting them. We separate now, each of us working our own end of the store—she among the Polo shirts, me among the jeans. It is probably worth noting that my identity as a woman has never derived from clothes; for me, the sense of self has always come from within. If, in keeping with my hippie sensibility, I have had a caustic relationship with fashion in general, that attitude is not ameliorated by the fact that the fashions I encounter in stores seem generally aimed at someone other than my middle-aged self. All around me are the twenty-year-old girls for whom all jeans are designed. The waists of their jeans ride so amazingly low that, if they were any lower, they'd be socks. It's a good look for them, less so for me, and, what's worse, I can't find what appears to be a good look for me, in part because I'm forty-six and in part because I'm almost six feet tall. Even the "long" size jeans fall well above my ankles, and, by the time I rendezvous with Grace, I'm surly. It's some consolation that she's nearly as surly as I am, having been unable to find a shirt that fits, and so the two of us head back out onto the streets of Freeport, ready to kill.

Luke and I pull up at a small island and tie the boat's mooring rope around a tree. Then we sit down on a rock and eat our lunches. He's got roast beef and a Kraft single on two slices of whole wheat, a Capri Sun juice bag, a plum, and a bag of pretzel goldfish. I've got a pita with chicken salad, a banana, and an iced tea. The sun is twinkling on the water, and we listen to the waves slapping the side of the boat.

Luke eats his plum. "You know, when you were a baby, you loved plums," I point out.

Luke looks at me, still surly from our fruitless expedition. "Maddy," he growls, but he doesn't mean it. Maddy is the name my children call me, their combination of "Mommy" and "Daddy."

When he finishes his lunch, Luke comes over and puts his arm around me. "This is a good day," he says. Then adds, "Except for us not catching any fish."

"We'll catch some fish," I say, but I'm in no hurry to get back in the boat. For a while we sit there with our arms around each other, watching the water.

Then we get back in the boat. "Come on, Maddy," he says. "They're biting."

"You know I love you, right, Luke?"

He rolls his eyes. "Duh," he says.

Grace and I go out to the Onion, a nice old diner in the center of Freeport. We both have lobster rolls and iced tea and ripple chips. We talk about her brother Tex, about her sister Bonnie, who died two years ago.

"Now that was a woman who could shop," I say.

"Jenny," Grace observes, "what she could do was buy. Anybody can buy. It takes an artist to shop."

I nod because, as always, Grace has hit the nail on the head. After Bonnie died, we found a storage unit filled with all sorts of stuff she'd bought in a panic, things she couldn't afford and didn't need—stacks of china, patterned silver, boxes of clothes she never wore, some of which had the original price tags still attached.

After lunch, Luke and I change our strategy, and it's not one that brings either of us much joy. After a whole morning of being skunked, it's time to fish with worms.

When you fish with worms, you stand a much better chance of catching something; in fact, in our lake, if you can't catch something with a worm, you might as well just get out of the fishing business altogether. This is the very reason fishing with worms is joyless. You're almost guaranteed to catch a fish, but the fish you're likely to catch is one you don't especially want to land. Bluegills—which back in my Pennsylvania childhood we called "sunnies"—are what you catch with worms, and their sharp spines will jab you if you don't carefully arc your hand down their back first. Once, it was possible to catch yellow perch in this lake with worms, but in the last few years the pike—which are not native to the Belgrade Lakes—have taken over everything, and eaten most of the yellow perch for lunch. It's not just the perch the pike have decimated, either—the land-locked salmon, for which this lake was once famous, are mostly gone now, too.

Luke and I climb into the boat and then drift among the islands. He's got a bobber on his line, and now he's staring at the waters of Long Pond, waiting for his bobber to disappear. We are surrounded by soft sounds—the lapping of waves, the wind rushing through the trees, the weird laughter of loons.

By early afternoon, Grace and I are doing the shopping equivalent of worm fishing, which is the Gap. If things don't pan out in the Gap, then we're off to Old Navy, or, god forbid, T.J. Maxx. There's no question we'll find something we can wear in one of these stores—but the clothes here are likely to be the retail synonym of bluegills. There will be the same baggy T-shirts that all the other moms our age are wearing, the same Capri pants, the same not particularly flattering jeans. We know that we will find things we need here, and that some of these things might even be cheap—at least compared to Ralph Lauren or Jones New York. But it's not the same, and, even as we head to the fitting rooms to try on things we know will fit, I can tell what Grace is thinking about. It's that perfect lime-green jacket she found before and lost. The one that got away.

We are surrounded by music here, that horrible, insulting, car-crash music that blasts in every store in America. For the life of me, I don't understand this, even though I love rock and roll, love playing music. But the tunes played in stores now are the kind you'd hear in a SoHo disco at 2 AM, and why this is considered the optimum music for shopping I have never understood. This music makes me feel old, and feeling old makes me grumpy. I hear the voice of my mother, shouting up the stairs. *Hey, you kids! Turn that music down! I can't hear myself think!*

Luke's rod suddenly bends again, and once more his line unwinds off his reel just about as fast as it can go. "Maddy," he says, "I got one!"

And this is no bluegill he's nabbed, either. It's another largemouth, as we can see when it surfaces and slaps against the water.

"Let him play with it," I counsel Luke again. "Try to tire him out a little first."

"Maddy," Luke says, as if to say, *I got it.*

I stand by his side, watching him work the fish. His tongue ticks out, Charlie Brown–style, as he concentrates on reeling in his catch. When the fish draws near the boat, I lean over the gunwale with the net, and slowly I draw it around the fish.

When we get it onto the boat, Luke and I just stand there for a while admiring the bass. It's a very nice largemouth, maybe seven or eight pounds. It's still thrashing around, the tail whipping back and forth.

"It's a feisty fella!" Luke says, bursting with pride.

"It sure is," I say. "A nice one."

We stand there for what seems like a long time—but what is probably less than a minute—enthralled by the bass, and then my son looks at me and says, "Throw him back now?" and I say, "Okay."

I take the fish—which Luke doesn't particularly want to touch—and gently wrap it in a towel, so as not to disturb the mucosal lining on his green skin. Then I take the hook out of its mouth, and bend down, and hold the bass underwater for a moment. It's been a traumatic couple of minutes for the fish, and it takes several seconds to get its bearings. Then, with a flip of its tail, it heads back out into the lake. Luke looks at me, older than he was a moment ago.

"That's the biggest one I ever caught," he says, with evident pride.

I nod, pick up my rod, and cast out again with my worm. Luke just sits on his chair, enjoying the sunshine, done now. A moment later, when I catch a stupid little bluegill, Luke just looks at me. "Oh, a bluegill," he says, as if recalling the word from a long time ago. "They're nice to catch, too, I guess."

Grace finds a pair of white capris in the Gap, and, if they're not exactly on sale, they're still a good buy. I find a peach-colored top with a built-in shelf bra.

I pick up some shorts and a khaki skirt and some socks, and we feel content enough, after the checkout, to head north. We stop off at the lobster pound on the way home and get a mess of steamers and some pound-and-a-halfers for ourselves and for Paddy and Luke, as well as a pound of butter. For a moment I think about the fact that in two summers I've gone from a size ten to a twelve, about the amount of food I eat that gets dipped in melted butter—but then I decide this is an insane theory, better off discarded. I know, in the long run, that I'd rather eat lobster than be thin.

We talk more on the way home, Grace and I, about our mothers and fathers and children. It's over an hour from Freeport to our house on the lake, and, after a while, our conversation peters out and we just drive along in silence. Now and again Grace looks over at me, her eyes still twinkling, her face still as beautiful as when I first saw it, twenty-five years ago.

The lobsters rustle in their brown bag.

There aren't a lot of days left in the summer, but there are enough. The next morning, the day is clear, and we all get up early. Grace and I put on our new clothes.

She sits on the dock as the boys and I cast out our lines. Grace looks at the three of us. "Hey," she says, drinking her coffee. "Maddy, Luke, Paddy. You know I love you, right?"

We look back at her for a moment. Mist is rising off the water. I say, "I do."

SHOPPING FOR BREASTS

Wendy Staley Colbert

W hat size are you thinking?" the plastic surgeon asked.

I sat shirtless in the oversize, faux leather examining chair as he eyed the twin slits remaining on my chest four weeks after the mastectomy. I slipped a C-cup silicone breast prosthesis out of one side of the bra I'd worn into the office. "I used to be an A-cup. Can you match this?" He palmed the three-dimensional, triangular blob and then pressed it against one of my incisions, using the tips of his fingers to hold it in place. "I don't see why not. You're tall—you can carry any volume you want. Let's go with a 350 cc."

As a cancer patient, I felt a little sheepish asking for bigger breasts. I worried I was selling out to our society's beauty standard. But another part of me wanted the fun, sexiness, and visual appeal of a larger bustline.

The doctor wheeled backward on his stool, opened a drawer, and pulled out a crescent-shaped expander. I had liked him immediately. He seemed practical, matter-of-fact in the face of my cancer, the way I hoped in my best moments to be. He explained the surgery would involve placing two of these, filled with saline, in my chest to begin stretching the skin and muscle to shape mounds that would eventually house the implants.

After being diagnosed with early-stage breast cancer at age forty-three, I viewed my choice to have a mastectomy and then reconstruct my breasts as a privilege. My grandmother died of metastasized cancer in her forties. My mom had a lumpectomy and radiation following her diagnosis of cancer in her forties. I realized many women with more advanced breast cancer didn't have a choice of treatment options. Still, I wondered about the function my new breasts would serve. I no longer needed them for any practical purpose, such as breast-feeding. I would no longer derive the same sexual satisfaction from them, since they would be numb and my nipples were gone. Would they be purely cosmetic, as the title on my doctor's business card implied? If so, what was the right size for me?

A couple of weeks earlier, right after I'd had my post-mastectomy drainage tubes removed, I'd visited Mary Catherine's, a boutique in Seattle that special-ized in mastectomy wear, to try on prostheses and bras.

A woman in her fifties in polyester pants and pink lipstick and bright white bouffant hair that flipped up in a curl once it passed her shoulders asked if she could assist me. I wondered if she was a breast cancer survivor herself. She led me to one of the changing rooms. I winced when a twinge of pain spiked across my chest as she helped me slip my shirt and camisole off. She asked me what size I'd like to try on. "Let's start with a C," I said.

As I waited, I glanced in the mirror and saw the two strips of surgical tape that remained over the horizontal incisions on my chest, and the tan lines from my pre-surgery trip to Hawaii that started at my shoulders and led to nowhere. The tan was fading, and my skin was beginning to peel off in little white flecks.

She brought in the first bra and a couple of boxes with different types of pros-theses. "Most insurance covers the standard silicone—see how heavy that is. If you want to pay extra, you can get this new, whipped silicone, which is in the same shape, but much lighter and more comfortable to wear. Since you'll only be using yours for a couple of months, though, you'll probably just want to go with the standard."

I nodded in agreement and she showed me how to fold the heavier prosthesis like a taco to fit it into the pocket in the bra. She gently slid the bra straps over my arms and up on my shoulders and hooked it together in back, and I slipped my shirt on over it. The effect was too pointy and conelike—more like what women wore in the 1950s. Next, please.

The next set I tried on felt more comfortable—I liked the way I looked in the mirror.

"Why don't I try on a D just for the heck of it?" I asked the shop lady.

D felt too big on me—I thought it made me look wider in my chest than I would naturally be. I settled on the second prosthesis I had tried, which was a full C-cup—one or two cup sizes bigger than I'd been just before the mastectomy and about the size I'd been in college, pre-kids.

As I thought about my ideal size in the dressing room, I tried to separate my own preference from the expectations of society, media, and men. Wasn't the purpose of reconstruction to replicate what you had lost?

I would never truly recover the physical part of what I had lost—my breast tissue and my nipples. I would never again feel the water from the shower running down my breasts. I'd never again get goose bumps on my breasts when it was cold. I'd never again feel the pleasure of arousal when a man caressed my nipple. I'd forever miss seeing the original version of my body in the mirror.

Some would view reconstructive surgery as an opportunity to "improve" on what I'd lost. But that thought made me sad because I loved what I'd lost. I loved my small and droopy breasts, imperfect as they were. They were mine. I imagined I would feel detached in some way from the new breasts that the doctor would create. These wouldn't be the breasts I had been born to develop, which had served me so well.

Getting cosmetically improved fake breasts without any feeling was some small consolation after the mastectomy. But I would have the awareness every day that they weren't mine. I wouldn't be able to take credit for any approving glances I received in the future because of them. It would be like someone complimenting you on your smile when your teeth are covered with veneers.

I knew what middle-aged women's breasts were supposed to look like. I remembered sitting on my knees on shag carpet on sun-drenched afternoons thumbing through a stack of my parents' *National Geographic* magazines. The image of flaccid, elongated tissue with a surprisingly turned-up nipple on the end stayed with me. After using my breasts to nourish my infant son for a year, I hadn't expected them to pop back up to their pre-baby bounty. The replacements the surgeon could give me would not look natural in any real sense. They would be fuller and rounder than middle-aged women's breasts, regardless of the size I chose.

Now I sat, bare-topped and scarred, glancing over the plastic surgeon's shoulder at creamy brown walls holding strictly aligned, framed black-and-white photographs depicting nature's perfection: sailboats thrusting through currents and mountain ranges piercing cloudless skies.

I asked, "Why is there this myth that mastectomy is such an emotionally devastating surgery?"

"Because it's mutilating," he replied. "It's more like removing a hand than an appendix."

Because of my family's history of cancer, since my twenties I'd imagined what course I would take if I received the dreaded diagnosis one day. I got used to the idea that I might be part of this clan of women who got cancer early, just the latest generation to cope, and knew early on that I would choose to have my breasts removed. I was less shocked than some women about my diagnosis when it came and less anguished about making the treatment decision. I didn't view the possibility as any more difficult than the issues my friends would deal with in their midlife. By the time we hit our forties, we've all known pain—it's been layered on us like so many coats of paint. Who's to say which heartbreak is the greatest: Losing a child or never having a romantic relationship? Surviving cancer or having a mentally ill son? All painful life events gouge deep furrows and cause emotions to bleed out of us—shock, sorrow, and dismay. Through these tragedies, we are constantly rediscovering ourselves, peeling off the personas we've created to fit in socially and reaching for the unaltered seed of self within us. We'll never completely know our raw core—never completely be able to separate the white of external influences from the yolk of our true selves. But we can ask the questions, keep on with the quest. In the quest for new breasts, my most surprising realization came as I sat in the plastic surgeon's office, flipping through binders of "before" pictures of anonymous women who had had mastectomies and chosen not to reconstruct. I was surprised at the depth of awe I felt. I respected those women most of all—and recognized I wasn't there yet.

I was still too reliant on society's expectations to forgo reconstruction after the mastectomy.

Why did I want new breasts and a larger cup size? For reasons of vanity. For my husband's sexual pleasure (since he'd be able to feel them and I wouldn't). And so I could deal privately with the emotional pain of removing my breasts by "passing" in society's eyes. I realized I hadn't chosen new, larger breasts after cancer solely to meet society's beauty standard. My new breasts would be more than cosmetic. They served a practical purpose. My new, larger breasts would be a reflection of the authentic me.

A CLOTHESHORSE IS BORN

Allison Amend

I am a female dandy. There, I said it. I own a closet full of the who's who of contemporary designer fashion. I wear couture and tell people I can't remember where it's from. The sale rack at Nordstrom, maybe?

It's not my fault, though. It's in my genes. Both my parents are clotheshorses. My father's law firm used to send a tailor around to the offices with a few swatches of fabric, a small style book, and a tape measure. He would walk into the busy lawyers' offices and they would not even have to stop working to be measured for suits. My father found this absolutely appalling, as shopping was one of the greatest pleasures in life, and he would brush past the tailor on his way to get his male manicure in 1980, years before anyone ever considered coining the term *metrosexual*.

I get it from both sides: One of my early recollections is of three generations of my family inside a dressing room where my grandmother was treating my mother to a new outfit. In my memory (suspect, often accused of misinterpretation) it was a 1980s polka-dotted delight: the blouse with a bow was white with black dots, the matching pants black with white dots. It was accessorized with a cherry necklace.

In my house, clothes were both secret and sacred. I thought it was completely normal that my mother hid the clothing she bought in my room so my father wouldn't see the shopping bags. I thought everyone's father was the person in the family you waited for while he primped and chose what outfit to wear.

Adding to my legacy, I was a child of aesthetic inadequacies. In my memory (again, not to be relied upon) I was a chubby child with unfortunate hair, bookish and sensitive. What could a mother do to help her daughter feel at home in her body? Buy her nice clothes.

So that's how it started. A couple of back-to-school outfits that cost perhaps a bit more than they should have. A nice dress to wear to prom (a black bodice and capped sleeves, a flared skirt that may have been too short). A few hand-me-downs from Mom that were a bit too fancy for a kid (a Krizia sweater with a fierce lion in a ring of fire, cashmere twinsets, a Chanel suit I was careful to wear only as separates).

Thus a clotheshorse is born.

I live in New York where my couture fetish has company. But I am a writer and a college professor and I spend most of my time in my writing space or on the inner-city campus where I teach. My sartorial savvy is lost on my colleagues. Most of them aren't remotely interested in fashion (as evidenced by their choice of wardrobe, which can often look as though they rummaged blindly through a resale bin or bought clothes in bulk). We enter academia for the life of the mind—if you worry too much about your body, other than as a vehicle for transporting your brain, you are somehow betraying the profession. My colleagues rarely comment on my clothing.

But I'm dressing for me, to make myself feel beautiful. For reasons best shared only with my therapist, I find my face and body grossly inadequate. What to do so that when I look in the mirror I like what I see? Buy beautiful clothing.

I won't pretend I don't like the attention, friends who coo over my new duds. I enjoy being the rare object of envy, and though I would perhaps prefer it be for something about me, rather than something I adorn myself with, I'll take what I can get. I have one friend who anxiously awaits the day when I get tired of something, so that she can have the third-generation hand-me-down. She rides to work on a bicycle in my mother's Nina Ricci knits.

And if I share the occasional secret glance with another fashion maven (women and gay men), it is because we are members of a secret society. We

KNOW. "Is that a Proenza Schouler?" someone whispers at a party. "I used to work for *Vogue*."

Yet when someone compliments me on my skirt (I almost never wear pants), I say what one is supposed to say: "Oh, this old thing? I forget where I got it."

But I didn't forget. I got it at Ikram, a famous high-end boutique in Chicago, known for its eponymous owner who dresses celebrities and socialites and politicians. And me. When you walk into Ikram, the door having been opened for you by the doorman/security guard (Ikram's store contains merchandise worth more than some jewelry), you are greeted by career couture assistants, groomed for years, who remember everything about you and drop whatever they are doing to help you. You are accompanied into a dressing room and offered Starbucks, which some invisible minion goes to fetch. Then you strip to your skivvies (I always save my best underwear for these occasions). You are welcome to look around the store, but it's futile, because they bring outfits to you. They're the expert artists, the clothes are their paints, and you are the mere canvas—who lets the canvas choose the paints? The clothes are then tailored so that they fit like proverbial gloves. Your hips are too big? They can hide them. Arms a bit thick? They'll put in a secret panel. Maxis become minis; bagginess turns into ruching. Offending lace disappears on command.

Years ago, my mother was in the next dressing room over from a gorgeous African American woman with amazingly toned arms (modesty is a virtue you are expected to check at the door, as you are adjusted and appraised by a cadre of eyes). The woman was trying to decide which dress to buy, and my mother, in her ineffable wisdom, told her to get both. That was Michelle Obama.

Money never changes hands; prices are rarely discussed. Your credit card is on file and the clothes come home with you without you signing anything. They are wrapped exquisitely in a ruby-colored hanging bag or a lacquer-red box, a ribbon revealing that . . . is she carrying . . . ? Yes, I think it is . . . an Ikram bag!

"Here," you're told. "You need this." Protest is useless—if you're told you must have it, it comes home with you, and 90 percent of the time it is the piece of clothing you wear most in your wardrobe. "Nope, take it off," you're sometimes told, or, rarely, "You can find the perfect leggings to match this at Blooming-dale's." Shopping at Ikram is what shopping must have been like if you were a member of the aristocracy in eighteenth-century France, except you're called by your first name and when you demand executions no one listens.

Recently, a friend dragged me to Filene's Basement. I say dragged because she had to convince me that I was capable of pawing through racks of discounted and irregular clothing, sorted not by size or designer but by chance. She negoti-ated the store like a professional big-game hunter while I stood by ineffectually. I cannot pick out my own clothes, it turns out. I don't actually like to shop—in a regular store I'm zaftig and disproportionate. I would have been embarrassed had I not been so overwhelmed (and hot: no one takes your coat in discount stores!). Eventually I came away with a pair of jeans, but the color has faded and they're not quite the right size.

Why don't I admit to my labels? First of all, not everyone's mother still buys clothes for her at almost forty. I'm embarrassed—but not so embarrassed that I won't accept her largesse. Second, there have been times when finances don't allow me to go out to dinner or to buy a ticket to an event, which is difficult for me to explain as I open my Chanel purse and stare at its empty cash compart-ment. I wish I didn't have to rely on labels to feel beautiful, but, if wishes were horses, everyone would wear Balenciaga.

And why couture—or, to be legally specific, high-end *prêt-à-porter*? (*Haute couture* is a term protected by the French government, the same branch that slaps people on the wrist for using the word *champagne* indiscriminately.) Oh, must I answer this question? The fabrics are exquisite, the cuts forgiving and flattering. My clothes are an investment. My closet has a few pieces that last for years. No frayed seams, no pilling sweaters. I tire before the pieces do. Buying H&M dispos-able trends, wearing them once, watching the dyes fade unevenly and the threads pull, being terrified of washing them lest they disintegrate just feels wrong, waste-ful, and careless, like throwing a plastic bottle in the trash when there's a recycling bin right there. I have to care about myself more than this, right?

I would like to tell a story now of how fashion saved my life. How I was dangling from a ladder high over a gorge and only the tensile strength of hand-woven Italian silk saved me. But that didn't happen.

Here's what did: Couture got me a job. I'd had a rough go of it—rejected novels, unemployment, failed love affairs. To cheer me up, my mother bought me the most expensive dress I've ever owned, an Azzedine Alaïa—emerald green with a unique scalloped neckline. It is fitted through the waist and then flares gently to just below my knees. It's exquisite. Sometimes I just take it out and look at it.

I wore it to interviews for academic jobs, where men with mismatched socks took notes on my theories of pedagogy and women in chinos asked me about my fiction. No one noticed my dress.

But in my Alaïa I felt beautiful. I sat up straight so that the neckline wouldn't gap. I crossed my knees and smoothed the skirt over them so that the pleats fell perfectly over my legs. The dress gave me a sense of worth. Even if I didn't get the job, even if the interviewers had forgotten more about nineteenth-century Anglophone literature than I had ever learned, I still knew more about fashion. From the looks of it, a lot more. And this knowledge gave me confidence. Confidence that must have shown during interviews.

Finally, I interviewed for a job in New York. And as luck would have it, the then-chair of the department was Italian, a sharply dressed, impeccably accessorized statuesque beauty. She gave me the once over and I could tell that she knew. She KNEW. And I got the job. Because of the dress? Let's just say it didn't hurt.

SEARCHING FOR THE MAGIC IN MACY'S

Jessica Machado

or my thirtieth birthday, my boyfriend offered to take me to Macy's. "You can pick out whatever" were his instructions. Lee's sweet-yet-strange proposal was a culmination of our urban, chosen destitution (we were in Portland, Oregon, living off my graduate school loans and his fourth-career sales job), my vocalized disappointment (he had shown up to my birthday party empty-handed), and a quick fix (he was trying to shut me up and had a Macy's card).

Still, it was a nice gesture considering the mixed signals I was giving about turning thirty. "Bring it, 3-o!" I told all my friends. "I can't wait to put my twenties behind me!" I said to people younger than me who reflected my fear that I was suddenly on a different plane than them. And most of the time, I did believe my own sentiments—a good part of my twenties sucked, and I was, in many ways, on the road to a better place. However, I wasn't necessarily in that place yet. Not to mention thirty was such a round, bold age, with all its curves and buoyancy, that it was hard to look past the "it's just a number" thing. Thirty was there, puffed up, bloated, signifying something.

Over the next few days, I thought a lot about what I could buy at Macy's to mark my shift into thirtydom. I came up short. "What do you think I should get?" I asked Lee as he drove us to the mall.

"I dunno," he said. "Oooh, wait, I got it." He flashed his boyish grin that, after six years together, could be endearing or infuriating. "Lingerie. You should get lingerie."

"Yes, red lacy thongs. That's what I want," I told him, rolling my eyes.

"Why not?" he kept on. "Go ahead, throw in some pink ones, too."

I turned to face the window. I could feel him looking at me, smirking, waiting for a reaction. This is thirty, I thought. Annoyed by sex, making predictable banter, creating an event out of a Saturday at the mall.

I'm not sure I ever imagined what thirty would look like on me. I know at age twelve I didn't think I'd live past twenty-four, as I feared being immersed in a young lady's cosmopolitan life and then suddenly getting killed in my apartment like *My Sister Sam* actress Rebecca Schaeffer (what can I say, twelve was a dramatic, susceptible age). At nineteen, I envisioned my ten-years-older self as an edgy Lois Lane type, perhaps married to a handsomely rugged paycheck-earning musician—if I decided to marry at all. At twenty-four, I evaded the whole notion of thirty—I was running around with my coworker-boyfriend Lee, getting drunk after our bartending shifts, sick of writing unpaid concert reviews, and hoping I'd eventually have my better shit together.

As Lee and I pulled into the dismal basement of the Lloyd Center mall, I did have some semblance of direction—I told him to park at the Macy's end, so we could get down to business. Upon entering Macy's, what you first notice is how average it is. It is not the Macy's of New York's Herald Square, with its eleven floors and thousands of brands and two million square feet. Lloyd Center Macy's is simply a department store. Tables of packaged button-up shirts to the left, polos to the right. An instrumental version of a Backstreet Boys song punctuating the machine-chilled air, a handful of elders shuffling to find the restroom. "Um, I think I'm gonna go smoke a cigarette," Lee said as soon as we walked through the doors.

I took the escalator to the second, all-encompassing women's floor: shoes, cosmetics, juniors, casual and formal wear. The possibilities of what I should get were overwhelming, especially since I hadn't had the opportunity to buy much for myself after giving up full-time work for small-time freelance jobs and fretting over school essays. Should I get a good pair of running shoes? Nope, too practical. A smart adult dress? No, too impractical (in Portland, a slim-fitting plaid shirt was about as fancy as the dress code got). A slutty top? Again, impractical and too obvious. That's when I saw it: perfume.

Every woman should have a scent of her own, I could hear my mom saying. My mom was southern, and some of her weird feminine-isms couldn't help but seep into my being. As a kid, I loved watching her stand in front of her bathroom mirror and put on Dior every morning—a spray on her wrist, rubbed together with her other wrist, then gently below her earlobes. It seemed womanly and glamorous, a ritual that made me want to be a grownup. Now that I'm thirty-five, I don't know a single woman my own age who wears perfume. But at thirty, figuring out what I should smell like seemed, at the very least, purposeful.

The perfume selection at Lloyd Center Macy's was vast—as opposed to the attractive-jeans section, which was the size of a cubicle—so I was not short on choice. And in 2007 there was definitely a trend happening in fragrance and that trend was celebrity pop princess. Hilary Duff had two scents; Paris Hilton had three. J-Lo had Glow, Miami Glow, Love at First Glow, and Glow After Dark. All of them smelled like bubblegum sweat. I headed for the more traditional section—Calvin Klein, Giorgio Armani, and my mom's favorite, Dior. But they smelt too mature, too faux bourgeois. That's when I stumbled upon Betsey Johnson's namesake fragrance. Here was a successful adult woman, spunky and weird, sporting dreads, doll makeup, and tattered floral layers, smelling neither too saccharine nor too stuffy. After a twenty-minute search, I believed I had found my scent.

I wandered around the corner and stumbled into Lee sitting on a lone chair in the work–casual apparel corner, legs spread, back hunched over, twiddling with his phone. I stood in front of him for a few seconds. Although we had been sleeping next to each other for most of our twenties, it still took him a while to acknowledge my presence.

"Oh," he said, looking up. "Found something?"

"I think so," I told him. He stood, ready to wrap this whole thing up.

"Don't you wanna know what it is?" I asked.

"What is it?" he asked, humoring me.

I shoved it at his nose. "Here, smell it."

"What is that? Horse musk?" he said, swatting it away. I loved eliciting his jokes, even though they annoyed me. They showed me he still cared.

"You ready then?" he asked.

No, I wasn't. A sudden panic came over me. It was like not wanting to leave the bar before I got a buzz on—except here, I wasn't even sure what kind of high I was looking for.

I scanned the room. It was a blur of khaki pants and billowy polyester blouses, the uniform of the traditional, boring working woman; I'd held but one single office job in my entire life. My eyes wandered past all the blazers and trousers, to whatever else could be out there. My feet followed. "Give me a minute," I called out to Lee.

I zeroed in on a display holding $75 flatirons. I'd only ever owned the cheap drugstore kind; my post-college hair life had been spent half-frizzy, half-dented with crimped waves. This was a better tool to become a refined woman. Never mind that this tool would be bought not with my own independent-woman money, but with dollars neither of us had yet earned. Lee and I were supposed to be—in the vaguest way that I'd explained to my parents—working toward a future together, a future that had ostensibly started when we moved from L.A. to Portland the summer prior so I could go to grad school. Only we'd never really discussed any next steps. "Dude, do you wanna, maybe, you know, head forward toward the Big M?" I'd asked him, referring to marriage in a middle school manner, a few months before my birthday. We were outside a friend's party and the weather had just eased into warm after our first long winter in Portland. Everything seemed hopeful and possible. "Yeah, maybe? Yeah?" he answered. He looked eager and excited, which made me look eager and excited; granted, we were both a little drunk. That was the last we ever spoke of it, neither of us thinking too hard about why we never did.

I brought the flatiron back to Lee. "Here, can I get this, too?" I asked. He shrugged and told me sure. This was too easy. "So, uh, how much credit do you have left on your card?" I knew I was pushing his limits, but I also knew his limit wasn't more than $500 and was probably already close to maxed out.

"I dunno," he said. "Maybe a couple hundred bucks?"

I gave him my *pretty-please* eyes. He gave me his *yeah-what* face. *Pretty fucking please*, my eyes pleaded. *Yeah, what*, his shouted.

"Dude, can I maybe have one more thing?" I finally blurted.

He exhaled. "Hurry."

I walked over to the shoe section and picked up the first two items I saw: a black riding boot and a burgundy lace-up bootie. "Do you have these in a size seven and a half?" I asked the saleslady, waving them in her face. I continued to grab and put down shoes while she was away retrieving my goods. Lee slouched in a chair. "Tick-tock," he muttered. "Tick. Tock." I ignored him, touching everything I could, as if it would trick my brain into satiation. The saleswoman came back out and placed the giant boxes in front of me. I frantically shoved my left foot into one style and my right into the other and, because of the heel-height difference, limped back and forth in front of every full-length mirror within the department's parameters. Did the riding boot devour my leg? Did the bootie make my hips look wide? I wasn't sure. I didn't know what I'd wear with either pair, but both were massive, dominating, weighted. If I could've swallowed them to make me feel full, I would have.

I told the saleswoman I'd take the riding boots.

About a step away from the register, I froze. "Um, let me just make sure this is what I want," I said to no one in particular. And with that, I was off again.

I scurried over to the accessories. I did a breezy walk-by of the purses, spun around one turnstile of earrings, and then another, before moving on to the scarves scattered on a sale table. Against my original plan and better judgment, I walked over to the juniors section. Maybe I wanted a slutty top after all. Maybe it would make me feel good the first time I put it on and walked into a bar, spaghetti straps baring my shoulders, the deep V of a loose blouse showing a hint of cleavage when I bent over. I'd feel young and undamaged and like everyone else who had the night and the world in front of them. Maybe I'd dance with a strange guy, touch the newness of his skin and hair, maybe I'd wake up in the morning and write my best paragraph yet and not have a hint of a hangover. I rummaged through the racks. Sleeveless polyester see-thru tops. Little threads hanging from the seams. Everything felt cheap to the touch. I didn't know what looked like me or the me I wished I appeared to be.

I came back to the register, defeated. "Okay, I guess this is it, then," I declared. It was the first time I'd stood still in more than an hour. Before me, on the counter, were workman's boots and what were essentially toiletries. "Do you think any of this stuff is weird?" I asked Lee.

He stared at me, cold in the face, exhausted. "Are you serious?" he asked. "Is this not really what you want?" He was gesturing at my prizes like a disgruntled game show host. I didn't know. "Dude, I'm not wasting any more time in this place," he told me. And with those words, I completely lost my shit.

"You waste time? *You* waste time?" I told him.

"Yes," he said. "I'm wasting time. You're the one who said you wanted to come here."

"That's because it was my only choice!" I screamed.

I could sense the woman behind the counter getting nervous. She started picking apart a stapler. I felt like yelling at her, "What? You've never been around a couple who's sick of each other before?" But more urgently, I felt like yelling at Lee, "Why, after six years together, is this my only choice? Why do I have to tell you what I want? Why, most of the time, do I not even know what I want?"

But the problem was I did know what I wanted. And it wasn't the same thing I did when I was twenty-four, when I was happy just to laugh, drink, and feel less alone in his company. But I couldn't admit that right then. So I stood there.

Lee opened his wallet and pulled out his Macy's card. "Are we doing this?" he asked. It was the most serious I'd ever seen him. I nodded.

"Your card is declined," the cashier said, barely raising her head from the credit machine. Lee looked over at me. "What if you take away the boots?" I asked her.

She hit a button and scanned the shoebox once again. *NEGATIVE 79.99*, the register read. She ran the card and this time it went through. She handed me my big, rectangular Macy's bag. "Have a nice day," she told me.

"Have a nice day," Lee mimicked as we walked toward the escalator.

"Now what's your problem?" I asked.

"What's your problem?" he barked back.

"You tell me."

"What?" he asked, confused and flustered. "God, this sucks!"

"What sucks?" I was baiting him to say it, to just say anything, so I didn't have to.

"*Ugggghhh*," he grunted loudly. "I'm outta here." He threw me the car keys.

I stood there, in the middle of the women's department, staring at his back for a second, before suddenly feeling overwhelmed. I stormed off in the other direction, to an immediate way out of the building. The first door I saw led to an employees-only stairwell. I walked through it.

Outside, there wasn't any soft rock buzzing or power-suited mannequins eyeing my outfit. Dusk was settling behind me. I sat down on the landing and put my head in my hands. And I felt the weight. I felt it there in my hands, and then I didn't.

This was the end of all the things we could never say and never be. This was thirty.

Jenny Moore

We shopped in the suburban sprawl thirty miles east of Los Angeles. My grandmother lived in a leafy college town, but to do real shopping we took the freeway to the malls, where concrete blocks of department stores sprang from slabs of parking lot, the buildings bleached so white by the sun that I could hardly read the names affixed to their top corners.

In my grandmother's car—she went through a series of sedans, one white, another gold, the last one peach—we drove to stores with names that sounded exotic to me, Buffum's and May Company and Bullock's. On the way home, for the afterthought of dinner groceries, we stopped at Vons, or we dined at Taco Bell.

On early outings, her goal was to buy me a dress to pose in for photographs taken while I knelt on a blue-carpeted plywood platform at Sears. Later the search was for a dress to wear to a holiday dinner or church. Eventually, when I was an adult, it was to treat me to clothes for a good restaurant, a job interview, or a date. Our shopping was grounded in her benevolence. Conveniently, it also gave us something to do together, especially when I grew too old for a visit to the arcade or an amusement park.

The unspoken agenda was my grandmother's mission to girlify me. She had raised two sons she adored but made it no secret that she had always longed for a daughter. She doted on her nieces and her friends' daughters. She tried to dote on her daughters-in-law, who each proved disappointing: my aunt was ill for years with breast cancer, and my mother was an inscrutable pioneer of intellectual discourse and women's lib and divorce.

And then there was me. The first granddaughter. Fresh meat.

The thing, and it really was a *thing*, had two layers: solid black cotton beneath sheer patterned rayon. The abundance of filmy material had a surprising weight, and spilled over my arms when I gathered it up. The pattern was aggressively floral. Huge splashes of flowers, blues and reds and golds, drenched a black background. Buttons ran up the front, topped at the neck by a floppy ribbon as wide as a lasagna noodle. Long broad sleeves billowed over tight cuffs.

And from the waist, wide floral pants flowed down to the ankle. I was in my last year of college. It was 1995.

My housemate Cindy held it aloft, standing in the doorway of my room. "*What* are you doing with a jumpsuit?" She stitched costumes for plays at the campus theater. She had a sewing machine and altered her own clothes. Her sense of style was funky, inventive, sexy, impeccable. She knew things about jumpsuits I would never fathom. "Where did this come from?"

"I didn't buy it," I answered. It seemed the less said the better. At least I hadn't worn it in her presence. "I've had it lying around for a few years."

I had tossed it into the Free Store box someone set up in our group house. When Cindy discovered it, she went door-to-door to find its previous owner.

"It's amazing," she breathed.

At that I felt a strange pride. Did she mean the jumpsuit possessed some mystique, some raw potential I had divined? There *was* something about it I liked. Perhaps what had previously seemed my unseasoned fashion eye was actually an astute fashion-forward vision. Perhaps only I, along with the designer, had recognized that the age-old uniform of mechanics, astronauts, and biohazard doctors could also be rendered into pretty casual wear, even in the grunge-fest of the 1990s.

"You can't throw this away."

Could she possibly want to wear it herself? "I keep holding onto it, thinking . . ." I trailed off, then finally confessed. "My grandmother bought it for me."

"It's so good." She began to giggle and didn't stop. "I'm keeping this," she announced, as if it were an artifact that was simply too inexplicable, too *sui generis*, too breathtaking in its hideousness, to let out of her sight.

When my grandmother flew east to visit us, her suitcase was a magical trove with gifts tucked into every possible crevice. Books, candy, toys for my brother and me. On tiptoe we peered over its edge, entranced by its bounty. She always waited until we'd opened everything else, when it seemed nothing else in the suitcase could possibly be for us, before she gave us the clothes.

"Try them on," she urged, not hiding her eagerness.

I would, eventually, try on the clothes, hoping desperately for them not to fit. They smelled of plastic and chemicals. Sometimes they still hung from plastic hangers, unwashed and stiff, price tags dangling from the armpits, dollar amounts carefully torn off or blacked out. The seams pressed in at the neck, the waist, under my arms. Labels sewn to the collar scratched my neck. If there were ruffles, they itched. The polyester layers were too cold or too hot. There were tights, like sausage casings waiting to swallow my legs. Usually, tragically, everything fit.

The bribes began early. We settled into a system that worked for both of us. I announced that I didn't want to wear the dress in question. She countered with a reminder that I needed to look nice. This mattered little to me. Mostly I disdained nice. I wanted to look like my older brother, whom I idolized. In the case of a particularly intractable stand-off, she waited until we encountered a true temptation. A toy inside a store window, or a movie or a chocolate bar. Then she reeled me in. In exchange for the desired item, I agreed to wear the dress she wanted me to wear.

Her payoffs were well-chosen, too otherwise forbidden for me not to surrender. My brother had his own arrangement and had no trouble honoring his terms. I was still learning, however. Once, I agreed and cashed in on her side of the bargain but later thought I could avoid delivering my end. Stern reprimands followed, and insistence that I honor the agreement. I knew that was fair; I just didn't want to. I longed for my mother to intervene on my behalf. She knew I hated dressing up this way, and I sensed a feminine appeal would be most effective. But my mom was at her own house and we were with my dad. He stayed out of his mother's negotiations, mildly disapproving of both sides of the transaction. This was between Grandma and me.

The price I paid was the unveiling. I would put on the dress, alone or with her help to zip the back or tie a bow. I felt scratchy, frilly, and starched. It was the prologue to the main event, when I walked into the living room and presented myself for inspection.

"You look darling," she'd say, thoroughly enchanted. "What a pretty dress for a little girl." My grandfather would add his praise, and my father chimed in, too, though less effusively as a way of keeping the peace with me. She'd hug me, and I'd feel a little better. I understood that the whole thing made her happy, that I was giving her something she didn't normally have.

But I couldn't wait to change. I did not enjoy being made the center of attention for this purpose. The *oohs* and *aahs* were meant to flatter, but I felt strange in clothes I hadn't chosen, and I didn't want to look pretty if it meant I was not myself. In those moments I felt a fraud and was too young to know why I felt discomfort inside as well as out. I was an easy mark. I endured it for candy.

She knew what we liked: things we didn't usually get, multiple varieties of sweets we could eat at our leisure, Archie comics, Bobbsey Twins and Hardy Boys books, a meal at a restaurant, a trip to Disneyland. She was attentive. She often explained to my father, when he protested that she was spoiling us, that it was her privilege, her right, to do so.

We knew she had money to spend. Not a ton of it, and not an endless flow, but plenty more than we usually had. She said over and over that it made her happy to give us things we enjoyed. Eagerly, we helped her find happiness. My brother and I grew skilled at the casual hint, the lingering glance or touch, a healthy dose of feigned innocence once she noticed ("Oh, *that*?"). We knew to wait for her to ask and we knew how to first demur, then graciously accept. We knew thank-you notes were part of our currency. It was a delicate dance and we learned every step. It was never clear who was leading whom.

When I was in high school she became truly weakened by heart trouble and extra pounds she couldn't shed. When we shopped she found a chair at each department store and waited, people-watching or reading a romance novel, while I skimmed the racks.

I'd be lost in thought until I'd hear her calling my name. She sounded urgent, the pitch of her voice making me fear she was having another heart attack and needed me to dig for the nitroglycerin tablets in the pillbox in her purse, or release the one in a locket she wore around her neck and somehow get it under her tongue before calling an ambulance.

I'd drop the clothes in my arms and run, and, when I reached her side she would look up at me, wave a hand toward a nearby rack of clothes, and say, "Red's popular this year." Or she'd point to the outfit on a mannequin and announce how cute it would look on me.

I'd study the item she indicated. "You mean the sailor suit," I'd say, under-whelmed by her choice even as adrenaline rushed through my limbs. Or the tan-gerine pants. Or the floral jumpsuit.

"Just try it on," she'd say eagerly, and usually I was so pleased she wasn't dying that I took the offending item to the dressing room. Other times I'd grow irritated and protest. She knew she could insist and I would comply. It was all part of the dance.

In the dressing room I would put on what she chose, scrutinize myself in the mirror, step outside to model for her, and repeat. The vestiges of my childhood embarrassment at this sort of modeling were faint, perhaps diluted because we were an hour outside L.A., where I knew no one. Here, I was outside my regu-lar life. I was only her granddaughter. And I liked giving her what she wanted. I wasn't in my eighties, in declining health, and far away from my family. If it made her happy to shop for me, who was I to refuse her?

Sometimes, I did refuse. She could rise to a stubborn, imperious grande dame, and I had her genes. I could dig in my heels when I felt strongly enough. I was still figuring out what I was about, who I was. But I wouldn't let her buy me clothes I hated.

"You really don't like that," she'd muse, and then sniff as if the vagaries of my taste had tainted the air. "It's adorable. But you say you won't wear it." Then she'd sigh.

"That's right," I'd say cheerfully, knowing I had prevailed. "I really won't."

Her lips pinched tight, but after a while she'd say, "I just want to get something you like."

When she was recently widowed and desperate for company, I flew down from college to spend a weekend with her. I was beginning to find her undiscerning consumption troubling in a larger sense. We didn't need material goods to connect. I insisted she didn't have to buy anything.

"What else do I have to spend money on except my children and grandchildren?" she asked, and immediately I felt guilty. She was grieving. Besides, what else would we do with our time together?

I drove her car and she directed me to a sparsely populated mall I didn't recognize. The store she had in mind targeted a clientele that was far beyond college age and had seen better days. Surely I could find an inoffensive item, I reasoned, among the slacks and muumuus. It took much searching in a department that skewed toward peppy prints and maximum coverage, but I unearthed a dress to try on: navy blue, ankle length, simple and serviceable—even, in the right light, a bit sheer and therefore sexy.

It was on sale, which posed a problem. It meant one dress could be turned into two for the amount she wanted to spend. This was not something she was accustomed to passing up.

"That's all? You have to try on more things."

"I'm not sure there is more here for me," I said, trying to be delicate.

"Of course there's more!" She was scandalized. "We're in a whole store full of clothes."

Off my game, I drifted away from her chair, sweating a little. If I could find an innocuous casual dress, maybe even something to wear to class, we could leave. I pulled an item off the rack for a better look: Was it a dress? A skirt? Tunic?

"That's gorgeous!" she gushed. I hadn't realized she was still watching me. "Try it on."

It was, I realized, a blouse and pants. Together. A jumpsuit. "Grandma, this really isn't my style. I'll never wear it."

"If it looks good on you, maybe it *should* be your style."

It was hard to argue with that. I wasn't even sure what my style was at the moment. I draped it over my arm.

She didn't approve that I'd had premarital sex (which wasn't a detail I'd offered up, God knows). She didn't approve that I had tattooed my ankle (she spotted it one summer day when I thought she wouldn't notice). She didn't approve that I took too long to write thank-you notes, or that I waited until I was thirty to marry, that I didn't get pregnant right afterward. She came from a world of trousseaus and girdles and waiting patiently while the men around her concerned themselves with the mechanisms of the broader world. She believed herself to be academically challenged because she hadn't been able to finish college. When in high school I told her I'd earned an A in precalculus, her response was, "Oh my, they let girls study that?" She marveled at me, sometimes admiringly and at times as if I were an odd anthropology exhibit. We found our common ground in stores and dresses and changing rooms. Shopping allowed us to show each other who we were.

She insisted I model the jumpsuit, though that wasn't what we were calling it; we were calling it "the black flowered dress." As I pulled up the pants and then slid my arms into the sleeves and buttoned it up, I scrutinized my reflection in the mirror: it was a true *outfit*. A garment. A full-on look.

There was something appealing in the wholeness of it. I admired its all-in-one efficiency. The floral was stylish at the time, or at least not vastly incongruent with the baby-doll dresses that were a trend among my peers. The layers were so full and flowing that it might appear to be a dress, in which case it had a more respectable, Laura Ashley vibe. Or so I convinced myself. I imagined myself striding across campus, wearing the right shoes with this almost-dress, turning heads.

Because I did look good. I looked hot, actually, in that thing. I was tall and thin. I had some nice sling-backs that would add more height. I would turn heads, but I couldn't be sure they would turn for the right reason. What if it was ridiculous?

I walked out of the dressing room to show her.

"Oh, isn't that *mar*-velous!"

"It's comfortable," I conceded, though in that instant I noticed the seam of the crotch stretching tight, pulled north by the waist and sleeves reaching to my shoulders—pulled, in fact, by every move of my upper body. I was just beginning to realize I had a long torso and that not all clothes were created equal. "I think."

"It looks comfortable." She narrowed her eyes at me. "Miss!" she called loudly in her urgent heart attack voice. A sales representative snapped to attention and hurried over. "Doesn't this dress look beautiful on my granddaughter?"

"Of course." The saleswoman's glasses hung from a string around her neck. "A lot of people are buying those suits these days."

I studied her to get a sense of how much she was faking. Never have I been as conscious of conflict of interest.

"It's nice," I hedged. "I'm just not sure I'll wear it. At school."

Grandma raised her eyebrows and huffed, a sure sign we weren't done. "Well, you've got to get *something* for school."

Back in the dressing room I turned in half-circles before the mirror, trying to check out how my ass looked (flowy and floral), how it felt to sit down on the little bench (I'd need to adjust the tight seam every time I sat, or else something really bad might happen) and how I looked midstride (the legs recalled the oversized swishing ribbons in a drive-through car wash). I tried to rearrange the seam between my legs. Most of my clothes were extra-large and baggy. Maybe this wasn't tight but just a change from what I was used to.

The bow at the neck was big but disappeared into the folds of the thing. It could have used a belt, though I didn't notice. This was neither a distant cousin of the pseudo-professional "pantdress" of the 1960s, nor a diluted glitzy-top-blended-with-flowing-pants à la *Charlie's Angels* in the 1970s. It wasn't even reminiscent of the shoulder-pad-armored power suits of the 1980s, nor did it somehow presage the strapless romper of the 2010s. Perhaps the outfit had surfaced only in that one store (Penney's? Robinsons-May?) in the early 1990s. Its sack silhouette and ankle-skimming legs made it an anachronistic garment of mystery. I was intrigued.

I grasped immediately that it was going to be all about how I wore it. I would have to own it, a challenge as I wasn't usually adventurous with clothes.

For a moment, looking in the angled mirrors, I imagined a new me, crossing the quad or the plaza, empowered, wearing a new style and shedding the things about me that I didn't like. I'd be bold and beautiful. I wouldn't care what anyone else thought. I wouldn't be self-conscious. I'd wear heels and they wouldn't hurt. Maybe Grandma was right. Maybe I did look marvelous.

I never saw her buy something that didn't deliver pleasure at the moment she purchased it. A sale sign drew her like a bee to honey. A teenager when the Depression hit, she was incapable of passing up a good deal. Bargains, particularly church rummage sales, were her preferred milieu. But she'd shop anywhere and she bought what was on offer, not necessarily what fit best or was most flattering. She shopped for her family, her friends, herself. Each acquisition was a gesture of love. It seemed to me she was always acquiring.

I couldn't keep up. I was raised to not be wasteful—of food, of time, of effort, and especially of money. As a child I learned money was confusing, for countless reasons including that everyone applied different rules. I already had two households, Mom's and Dad's, which had different spending habits. Both were founded on restraint, out of necessity, but the definition of restraint could shift. My mother's parents didn't have extra money, and they had too many grandchildren to buy gifts at every visit. Instead they plied us with homemade cookies and trips to the park and games at their dining table. My father's father was a very careful spender, appraising every purchase with cool calculation. My grandmother had scrimped much of her life, and so she bought cheap, preferring quantity. As a girl I never noticed that much of what she bought was unnecessary or redundant, nor did I care about quality. I was too caught up in what I wanted her to buy me.

In the dressing room I tried on the jumpsuit once more. Just to see. There was something about it. Something alluring. I imagined leaving my dorm room in it, walking through the halls past the granola students I lived with, kids who were less mainstream than me, who bartered secondhand hemp clothes and claimed to abhor consumerism. They wore Tevas and grew dreadlocks and baked bread naked. Among them, in this, I would stand out.

More than that, I wanted to wear it so that I could be the person who could pull off wearing it. If I could be bold *and* truly own the look, I'd be greater than the outfit was alone.

I left it behind in the dressing room. I wasn't that person.

At the counter, my grandmother handed the serviceable navy-blue dress to the saleswoman. "Where's the other one?" she demanded.

"Which one?" I asked, though I already knew.

"That dress with the flowers."

"It's not a dress. I really don't think I'll wear it." Appealing to her practicality often worked. And I did mean it. I wasn't bluffing to get her to buy it for me. Yet we both knew the steps of this dance.

"But it's so pretty on you." Her voice approached a scold, as though I were wasting the gift of being young, when clothes fit without effort.

"Thank you, Grandma. But I don't think I'll wear it."

"Well you can't wear it at all if you don't have it. I'm buying it for you. Go get it." She looked at the saleswoman. "Wait a minute, Miss, we're getting one more."

It was easier, at that point, not to argue. I returned to the dressing room, both sheepish (she'd been so generous to me over the years; it was rude to turn down the gift) and annoyed (she wasn't listening to me, and who would I be kidding if I wore that jumpsuit?).

The siren song of flattery was taking hold. Two people, albeit biased, thought I looked good in it. I thought I might look good in it. Maybe this was an opportunity. If we were all wrong, I reminded myself, I didn't have to wear it. All I had to do was take it. Grandma would never know what I did with it.

I thanked her, as always. I allowed her to give me something she wanted me to accept. It made her happy. I also thought that I might decide, one day, to wear it.

The time came that we needed to move my grandmother out of her home into a single room at the nursing home. This meant sorting through the contents of her entire three-bedroom house, the prospect of which had been weighing on her for years.

She was wheelchair-bound by then, and she sat in her chair at one end of the kitchen table, going through her jewelry collection with my father.

The rest of us spread out. My uncle tackled my grandfather's office, untouched since his death. A cousin went through Grandma's clothes—dresses, blouses, pants, sweaters. The number of hats alone was tremendous, stacked and crammed onto closet shelves in an architectural feat of storage.

I helped with the jewelry at first. It was her biggest weakness by far—especially diamonds, the birthstones of her family members, and anything in the shape of a butterfly. There was an enormous quantity. Cases, trays, and chests full of small boxes, each box holding a single item. More than we could go through, in several days, though we tried. My father sorted for value, studying each item with a magnifying glass and separating out the gold and sterling from the costume and straight-up junk. I gave him the gold I found and organized the rest as quickly as I could, setting aside things I found appealing or that were clearly designated for someone in the family. Cameo brooches went to a cousin. Opals were for my brother, born in October.

When I needed a break I worked elsewhere in the house. I'd already helped my father's cousin go through the handbags, shoes, and bed linens. We had taken the clothes my grandmother needed to her new room, and the rest of the pile was going elsewhere—where, none of us wanted to think about. After we returned to our homes an estate sale company would come in to sell the remaining furniture and the jewelry and all the other things we couldn't get through.

I scanned the kitchen cupboards overflowing with snacks and sweets as well as dishes, the bookshelves full of volumes on jewelry and the British royal family, the Nora Roberts and Danielle Steele novels and stacks of *People* magazine. It was impossible to be methodical. I just had to dive in.

Grandma's voice rose heatedly when she couldn't find something, which occurred at regular intervals. It agitated her to see all of us opening her drawers and cabinets and dismantling her home. She accepted that she needed to get rid of things. But that was much easier than having us there doing it.

Each of us filled boxes to ship to ourselves and others. China earmarked for me, silver for my brother. There wasn't just one of anything, even sets of china and silver and stemware. Table linens, videotapes, picture frames, blankets, tchotchkes, a silver tea service. Jewelry, jewelry, jewelry. We were initiating the grand diaspora of a lifetime shopper.

In one bookcase I found a series of photo albums, the kind from the 1980s with plastic that peeled off to expose adhesive-backed pages onto which you could attach snapshots. They were filled with pictures of trips my grandparents had taken, mostly to Scotland for my grandfather's ancestral research, locations painstakingly written in her hand on the back of each photo and then arranged chronologically.

No one had looked at the albums in years: pages of shots of my grandparents standing outside castles and seated at group dinners with Scots to whom we were vaguely related, my grandfather wearing a kilt and Grandma in her tartan skirt and white ruffled blouse and tam, a larger version of items she'd given me when I was in grade school.

When I brought the albums to my grandmother, she glanced at them quickly and said she didn't have room for them. Her husband had been dead for more than a decade. Her sons didn't want them either. Neither did anyone else. I wanted to want them. How much time had it taken her to carefully label and organize the albums? I could envision her, much younger, dutifully preserving the memory of her transatlantic journey. Suddenly I felt certain that she had needed to search to find ways to fill her time.

On that exhausting trip I realized she was a collector, not just of jewelry. The house contained copious quantities of hats, Hummel figurines, Elizabeth Taylor books, thimbles, stationery, handkerchiefs, butterflies, embroidery. She had stockpiled candy and hotel soaps and shampoos. She kept drawerfuls of gifts on hand for emergencies.

We discarded—the estate sale company sold—a huge amount of the jewelry. There was more than any of us could take away. I packed four full jewelry cases, each about the size of a toaster oven. She gave me a few of the pieces I loved most: her turquoise squash-blossom necklace and an antique bracelet. I also took a pair of clip-on earrings made of bright yellow feathers the size of my hand, and ropy chains that now recall the look of a blinged-out aspiring professional athlete. I took Irish and Belgian tablecloths and embroidered cocktail napkins, her set of Lenox china, a quilt stitched by a great-aunt, a vintage hatbox, pictures of my parents' wedding, an overstuffed sewing box she'd never used because she was so bad at needlework, cut-glass saltcellars, hand-painted dishes from Japan. I took handbags and a cloche and a cape.

It was easy to give away her Christmas sweaters and earring sets still tagged "$1.00" and the ceramic animals and gold-rimmed keepsake boxes she had ordered as gifts from catalogs like Lillian Vernon and Harriet Carter. This was the shopping that had filled her recent days. It was much worse to throw away those photo albums. She had collected experiences, I realized, as much as she had collected all these things. As we moved her out of her own life, she seemed lonelier than I hope I'll ever be. I laid the albums gently in a trash bag and quickly tied it up though it was not yet full. I couldn't bear to look at them.

I wore the jumpsuit once, on campus. I turned in front of the mirror for a good long while, sure that if wearing it were a mistake some part of my brain would scream that out to me. When no message came I inferred that I looked passable. I was ready for a change, ready to be bold. I rode my bicycle to the coffeehouse. The breeze cut through the sheer rayon and I wished for a warmer layer.

I sat with friends, wondering if anyone would comment on my clothing. I was more comfortable sitting down than standing up because I was painfully on edge, expecting either admiration or ridicule. Slowly, it sank in that neither would arrive. With some relief, but mostly dismay, I realized that most people didn't look at me twice. Those who did made no comment. I'd prepared for a sensation—any sensation—and there was nothing. I became so distracted by whether I looked good or ridiculous and who might notice and why that finally, furious with myself, I left. Riding my bike hurt like hell because of that one wire-like seam I couldn't adjust.

It was a relief to change into my usual jeans and T-shirt. Even so, I chastised myself. I had not made the black flowered outfit my own, nor had I mocked it with self-aware irony. I had not owned it in any way whatsoever. I had attempted the look and wound up in no-man's-land. I was still confused. Still me.

I kept it for a few more years, hanging in the very back of a dorm closet or rolled up into the back of a drawer. Each year as I moved from house to house I stuffed it into a corner of my suitcase, and each time I saw it again it stirred up a litany of thoughts: *It's wrong to throw away a gift. She thought it looked good on me. It doesn't look bad on me. It made her happy to buy it. It doesn't actually fit.* I worried that once I discarded it the perfect occasion for it would arise, or the jumpsuit would careen back into fashion.

At the beginning of my last year of college, heartsick after a breakup, I became hard-hearted about getting rid of extraneous things. Items were appearing in the new Free Store box on the landing: textbooks, a few cassette tapes, old tie-dyed T-shirts, a hat, a single flip-flop. Everybody was purging as they unpacked. One or two decent things donated to the Free Store were quickly repurposed, while the rest were simply inspected and passed over.

When I was hanging clothes in my new closet I found the jumpsuit. It was time, I reasoned. I was tired of resenting it and tired of carrying around aspirational clothing that wasn't even in style. It was time to be the person I wanted to be. An ill-fitting jumpsuit was not going to get me there. Relieved and just a little guilty, I took it to the Free Store.

Cindy wore it once that year, parading down the stairs as the rest of us watched in convulsions of laughter. She accessorized with high-heeled lace-up boots and a bike helmet. With the jumpsuit we celebrated the pinnacle of the ridiculous. I still have a photo; she'd tucked up one leg of the thing to show off the boots.

After my grandmother died we had to clean out her room at the nursing home. My brother was there that time, and my two cousins, and my father and my uncle and his second wife. It took half a day, and we were on deadline to clear out quickly so her room could be filled by another resident. The process was noticeably calmer than the last time because she wasn't there watching us do it.

The closet was jam-packed. She'd crammed in as many clothes and hats as she could, stockings and purses and coats and dresses, more than she'd had a few years earlier when she moved in. Her Smith Corona typewriter sat high on the shelf. It was too heavy for her to retrieve and use, but she'd insisted it be kept there.

When I returned home after that trip, more boxes were being shipped from the West Coast. My own baby pictures and school pictures, letters and cards I had written to her, the typewriter and a box of typewriter ribbons I'd found. My father and uncle agreed I could take an art nouveau ring with diamonds I'd always admired, as well as the first necklace my grandfather ever gave her. I took two daily journals she'd written in during their courtship. These were the items she had wanted to keep with her, close by.

One thing I'd been sure to carry safely tucked in my purse: a small ring box, holding the diamond ring and gold band that my grandfather had given her at the beginning of their fifty-year marriage. A slip of paper inside read simply, "For Jenny. My engagement ring." She would have added the wedding band to the box after wearing it on her swollen fingers became physically painful.

Her marriage was traditional in the classic 1950s mold; I remember my grandmother serving my grandfather his breakfast while he read the newspaper and she remained in the kitchen or ironed his shirts. It's not a dynamic I can fathom for myself, not something close to the wife I was when I was married. But they loved each other and I loved them, and even before I was divorced fifty years of marriage seemed an accomplishment I'd only ever be able to guess at.

The rings are too small for me. They don't even fit on my pinkie finger. She wore them as she cooked oatmeal and wrote letters to pen pals and fastened her other jewelry and opened her wallet to buy things for her family and for herself, her mottled hands with her manicured nails growing shakier with each year.

When my uncle handed me the ring box and I read my name in her handwriting, I couldn't speak. My throat was swollen with grief and pride. We hadn't always understood each other, but she was honoring me, the eldest female of the next generation, with one of the most powerful symbols she possessed. It felt like an ancient message, a birthright more potent than any item on sale in a store.

All those dresses she bought for me were her attempt to make me as like her as she knew how. I'd tried to surrender fully and I'd tried to stubbornly resist, and both were equally futile approaches when who I really was lay somewhere in between. We were finished trying to bridge the gaps between us in a store. At the end she gave me something she wanted me to have, and it hardly mattered that it didn't fit and I would never wear it. She gave it to me and I took it.

MY MOTHER'S CLOSET

Kerry Cohen

his story begins in my mother's closet, when I was eight. It begins with the scent of my mother's clothes—all Prada and Yohji Yamamoto and Adrienne Vittadini and Ralph Lauren—their well-made fabrics against my palms, the feel of silk and wool and good cotton. It begins with my mother's care for them, how she treated them as she would expensive art. Indeed, she called her clothes "pieces." Once, when I was much younger, I made the mistake of cutting up one of her sweaters. I didn't know. I had found the cashmere length of it in a trunk in her sewing room. I thought it was scrap, and so I used scissors to cut it into a blanket for a doll. My mother was furious. She was enraged. She couldn't even look at me, she was so mad.

"My sweater!" she yelled. "My sweater!" As if it were her baby girl, her child.

I ran from the room, tears streaming. I waited for her to come and say she was sorry. She never did.

When I was ten she took me into Manhattan, across the George Washington Bridge where you could look out the car window and see the cityscape, the Hudson River deep and white-capped and dangerous. We sped down the West Side Highway, excitement building, into Midtown, where we drove around and around to find a parking lot. My mother was often agitated. She cursed at people, told them to go back to the suburbs, even though that's where we just came from. Once out of the car, she nodded toward other people and spoke under her breath to me—that one was wearing the wrong outfit for her body type, this one's hair was styled too young for her age, another was wearing a tacky cut-off shirt or cheap lipstick. My mother had something to say about everyone. Inside Bloomingdale's, though, everything changed. There was Chanel No. 5 in the air. The lights were brassy and warm. At the makeup counter, my mother made me wait while she tried different eye shadows and lipsticks. She glanced at the new Prada bags. She took me to the juniors' section and picked out items for me to try. Only certain brands were allowed. Everything had to be well made. She favored Polo and Laura Ashley. Never Guess? or Jordache or Gloria Vanderbilt, which were low class and poorly made and beneath my mother's sense of who I should be. She bought me the three-step cleansing pack from Clinique. Then, we went to the women's section and bought my mother new blouses and skirts. She tried on shoes. We left with crisp bags, our items folded carefully inside, smelling of sweet perfume. We stopped at a café and drank diet sodas.

By the time we drove back over the bridge, the sun had begun to set, and the lights to come on in the city. They appeared slowly, like stars in a darkening sky. I watched them for as long as I could, until they were out of sight. At that time my father was having an affair. It was no secret. In fact, he made no attempt to hide his affair because he wanted out. But my mother paid that no mind. She dragged him to counseling sessions. She acted as if everything was just fine. And, of course, she shopped. The fact of their unhappiness together, though, was unavoidable. I heard them arguing at night. My room was next to theirs. I lay in bed, my body stiff, waiting for her crying to stop. Only once it did would I relax into sleep. In the daytime they floated around one another like ghosts, barely there. My father would walk out the door in the morning without a word.

He moved out a year later. Every other Wednesday he took my sister and me out for dinner, and every other weekend we slept at his apartment. There were girlfriends and electronics and Doritos. There were Vienna finger cookies. There were many things that weren't allowed in my mother's house. My sister became my mother's protector, while I became my father's friend. He was fun. He was freedom. He was *things*, like Atari and computers and junk food, like sheets with only 300 thread count, board games and *People* magazine and Foreigner. He was all the things my mother abhorred.

It was only a year and a half later that my mother left us so she could attend medical school in the Philippines. She had grown up with a doctor father, and then she was an engineer's wife. Now, who could she be without money and the standards she'd set up for herself? Later she would move to Chicago to finish medical school. The point is, she left us for good. I have no memory of that year. It comes to me in flashes, like a series of photographs in my mind. Moving into my father's new apartment that would accommodate his daughters. The hot pink color I chose for my room. The swimming pool at the apartment building. A boy with shaggy blond hair and red shorts. Out the window of my new bedroom was a perfect view of the George Washington Bridge and the Manhattan skyline, a beacon. On weekends, I begged my father to bring me to the department stores as my mother had, and because he was always feeling guilty—for breaking up the family, for his sense of his own inadequacy as a father—he did. This time, I was free to buy what I wanted. I bought Guess? jeans and the cutoff shirts my mother had judged. I bought Bonnie Bell lipstick and concert T-shirts. I bought nail polish even though my fingernails were bitten to the quick. The shopping bags were like weights that pinned me back to myself. I am here; I am here.

When I was blue or on edge or just bored, my father drove me to the River- side mall and set me loose, to help me feel better. It was his way. He met me at the checkout counter, shaking his head. "Daughters are so expensive," he said to the clerk, who smiled and nodded as she folded up my purchases. She wrapped them in tissue, placed them in the bag, and then walked around the checkout counter to hand me the bag. So ritualistic, like a tea ceremony.

My mother called, and I sat stiffly, gripping the phone, while she told me how much she missed me, how she hoped my father was at least trying to do right by us.

"Do you love me?" she asked me during those phone calls. "Do you?"

"Yes," I said, though I feared that I didn't.

In the summer, she flew my sister and me to the Philippines. I didn't want to go. I couldn't envision how I could be on this side of the world, and then the other, and that somehow I would still be alive and make it back home. And, also, I didn't want to be with my mother, with whom I'd have to disappear, with whom

I had to go silent to accommodate who she was. I considered faking illness. I considered outright refusing. But, in the end, my sister and I boarded the plane at JFK and traveled to Manila via Japan. When we arrived, the air was muggy and foreign. My mother waited on the tarmac, which was where we'd landed. I stepped off the plane, wearing my favorite jean jacket that had patches of heavy metal bands sewn on. I wore a bandana around the thigh of my jeans, and I'd grown out my permed hair so it covered my eyes. To my mother, I'm sure, I was as unrecognizable as this place where she now lived was to me.

Our first stop was the beauty salon, where my mother had them remove my chipped nail polish and cut off my hair so that it looked more like hers. Then, she took us shopping. We drove through the Manila countryside, past huts where entire families lived, the smell of burning garbage at every turn. At the market-place we sorted through barrels and trays of shell jewelry and beaded purses. We bought hair accessories and scarves and tiny wishing dolls. When it was finally time to return to the States, my sister and I filled our suitcases with the things of my mother's new life. My mother made sure of it. Back home, though, I never touched those things again.

When it was time to leave for college, my father gave me a credit card to use for emergencies. I shopped the J. Crew and Tweeds catalogs every time a new one arrived, the colors and cuts crisp and bright and promising. This *was* an emergency. My need felt urgent. I could not have enough. There was never going to be enough. But my father called.

"I got a six-hundred-dollar bill," he told me. "Can you tell me what happened?"

"I'm sorry," I said because I didn't understand what happened. "I'll stop."

But I didn't. And then next month he called to tell me he had canceled the card.

I went to graduate school. I got jobs. I grew up. I bought a house, and I got married. My father, always guilty, finally felt let off the hook. He assumed another man could buy me things now. And I did—kitchenware and computers and clothes to wear to work. When my son was born, I bought him a co-sleeper and three slings and a food mill to make my own baby food. And then, while I was pregnant with my second son, we learned that our first baby, Ezra, was autistic.

This is not a tragedy. It is not even something bad. But at the time, I didn't know that. Everything I'd heard about autism told me otherwise. The world I thought I had built for myself, so different from the one I had growing up, crumbled. I didn't know who I was as a mother, a wife. My husband Michael and I turned away from one another, lost in our separate grief. And so, I shopped. Nothing was ever, ever enough. I wanted something different, something more. I wanted that feeling—a high, really—when I swept my hands across the fabric of something in a store, when I tried on boots, that ache of wanting in my throat, when I saw something in a design magazine. I wanted those bags weighing my arms, the knowledge of things inside. I couldn't have what I truly wanted, not really. I couldn't go back to Michael and me before. I couldn't understand how to be a good enough mother to my son. But I could have this. This, I could have.

After our second son arrived, we walked through the fourth house in five years that we would buy. Concrete counters and stainless appliances. A heated floor in the master bathroom. Walk-in closets. I don't know why Michael allowed it. I don't know why he didn't tell me to stop. But he stayed silent, and I bought more and bigger. I renovated the basement, the kitchen. My debt increased with my despair. By the time I was done with all the buying and selling and augmenting, the housing bubble had popped, and we were in serious trouble.

"What happened?" Michael asked me one night. He meant to our money, to our comfortable lifestyle. But I think he also meant to us.

I told him I didn't know, but I did. It had been my fault. I'd driven our finances into the ground. And with it our marriage.

When we separated, we did so without anger. We were defeated, but disconnected. I had pushed him away.

Sometimes I go into my closet, which is still full of clothes and shoes. I admire their patterns, the feel of the fabrics. I touch their arms, like suspended children. I wonder how I might have done things differently. In my trying to get so much, I wound up losing much more.

But my children—I have them. Ezra goes to my closet and slips on my Frye boots. He clomps around the house, his small body in my big boots. He sings, stomping out a beat, and his brother and I laugh with him. Despair, I know, is utterly unnecessary. Much later I find my boots discarded on the floor near his bedroom. They lie at an odd angle to one another and on their sides, like corpses. And I pick them up to return them to my closet.

I DREAM OF DEPARTMENT STORES

Kelly Shire

i dream of department stores. Usually they arrive as daydream, reverie, or flash: I'm walking across my living room or sitting at a red light and for a second I'm transported and entering the Broadway again through its glass double doors. Or I'm downstairs at the May Company with my mother, sifting through the sale bins of bright scarves and belts. A whiff of fresh caramel corn hurtles me down a portal to the popcorn and candy case in the middle of Sears.

Sometimes I literally dream of department stores, and I wake in my bed relishing those seconds of clarity before the memory dissolves, the sensation of walking familiar aisles again, edging past perfume counters in a dream mashup of old homes and stores and faces that are all totally inaccessible to me now in my waking reality.

There was a net of women I grew up shopping with on Saturday afternoons— my mother and her two younger sisters, Becky and Mary Ann. During the week, I'd accompany my grandma to the same stores and shopping centers, sometimes alone and sometimes with her younger sister, my great-aunt Elizabeth, or *Licha*, the Mexican American nickname that she actually used. My grandmother's given name was the Spanish *Esperanza*, which she was called as a girl (or *Espie*, again a nickname), but, by the time I was around, she was Hope, and that was all.

In my earliest years, only my mother was married and her two sisters were both single working girls, both employed at the tall black Bank of America building in downtown Los Angeles, then the highest skyscraper on the skyline. My aunts shared an apartment in Downey, the same town the Carpenters hailed from, and where they owned two apartment buildings named for their hits: "Close to You," and "Top of the World." Becky and Mary Ann didn't live in one of the Carpenters' buildings, but theirs was a similar complex, as Downey contained grids of streets with the same type of early 1960s designs, small complexes of a dozen or so apartments with balcony patios filled with Hibachis and bicycles and trailing spider plants.

Driving past one of the Carpenters' apartment buildings made me feel like the brother-sister duo were family acquaintances. My dad played their *Gold: Greatest Hits* 8-track on our weekend road trips and, better yet, told the story of how in his job as bar manager at one of the many dark lounges in the area, he had auditioned the two, before they became famous, for a gig but turned them down, simply because he thought it was weird for a girl to play the drums. (I have no proof of this story beyond its endurance over the years and that, despite his preference for the company of women, my dad had a wide chauvinist streak.)

On countless Saturdays my mom and I ate and dressed, and left my daddy sleeping after closing his late-night shift at the bar, and drove to my aunts' apartment. Then we'd all go shopping. They were all working women, attractive and young and with money to spend and reasons to spend it, and, if they were all stocked up on new pumps and sandals and office slacks and necklaces, there was always me, the first child, grandchild, niece, the one child always there, and children are always growing and needing something new. Also, the promise of something new was mostly what kept me in line when I got bored and started whining to leave, or tried hiding within the round racks of clothes.

Just as I learned the art of shopping from this trinity of working women, so it was that we shopped primarily at a trinity of nearby malls. There was Stonewood in Downey, and the Quad and Whittwood, both in Whittier, the town adjacent to our family's hometown of Pico Rivera. Our shopping trips began and ended in the large two- or three-story department stores that anchored the shopping centers, but we browsed the length of the centers, too. Both Whittwood and Stonewood had the Broadway, the department store that was the favorite of and most frequented by my triumvirate of tastemakers. The Broadway was firmly middle class, unlike the high-end Bullock's Wilshire in downtown L.A., where my aunts sometimes shopped during lunch, yet it was still more upscale and quietly sedate than the jumbled racks and fluorescent glare of Sears and J.C. Penney. The Broadway had a café on the first floor, more tea room than coffee shop in atmosphere, that served club sandwiches and chicken salads for lunch. Upstairs, at the left end of the children's clothing department, was a bustling hair salon where I endured my mother's first attempts to find a style and cut to suit my massively heavy, curly hair. Over the years I would also grow to prefer the Broadway over its competitors, but, when I was small, my personal department store of choice was Hinshaw's.

Hinshaw's was one of two anchors at the Quad, the other being the May Company. The Whittier Quad was the smallest of the shopping centers we visited, and unlike the other two, was not open air but enclosed for the short length of its single-story promenade. Hinshaw's was a small chain of department stores (truly small, as there was only one other store, in Arcadia, east of Pasadena).

I grew up eating dinners between my parents in leather booths, in the dark, upscale restaurants where my daddy managed and tended the bars, and in the sort of upscale coffee shops that on one end served reuben sandwiches to families, and on the other had separate entrances that led straight into a dim lounge, where one could order a gin and tonic alongside one's sirloin steak. But for lunch, I sat beside my grandma and the women of my family at the Trolley Stop, the in-house luncheonette downstairs at Hinshaw's, where I consumed countless meals of grilled cheese and hotdogs alongside chocolate milk in plastic ruby tumblers. Hinshaw's was mostly the domain of my grandma, her sister Licha, and her daughter Barbara, a few years my senior. It was a treat for my grandma to shop on a weekday afternoon, a symbol of her freedom to do as she wished with her day. She had learned to drive late in life, only a few years before I was born, and Licha had never learned at all, so on these weekday trips we would first pick them up at their little white house and then my grandma would slowly, carefully navigate the long, lime-green boat of her Monte Carlo across town to the Quad.

The Trolley Stop, its entrance crowded with barrels of cheeses and candies and mustards from the Hickory Farms shop beside it, wasn't Hinshaw's only charm. At Christmas the store erected four walls and a miniature door containing the Holiday Shop, a secretive enclosure where children could browse and choose gifts while parents waited outside. At the secret shop I bought narrow boxes of handkerchiefs for my grandpa, squat bottles of English Leather for my dad (who actually wore Aramis), and all manner of painted knick-knacks and boxed jewelry for my mother and grandma. The low shelves had a limited inventory of gifts to suit allowance-sized budgets, but I took a long time, relishing the opportunity to put all my window-shopping training to good use.

On Saturdays after Becky and then Mary Ann were married, both to men with white-collar sales careers, we'd congregate at my grandparents' house for the pre-shopping. My aunts and mom, after a perfunctory knock while turning the knob and opening the front door, inhabited my grandparents' house as if it were their own. It had been their home for so many years already, after all. They opened the refrigerator and made sandwiches, crowded into the narrow galley kitchen. They sat at the small dinette table and helped themselves to coffee (or brewed a fresh pot), or they sat on the blue-flowered couch and love seat and caught up on small talk, despite already talking on the phone earlier that day. Such small talk, such minutiae of daily lives, for what else was there to possibly discuss, when they talked on the phone during the week and saw each other almost every weekend? There was family gossip, the cliff-hangers on *Another World*, my grandma's soap, the local news. My grandma had no interest in her daughters' work lives, so when talk turned to Mary Ann's office politics, or a firing at my mother's job, my grandma would pretend to listen for two minutes and then clear her throat, rise from the sofa, and go into the kitchen. There, she'd open and offer me a pack of Van de Kamp danishes or start making grandpa his lunch.

Eventually the small talk would wind down, and the women would gather sunglasses, keys, and purses. Always we'd stand waiting while one of them lingered in the bathroom, freshening her lipstick before piling into Mary Ann's car to go shopping. "Stonewood?" she'd confirm as she turned the key in the ignition, and then we were backing out the black asphalt driveway, waving good-bye to my grandpa, who watched us from the front porch.

The men worked hard during the week. My grandpa was a foreman at the City of Whittier water department and my daddy walked his nightly miles behind the length of a polished wooden bar. On the weekends, they did yard work and the house chores requiring tools or the spraying of WD-40, and then relaxed by visiting the barbershop or sitting out on the back patio with cold cans of beer. Unless it was a birthday or barbecue at our house, they didn't associate with each other. Our shopping trips were the business of the women, as was the care and keeping of family ties.

I dream of department stores, that world of plush patterned carpets and per-fumed air, a world no longer my world—surrounded by family, by that suffocating close net of females who cared for me, spoiled me, were committed by proximity and blood to catch and hold me in their net when the world turned on me.

Except it was not the outside world that turned on me. The world, that scary mythical place depicted on the TV shows we watched, on the local news that showed us hillside fires and freeway serial killers and the bosses and teachers and landlords and coworkers who made up our family's distant universe—in the end, that place did me no lasting harm. Friends come and go, the net taught me. Their value barely extended past lunch tables and the office.

My grandmother did not have any friends beyond her older sister, Lillian (*Lili*), and her younger sister, Licha. There was tension between her and Lili, who lived in Los Angeles proper, some jealousy or disagreement about their father from decades past that still riled my grandma. Despite her standing as a typical woman of her era—she was a homeowner and homemaker who'd never worked, beyond a job in her teens at a local orange-packing plant, the mother of five children who'd all graduated from high school, mother to two sons who served in Vietnam and who both returned home apparently unscathed, wife of a hard-working and even-tempered husband—still, she suffered from both a debilitating self-consciousness and a deep-seated mistrust of everyone, including (and especially) her own family. She gossiped about both of her sisters viciously, their husbands, their looks, their houses. When her daughters were grown, she did the same to them. My grandma hated to stand outside her own house, especially in the front yard. People might see her. People might talk. Who? Neighbors. Others. Them. They would talk, she knew. Because she talked about them.

My grandparents' ranch house, purchased nearly new in the early 1960s, boasted a wide front window, nearly floor-to-ceiling in height, that looked out on the driveway and quiet street. The window was formally dressed in thick pleated beige drapes over white lace sheers from J.C. Penney. Every day, my grandmother opened her drapes about two feet wide, both to let in the south-facing sunlight and to signal to the world that all was well inside. The window was not for looking through. As a toddler and into adolescence, I was scolded whenever I played hide-and-seek between the drapes and the wall, or pulled the curtains too wide, or simply stood at the window too long. Neighbors would see me, I was reminded, and assume that I was spying, no matter that the window was set back at least fifty feet from the sidewalk, behind the raised brick flower bed. Looking out the window was never an innocent act, and my family was well-skilled at learning the specific rattle of every member's car engine as they pulled in for a visit. That's how we knew who was coming over—not by looking out. On the rare times there was a commotion or real reason to look outside, one could always just open the front door and stand mostly hidden behind the screen. But my grandmother's window, the very definition of a picture window—that view was off limits.

The net that held me shifted over the years, expanded to contain my sister, nine years my junior. It stretched to contain Mary Ann's growing ego and bossiness that accompanied her series of promotions at the bank, until she was crowned vice president of a large department. The net absorbed Becky's frequent melancholy and burgeoning shopping habit that bordered on addiction, her closets stuffed with blazers and blouses and patterned dresses with gold buttons. Their tags dangled white, still attached, in her dark mirrored closets. Her small house with the Olympic-sized pool in Orange County smelled pleasingly of new clothes, leather shoes, and shopping bags from tony shops at Fashion Island, the outdoor mall in Newport Beach.

The net of women morphed to accommodate the crisis in my immediate family of four. After more than a decade of bartending and dreaming of Hollywood glory, of scheming for other careers that might bring more money and happiness, my dad craved change. There had even been a brief plan to co-own and work in a welding shop, although to picture my dad trading in his elegant uniform of dress shirts and slim black slacks for the workaday grime of a welder's attire was hard to imagine, even for an imaginative child. In the end, spurred by his brother's lofty talk of the future of solar power, my dad moved all of us two hours north and a world away to dusty Bakersfield. For the first time in her life, my mother lived apart from the security of her family and sisters, away from her hometown and the surrounding cities that were all she'd ever known.

It didn't even last a year. Mere months after packing us off to Bakersfield, to the new house in a neighborhood so new there weren't yet houses across the street, my dad realized that selling solar panels was not his destiny, after all. Or perhaps the need for change went deeper than mere employment. Whatever—in late winter, after Christmas, my dad up and left town in our aqua Ford Pinto. Left the state, left the West Coast, left the bank account and cupboards quite bare. We didn't learn just where he'd gone until he returned, many, many months later, when he drove the Pinto up the driveway of my grandparents' house, where my mother, sister, and I had moved a week after he disappeared.

My extended family absorbed this turn of events as my grandparents welcomed the three of us into their home. The first time, it was a shock and a shame and a tragedy, but there was also sympathy and embrace. When my father returned six months after disappearing without a note or phone call and driving to Florida and back, my mother, after meetings in rooms and restaurants, agreed to take him back. And her decision was swallowed. Approved, even: a family should stay together.

And then my father pulled nearly the exact same stunt a year later, this time while we lived in southern Orange County and he tended bar at an upscale seafood eatery in Dana Point. One could not place the blame this time on the failure of clients to purchase solar heating for their new pools in Bakersfield. This time, clearly something darker and more troubling was afoot, and, while the bulk of the blame lay at my father's absent feet, somehow my mother and I were guilty, too. At least that was the judgment delivered through my grandma's tightly pressed lips, my aunts' silences, or their husbands' offhand comments. We who persisted in loving my dad shared the blame, we who loved and forgave him and still laughed when he poked fun and made arch comments about my mother's family, that family who had taken us in and kept us afloat when he had run away. Twice.

It was the same house that had once contained my mother and her four siblings for years, and yet the addition of us three females now made the house shrink. There were five humans in a thirteen-hundred-square-foot house that was in many ways my first home, the house that had remained my one constant over years of changes and moves. Now this house became a rat's maze where I tried to navigate a space large enough to hold me in my grief and confusion. A space in that house where I could escape my grandmother's sudden, inexplicable furies.

I had changed in the year and a half since the first time we'd had to move in with my grandparents. That time, there had been comfort—everything may have been wrong and different and stricken, yet at the same time I was perfectly safe, held in the net of family and familiarity. The first time my father left, there were afternoons of easy hugs, and evenings spent lying on the couch, my head in my grandma's lap watching TV while her fingers wove through my hair, picking off the nervous scabs that had erupted across my scalp. Same streets, same house, same smoggy-blue skies crisscrossed with overhead telephone wires. I stood alone outside and watched the ever-present crows stalking across my grandfather's dichondra.

But in the year we'd been gone in Orange County, everything had changed. Or rather, I had changed. I was no longer the chubby fifth grader who'd set up her Barbie ski lodge in my grandparent's spare bedroom, crammed with my yellow furniture. When I returned again to the spare room in the middle of sixth grade, the baby fat had gone, as everyone had always assured me it would. In its place I was smooth-cheeked and long-legged and needed to wear a grimy, thin bra that no one ever remembered to throw in the wash. I'd left yet another elementary school in midsemester and enrolled for a second time at the school a few blocks west of my grandparent's house. In my crisp white shorts and pastel polo shirts, I was an exotic bird blown inland from our house near the coast. The Mexican American *cholas* in their gray cords and navy windbreaker jackets threatened to kick my ass, daily.

Except for new, less beach-preppy clothes, I wanted for naught, except the intangible things I craved daily: conversations, attention, answers to questions I wasn't able to ask plainly: why, again, and where, again, and when, again, and was it me? And why was my grandmother so furious this time? Why did she stalk me through her house while my mother worked at her new job, while my sister attended preschool, while I busied myself with a dust rag and can of Pledge, hissing, hinting things about men in her stories, about running away from her father? Why the fit when she saw me, *caught* me she claimed, sitting on my grandpa's lap that one last time, before I was held at arm's length forever after?

My mother, the eldest child, the supposed rebel, came home from her new job craving silence, ease. She took in her mother's rants, sighed when I cornered her in the back bedroom as she slipped off her workday pantyhose. She played nice, made dinner-table chitchat, ignored the hostility of her mother's sniping, ate humble pie when my grandmother slammed down cups of lime Jello onto the lace tablecloth before us all. Only my sister, adorable and feisty at three, could break the tension with her chatter. Saturday shopping trips continued, though now as I trailed behind my mom and aunts, I seethed with adolescent rage at all they hid in flattering each other's purses, in all that went undiscussed in their vapid hours spent admiring shoes. My patience could no longer be bought with patent leather T-straps or Hello Kitty markers; rather, my mom urged me to show gratitude for the things my aunts bought me. Stricken by all that I needed and was refused, I hated how any passing stranger could size me up and accurately state that, clearly, I wanted for naught.

Although my father eventually returned again to Southern California, it took longer for my parents to reconcile. Whether this was because my mother felt legitimately torn about giving my dad yet another chance, or whether she just needed to give that impression, our second stay with my grandparents lasted much longer than the first. In truth, my parents' offstage decision to reunite when I was halfway through the eighth grade stemmed from a mix of ultimatums, promises, and the pressure to get away from my grandma and her nightly assaults of innuendo and vague threats of how someday soon *the truth would come out*. In the end, my parents stayed married.

Our family of four lived together again, in a small apartment complex on a busy street barely a mile from the house we'd lived in before the move to Bakersfield. Whittier—home of the Whittwood and the Quad and the historic Uptown district where I would soon love to shop, shoving a five-dollar bill in my jean shorts and walking on summer evenings to the crammed used bookstore, or Lovell's Records. Though my parents were lifelong renters, we'd never lived in an apartment before, always houses with spacious yards and tidy front entries. This is only temporary, they insisted when I questioned the choice of a second-floor apartment over a real house. Yet once settled within the Beverly Arms, my parents stayed put. The large three-bedroom unit with its rear views of rolling green hills, and the sprawling ranch homes tucked high within them, remained home for decades. Occasionally, my dad dreamed and schemed of relocating to small, scenic towns in the west: Prescott, Arizona, or Bend, Oregon. On vacations, we took side trips to explore these towns but never made real plans. Clearly, my mother wasn't moving anywhere too far with my dad ever again.

I was born into a net, closely knit, woven of history and genetics by a clan of women, each with their own secrets and scandals and dreams. I had a closely knit family, and then awoke from the long spell of childhood to find that maybe, after all, I didn't.

And so I dream of department stores, of afternoons at the May Company spent following behind the women, learning how to hold a blouse or shoe aloft and consider it, how to lightly run a finger through shimmering necklaces at jewelry counters, training my eye to find that one, there, that will tell the world who I am or aim to be.

I dream of drowsing among the circular racks of bright clothes, half here on this plane, half dazed with boredom and lost in my imagination. Years and years of shopping, and I can recall only a handful of items bought and treasured: chubby Bonne Bell Lip Smackers, a pair of white patent leather Easter shoes, a patchwork gypsy sundress I loved but that stretched snug against my middle. The carefully chosen loot is gone, but in my mind's eye I still ride the escalator at the Broadway, still see my hand upon its dull beige rail. I can step off and navigate my way expertly through its departments: the juniors section to my left, the infant and toddler section to the rear right, where my mom once won a drawing for free diaper service when she was pregnant with Kathy.

I can hear the hushed piped-in Muzak, interrupted now and again by the *ding, ding* chime of the in-house paging calls. The women's lounges in our department stores were quiet and dim and boasted a front room with a long couch, potted palms, and a wide vanity mirror with a white leather stool. On the side table was a telephone. If one so desired, you could simply choose to stay in the lounge all afternoon and hold forth from those headquarters.

Beneath my hand I can feel the plush green velvet ropes at the hostess counter of the Broadway's elegant coffee shop, where I was delighted to learn in my broke twenties that a club sandwich could simply be charged with a swipe of my store credit card. I dream of being back at Hinshaw's and the Trolley Stop, eating lunch with my grandma's petite weight impressing the red vinyl booth beside me, before I was exiled from easy exchanges with her, before my grandma's presence in her coordinating outfits filled me with dread.

I dream of those days when the net of women was intact and filled with good intent, back when I believed as much as my grandma that blood was thick and prophetic and would hold us all, gathered not around her dining room table but the circular tables at the Broadway coffee shop with their starched white tablecloths. The hostess had to seat us at the round tables to fit us all, our party of six, my mother, aunts, grandmother, and sister. We sat in the center of the dining room, shopping bags at our feet. I can almost make out the ease of our chatter, the satisfied winding down of another excursion that began like so many others before it, years of Saturday afternoons that started with a phone call and a tacit, unspoken gathering at my grandparents' house. I strain to hear the words that someone will inevitably utter and rouse us from the couches and the danishes and the gossip: *Let's go shopping.*

Ophira Eisenberg

he Bloomingdale's salesgirl must have made a mistake when she told me the price of the shoes, but I didn't want to embarrass the poor thing by having her repeat her error *again*, plus I was in a rush, so I let her take the credit card from my fingers and continue with the transaction. I'd figure it out after the party.

The "party" was the White House Correspondents' Dinner. I had received a last-minute invitation even though I was neither a reporter nor a celebrity, but rather the host of a new NPR trivia show called *Ask Me Another*. The public radio powers thought it would be nice if some new blood attended the event—either that, or some rich executive forgot that he'd already promised to attend the grand opening of his daughter's vineyard on that same night. It really didn't matter to me—I couldn't believe I was going. I couldn't believe I was going to be in the same room as the president of the United States! I couldn't believe it was tomorrow.

Of all the things I'd accomplished in my life, it was this invite that impressed my family the most. I was raised by immigrant parents who worked hard to make us middle class, but it wasn't until I moved to New York that I realized we were comparatively poor. I even felt inferior in the Ivy League NPR world, worried that they'd find out I didn't read Thoreau closely enough. And I didn't have smooth hands. It's lonely being a blue-collar nerd. I called my boss's twenty-something assistant who arranged my travel to Washington, D.C., and asked her about the event's dress code.

"It's black tie. Ophira, this is like the Oscars," she schooled. "You need to do it up!"

I'd never purchased a formal frock in my life. I didn't even know where to start. My mother sewed both of my prom dresses and I got married at City Hall in a sundress I bought at Anthropologie. Yes, I was that girl.

I asked if she had a suggestion as to where I should shop. She tossed out Neiman Marcus or Nordstrom and I had to break it to her that New York doesn't have the space for those warehouse-sized stores—we cram seventy condos and twelve Chase Banks into a would-be Nordstrom lot. She thought for a moment and then said with a degree of confidence that verged on condescending, "Oh— you should just call Saks and get a personal shopper."

"Normal people can just do that?" I asked. I didn't grow up on a farm, but all of a sudden I felt like I could smell the barley fields on my imaginary overalls.

"Yes, of course!" she said. "Anyone can do it."

Well, I *was* anyone.

When I first came to New York, I automatically assumed that I was cut off from 85 percent of the stores in the city. I would walk through Soho, just to feel insignificant, and gaze into minimalist boutiques to watch the upper crust shopping. I would never be them. I had to hold back from accosting people lounging at cafés in the middle of a weekday by yelling, "What exactly do you *do?*" As far as my clothing was concerned, it was purchased outside the city at outlet malls and chain store mainstays: H&M, Banana Republic (but not the BR line—don't be crazy), and Urban Outfitters. I distinctly remember after a couple of months of living in New York and working as a telemarketer, I purchased a red tank top at Club Monaco for sixty-eight dollars. I bought it because my friend Kelly guaranteed me that "it looked amazing" and I wanted to please her. At home, I treated it like a Ming vase, saving this tank top of all things for special occasions. The few times I did wear it I was uncomfortable, worried that I'd wreck it, rip it, or irreversibly stain it. I definitely had an S&M relationship with my clothes: The more expensive they were, the more they dominated me.

After locating Saks on Google Maps (I've lived within three miles of it yet had no idea where it was), I called to request a personal shopper. The receptionist cut to the chase and asked me how much I wanted to spend. I stuttered and said, "A thousand dollars?" The amount sounded exorbitant to me, as if I were doing an impression of Dr. Evil from Austin Powers. Was that enough? Was it too much? I'd never spent more than four hundred dollars on anything in my wardrobe—so I had no gauge as to how much these things cost. She said that *might* work. I hung up the phone and calculated how long I'd needed to work to pay for a thousand-dollar dress, and then sent out some emails for roadwork and freelance gigs.

At 4 PM, I showed up and met with an older man with slicked-back hair in a tailored suit. He spoke in an accent that was half French, half Italian, and 100 percent fake. He looked me up and down but settled on down.

"Go around the store and pick out some things," he commanded with a flick of his wrist as if he was shooing me away. It seemed a little antithetical to the personal shopper experience—I mean, wasn't that his job? I grabbed a couple of sequined numbers, but he shook his head and put them back on the rack. He held up a plain black wool dress and asked, "What's the occasion, again?" He made it clear he was already bored before he heard the answer.

"I'm going to have dinner with the president," I said. "Have you ever heard of the White House Correspondents' dinner?"

I am not one to rub someone's face in a thing, but I had to defend myself.

He smoothed his hair and remarked that he was unfamiliar with the occasion.

Oh, is that the way we're going to play this, Pierre Corleone?

"Well it requires something fancier than that," I told him. He wasn't backing down.

"Well, I don't know your ranking at this affair and I wouldn't want you to show anyone up."

Oh. I get it—*the help* should never overshadow the people who actually belonged at the event. I had to hand it to Pierre; he knew just where to pinch. It was clear that I wasn't his usual brand of clientele and, even worse, I'd worked in retail for years myself, so this guy and I were not that much different. That was the problem.

I said ciao and he gave me his business card for "when I changed my mind." My only other idea was to go to the top floor of Bloomingdale's and buy a dress off the rack, which I accomplished in about thirty minutes, no problem. It was a black-and-white dress, tight and form-fitting, but overlaid with flowing white gauze that fell to the ground. It wasn't the flashiest gown on the planet, but I liked it and it was even on sale, marked down to three hundred dollars. That meant I had money left over for shoes.

I descended one flight of stairs to the Shoe Salon and looked at the different brands, completely lost as to what would work. A black shoe? A sandal? A wedge? How did I make it through the world as a girl this long? I grabbed a salesgirl and pleaded for her help. She seemed reluctant at first, too busy for me, but when I tore out my dress and said, "Just something to go with this, please!" she gasped and caressed the long gauze skirt. "It's beautiful! Modern yet airy! I love it!" A woman sitting across from us with a face full of fillers, trying on Gucci loafers, asked where I would be wearing this dress. Having learned my lesson, I answered with an apologetic question, "The White House Correspondents' Dinner?" Her eyes bulged. "What? That is so exciting!" she yelped and hit the edge of her chair with a manicured hand. Both salesgirl and the filler woman started telling every shopper around them, "She's going to the White House Correspondents' Dinner!" which prompted another sales guy to gravitate toward the excitement. He established himself as the gay sales guy of the floor, and therefore the final word on all style choices and purchases. They all scurried around the salon, shoes flew through the air, and footwear options were heavily assessed and discarded. Finally, the gay sales guy presented a delicate, blush-hued sandal encrusted with tiny gray and black rhinestones. We all stood back and collectively sighed. "They're perfect," he said in a dramatic whisper. My shopping group and I nodded in agreement, and for a brief moment I felt like I belonged. "Okay, I'll take them!" I said, dizzy on a shopper's high, and my teammates almost cheered. The salesgirl whisked them away to ring them up, while the sales guy and the filler woman consulted me on what I should do with my hair. I was actually having fun. This was *really* shopping. I got it for the first time. With my credit card in my outstretched hand, I asked with a big grin, "How much are those shoes anyway?"

"Ah, let's see. Oh! They're on sale! One thousand, one hundred and forty-nine dollars."

Ha. Hilarious. That can't be right. Only a shoe plucked off Lady Gaga's foot could possibly cost that much. It was ridiculous. Were those rhinestones actual diamonds? Were the shoes assembled with adult labor? Did they come with a lease to an Upper West Side apartment?

It was my last chance to say something, but I didn't want to ruin the momentum or tarnish our temporary friendship, so I let her carefully insert each shoe into its own individual cloth bag and tuck them gently into their blazing yellow Fendi shoebox crib. I punished myself internally for being such a pushover. Last week, I let the girl at Jamba Juice talk me into two extra boosts in my smoothie. It was like that all over again . . . times a thousand. I barely owned them and these shoes were already walking all over me.

"The receipt's in the bag," she beamed.

"Great. Thank you so much for your help." I smiled, stunned.

I left the shoe floor feeling worried that security would grab me any minute, rip the shopping bag from my hands, and arrest me for being a fake. We all knew that those shoes were too precious for my kind. But the alarms didn't sound and I made my way home on the subway. That salesgirl must have been wrong, I kept thinking. How could four strips of leather and some rhinestones cost that much? Whatever, I'd figure it out when I got home.

When I finally got into my apartment, I fished out the receipt to see how much the shoes *really* cost and couldn't believe that the salesgirl nailed it. I looked at the yellow Fendi box. How could they possibly be over a thousand dollars? There weren't enough raw materials in their construction to justify the amount. You couldn't even really wear them *outside*! Did I just get scammed? Would savvy shoppers tell me that only suckers and rich oil barons from the Middle East pay retail prices for such things? I mean, I worked in public radio, for God's sake! I felt like a heel.

I could pay for them, of course; I had money in the bank, but it would set me back for a while. And it was irresponsible. Shouldn't I be doing better things with my money, like saving for retirement shoes?

But I wore the sparkling sandals to the event, disappointed that my long gown didn't allow for more foot exposure. No one complimented me on them or even noticed them. For one thousand, one hundred, and forty-nine dollars, I could have hired two handsome ab-ulous men to carry me around the correspondents' dinner. That would have gotten some attention. Then again, no one complimented me . . . period. Compared to everyone else, I felt like an excited jester, bouncing around, taking photos, devouring the bread rolls, and stashing programs, place settings, and napkins in my purse for my scrapbook.

As I sat with my legs crossed at the table, laughing at President Obama's speech, I periodically glanced down to admire my shoes, mesmerized by the rhinestones glinting in the ballroom's overhead light. And I will say this—at the end of the night, after standing for hours, I never noticed that my feet hurt once.

I returned to New York, and, as if under a spell, promptly threw out the golden shoebox and paid my credit card balance weeks before it was due. It was a combination of wanting to cover up what I'd done and remove the option of returning them. I wanted to believe that I *could* have those shoes, even though I could feel them mocking me from their pocket in my shoe rack. "Will you ever feel adequate enough for us?" they teased. "Will you ever be able to wear us without feeling shame?" I desperately tried to justify their purchase in my head. Maybe I could rent them out to friends? If I broke one, could I take Fendi to small claims court?

I want to justify owning them. I want the shoes and I to become equals. I've worked almost every day of my adult life, and I should be allowed to have nice things at this point. But the pragmatist in me has decided that the only way to make them worth it is by wearing them one hundred times in my lifetime, so that's only ninety-nine more occasions. Those stupid shoes are motivating me to have a better life, and, hopefully one day before it's all over, I'll donate them to Goodwill because I will have reached my goal. How painfully middle class of me.

RANDOM SAMPLING

Kristin Thiel

can't stop thinking about the running shoes I won recently. They're still in the form of a gift certificate, but I'm experiencing something mildly akin to phantom limb syndrome: I keep feeling those new shoes on my feet. I see their color, a blue hue natural only to underwater and equatorial jungles. And I am surprised when I look down and see my old pink-accented pair (a color natural only to, unfortunately, the jungle that is the hinterland of Barbie's Dreamhouse), their cotton-candy sweetness worn away on the inside at the base of my Achilles' tendon.

I'm not one of those people who never wins anything. But I am one of those people who, despite coming from a practically minded midwestern family, believes in luck. And the idea that, maybe, just maybe, two events beyond my control—the winning of those shoes and the losing of something much more serious—might cancel each other out and become somehow then a life controlled.

Nearly six months before I won these shoes, my partner of almost twelve years ended our relationship. To me, then and still, his decision seems as random as my winning of the running raffle. His reasons are understandable—I agree we had issues that needed to be corrected. But that we could not work through them is unexpected and feels out of character, outside the pattern I thought we formed.

The end had been coming for three months, the time between his telling me about his unhappiness and our final conversation as a couple. One of the many things I learned about the man I thought I knew so well was that he delivers horrible news when I'm comfortable. That last night I was well fed and happy in bed, reading a good, fun thriller, *City of Veils*, the protagonist one of the few women in a Saudi Arabian medical examiner's office. X joined me and perched on the bed, on top of the covers. I would have known what he was going to say even if he hadn't sighed and hung his head. I made my face stone. I fixed on the round chip in the paint on the door, the round doorknob, the round screw on the doorknob plate. I heard his choked crying, and then turned my hearing away. I kept myself stone.

After a while, I did not care about his words. I was thinking, *This is how I'm reacting to the end of my marriage. I'll remember this forever. He is my friend, and he is hurting.* I leaned forward and, without looking at him, hugged him. The orange walls were so bright in the bedside light. I released him, scooted over. "Come on, come to bed; it's late." He protested. I said, "Are you protesting me?"

"No," he said, "it would be very comforting to me."

"Then get in," I said.

And he got fully naked for the first time in a long time with me, and he climbed in bed next to me, and we lay on our backs, holding hands—a position we'd taken many times before.

It's like we're about to walk forward together, I always used to say. *Into sleep.*

When I won the shoes, I'd attended nearly all of the Fit Right NW First Thursday Urban Adventure Run events for three of its four years of existence. A core group of friends and others who rotated in and out joined me in this monthly free scavenger hunt through Northwest Portland, receiving for our efforts each time free beer and the chance at a variety of prizes in the free raffle, a DJ spinning dance hits while we waited expectantly for our numbers to be called, or, for some of us, not so expectantly. I didn't ignore my tickets in order to double-fist from plastic cups as some of my friends did—"We never win anyway, so why bother paying attention?"—and I stayed through the bitter end, come rain or come shine, of each raffle, hoping for one of the lightweight prizes I'd just give away at the next birthday party (a sporty-looking photo frame), the prizes, I'd joke, that were more punishment than treat (a discount on an upcoming 50K), the prizes I'd never ever *ever* use or give away (the brand-name Muscle Milk is on my list of gag-worthy words—muscles excreting a creamy liquid).

A month and a half after X ended our relationship, we were still living in the same house. We had entered the Christmas season also known as December, and I had this grand thought: X and I would do a final month together—as in those movies when someone gets a terminal disease, and he and his lover know he'll be dead in thirty days, so they live it up. A last hurrah! We'll eat at our favorite places, watch movies together, laugh—Wasn't that a good time? Wasn't that?— and then we'd say goodbye at the end, cleansed. Yes, I really was thinking that. Our cohabitation from October 15 until then had not been all roses and rhododendrons, though we certainly had done our damnedest to cultivate something other than weeds: me melting the marshmallows for the Rice Krispies treats he was taking to the party I was no longer accompanying him to, him driving me to work. We hugged each other and asked how the other was doing—but it turns out he didn't think my idea of a last-hurrah month was so grand at all. Worse, he didn't really think anything of it—neither embracing nor recoiling, he was genuinely confused. Why would we do *that*?

The day after I won the shoes, I wrote this email, which even referenced that perennial winner Barry Manilow, to everyone who'd ever attended one of the First Thursday runs with me:

> After three years, almost the entire life of this event, WE FINALLY
> WON! The grand finale, no less, free-pair-of-shoes prize! And by "we
> won," I mean, I'm getting the shoes, but I'll keep referring to the win
> as ours. Because why would I keep doing this monthly thing without
> my friends?
>
> [singing] Looks like we made it!

That night was the first time I had seen my ex since I moved out of our house. Our mutual friends admirably straddled the line between us as we stood waiting for our raffle numbers not to be called. He and I admirably avoided eye contact with each other. He had grown the beard that I'd always encouraged him to try and that he'd always refused. When my raffle number was (surprisingly) called, I have no idea if he smiled or joined in the cheering, but he did move quickly to be the one outside the frame, snapping the photo of our friends, my ticket, and me.

When a major life change happens, perhaps especially when it is foisted upon a person, that person sees connections everywhere. I was so ridiculously happy about winning those shoes that it buoyed me for days, a couple of weeks—I still feel a lift when I recall it. Thinking about it so much and knowing X was right there (but for the first time in a long time in my periphery), I connect the two. Two random happenings: how they mirror each other in many ways.

Consumer power may in many ways demonstrate the broader control females are finally experiencing (be it temporary or more systemic). After all, if we can buy our own shoes, clothes, even diamonds, as Destiny's Child sang in "Independent Women," we are also people with jobs and financial wherewithal, buying our own tickets to important places, wearing what we bought, and influencing people with the items we carry—and with the knowledge that earned us the money that allowed us to buy those items. Now, there are houses that Jill built.

X and I used to go shopping together all the time. I'd be his helper at the hardware store and the grocery store, and he'd encourage me through the shopping excursions for new clothes that I usually dreaded completing. (Yes, there's one thing we needed to work on—my reliance on him and his overly helpful nature.) I used to not-so-entirely joke that I wished he were a woman because he had a male-dominated career and brought home a much greater share of the bacon than I did (in my girly creative-arts career), and I hated how 1950s that made our couplehood appear. But X was the gatherer as well as the hunter, and that antiquated our relationship just as much. I let him have all the control. He may have been picking through produce and exclaiming over herbs, traditional female activities, but I was daydreaming an aisle behind. I did so because my paycheck wasn't as big as his—I didn't feel I'd bought a full share of the decision.

When we split, one of the things X did was make a list of our big possessions—furniture, appliances, art—and their resale value. We'd divvy via emotion—who loved *Maria*, the painting, more? The other could have the tapestry purchased on the same trip—but the dollar signs would help equalize, break ties. During one of these exchanges, I slid from the love seat (ultimately, mine) to the floor (ultimately, his) and just lay there, looking up at him on the chair (I don't remember who got that one; I don't remember which one it was, don't remember anything but his face), pressing my palm against the scratched, aged wood.

"Sometimes I wish you'd chosen the house," he finally said. "I just want to fill the car with whatever it will hold and go and be done."

I couldn't believe his wish, not only for its cutting finality but also for how carefree it was. Stuff was all I had anymore. This stuff. It also was never mine: His income had allowed us the month in Oaxaca, during which we dined under Maria's gaze and, at the end of our trip, asked a more advanced language classmate to accompany us for the request to purchase the painting from the restaurant. His income had bought us matching furniture. His name was on the deed to the house. I contributed, but on my own these things would have been realized much slower, or not at all, as single me surely would have at least some different priorities than partnered me. True to X's word throughout the years, at the end these possessions were ours, not just his, and divided as such. And I clawed for them and then clung to them, all the while wishing just as much simply to possess his attitude about them.

Just as shopping wasn't always done in orderly malls, consumerism also wasn't always controlled—think of the early-twentieth-century outdoor stalls of New York's Lower East Side, the traveling carts of wares, of bazaars, of haggling—and even today it still isn't.

"Great shirt," I told a friend recently. "I went into Goodwill for a colander," she said, "and I saw this shirt. I knew it would fit me, so I forgot the colander and bought the shirt without even trying it on."

In Portland, Oregon, people dig through the Bins, a Goodwill branch that sells the donations that no other Goodwill store will take, displaying its treasures and trinkets (and plenty of dirty, broken tricks) in heaps. The idea is to find something useful to you, but, in such craziness, there has to be some shopper appreciation for the random, the out-of-control. Like the joy of finding treasure in a pile of junk.

My life after the breakup is hardly the only one careening toward the unknown.

We all are made of soft tissue and fragile bones and, of course, mostly water.

Most of us are three months of paychecks from homelessness.

Most of us have crazy relatives who may swoop in at any moment.

Most of us have pets and children who behave like pets and children.

Most of us have lives precariously balanced against the whim of other precariously balanced lives, so that even if it's another life that topples . . .

While moving after my breakup, I made a couple of trips to Goodwill, and, regardless of whether my things make their way to the Bins or to a more selective outlet, they're all usable things—good things, even. I cast them off because I could not bear (practically or emotionally) them anymore, but someone else will see them anew, will have room for them, will speak their language.

"Reflecting back," X said of our relationship's dissolution, "I think this has been coming for longer than we consciously knew. But now we're both able to handle moving on."

An item at the Bins may be perfect, not for you, affordable, or too much for what it is, but earned money still exchanges hands for it. Every errand, for a new thing or for a new life, puts choices around spending—of money, of time, of emotion—in front of us. Now all my choices are wholly mine, including how to make future relationships even more sustainable.

Since starting this essay, I tried on shoes to choose which pair I'd buy with my gift certificate. My careful research included running on the store's treadmill and reviewing with store staff a video of my running to determine my unique gait, which led to a staff person choosing three pairs of shoes I should try, which led to him measuring both of my feet (one is longer than the other), which led to me trying on each pair and running in each pair—which brought me to two options, one being the blue pair I'd dreamed about and one being a charcoal-and-fuchsia-and-lime pair. As I tugged my heavy socks and boots back on and the clerk repacked the running shoes in their boxes, I confessed that I wouldn't be spending any money that day—as I had won the grand prize at the previous First Thursday run.

"You did?" he exclaimed so joyously that I myself had to laugh. "This woman won the shoes at last month's run!" he cried to another staff member returning from the storage room.

"She did?" she beamed, and I laughed some more. This happened again at the register: "Congratulations!" "Wow, the winner!"

To be praised for sheer good luck. When I won the shoes, those gathered cheered, and the announcers asked for my name to shout it back to the crowd, and strangers high-fived me as I returned to hugs from my friends and my ex taking our photograph. Winning is about luck, but it's also about attention, being singled out for a prize. And I said "Cheese" for the one who had singled me out for rejection. I gave you my time, my energy, my enthusiasm—you gave me a chance, and then a win. Bartering is at the heart of every transaction.

I surprised myself by choosing the pair of shoes I hadn't known existed before my shopping trip, the pair that exploded with 1980s-inspired color. Though the shoe expert assured me there was a distinction between the shoes' weight and soles, outside the colors, I couldn't tell the difference. But doing something out of character—yet at the same time very much within my control—felt right.

STRIPPED DOWN AND REDRESSED

Randon Billings Noble

et me start with a confession: I'm no fashionista. In fact, my look is pretty beat—Beat Generation, that is. I'm most comfortable in a T-shirt, jeans, and boots. Basic, but not sloppy. Fitted, but not fancy. I'll wear a scarf or a watch—a stainless steel Swiss Army or a chunky plum Zodiac—but rarely jewelry. I like to look at fashion magazines —but I almost never follow the trends.

Before I got pregnant, I was tall and thin. Pretty much any pair of jeans and any T-shirt looked good—or good enough—on me. I didn't have to worry about rises and cuts and necklines. Low, boot, crew—it all worked for me.

Then I got pregnant. With twins. People started asking me when I was due when I was only four months along. I didn't know during my first trimester that my waist was destined to double in size. I didn't know that during my last trimester I'd be pretty much housebound, stripped down to a maternity tank top and two receiving blankets pinned together to make a loincloth because nothing else fit and I was too hot (in February) to wear much else.

I had mixed feelings about this pregnancy. It was planned, but the twin part wasn't. We had no history of twins in our family and no help conceiving them— no fertility treatments, no medical intervention. It took almost the whole nine months for me to reconcile myself to the idea, and it was sometimes difficult to participate in all the happy baby conversations and preparations going on around me. The only part of pregnancy that I truly enjoyed (other than eating lots of cheeseburgers with milk shakes) was shopping for maternity clothes. Shopping for maternity clothes was all about me—not the imminent twins, who, I feared, were destined to take over (and thus destroy) my independent life.

Usually shopping—clothes shopping—is about trying on selves or lives as much as an outfit. Who will you become while wearing this dress? Where will you go? Who will you meet? What new life will unfurl before you? Perhaps you will wear this red sheath to a museum opening. Perhaps you will throw on this gauzy shift to prevent a sunburn at a European beach. Perhaps this is the little black dress you'll be wearing at the New Year's Eve party where you meet your future spouse. . . . But pregnancy is a finite state, and shopping for maternity clothes doesn't lead to these exploratory avenues. In the first trimester it might be about showcasing your new bump. By the last I was just trying to cover it.

I decided to hit the Gap—a place where I had shopped for nonmaternity clothes, a place that wasn't Mimi Maternity or A Pea in the Pod, a place where I could still sort of pretend I wasn't entirely pregnant after all, where I could keep a bit of psychic distance between me and the twins I was carrying.

I tried on "sexy" boot-cut jeans and long cowl-neck tunics. I tried on full-panel leggings and empire-waist dresses. I chose odd colors I didn't usually wear—plum pants, a fuchsia-print dress—because I thought, what the hell? I'm only going to be wearing this for six months at best. My belly was high and round and hard, my arms and legs still slender and muscled. I looked great. I bought it all.

For months—less than six, alas—I loved my wardrobe. But I kept growing. I grew the twins and all their accoutrements—placentas, umbilical cords, amniotic fluids. I made more of my own body, too: more blood to pump through more vessels, more skin to cover more abdomen, more miscellaneous swellings in my ankles and under my jaw. All too soon I grew out of my maternity clothes and into the tank top and loincloth.

As my body grew, I felt my self diminishing. I no longer did the things that made me me. I didn't make a pot of tea to drink slowly throughout the morning; I didn't go to aikido classes in the afternoon. I didn't make French toast breakfasts or take evening walks around the neighborhood. I didn't do crossword puzzles, read Russian novels, teach writing classes, write essays.

Instead I spent a lot of time sitting in my living room in an Ikea Poäng chair. I read all the Sookie Stackhouse novels I could get on my Kindle until reading felt too difficult. Then I watched whole seasons of shows on streaming video—science fiction like *Firefly*, addictions like *The Wire*. I had read that women's brains can shrink up to 8 percent during a pregnancy. I became convinced that, with twins, my brain had shrunk 16 percent. I tried not to think too much about the future, about my brain regaining its capacities, about my body subsiding into something more recognizable. I carried the twins but I let nearly everything else go. And still my body grew.

When the twins were born they weighed nearly eight pounds each. I had carried over fifteen pounds of baby all the way to term. That evening I looked at them in their little hospital bassinets and thought, *They're people—two little people*, and it felt like an epiphany. Once I had finally met them, they were no longer the squatters who had hijacked my body and colonized my existence. They would change my life—more than I could possibly imagine that long first night—but somehow I was certain that they wouldn't destroy it. And I was right.

When my belly finally started to shrink from its Henry VIII proportions, I had to go shopping again. I had hoped that my first-trimester clothes would fit my "fourth" trimester body, but instead of a high, firm baby bump I had a low-slung cross between a brain coral and a yeast dough. My early maternity clothes looked terrible, and my prepregnancy clothes were too small. I was back at wardrobe square one.

Once again, I hit the Gap, first online because I wasn't getting out much, and then at a store with a grimly lit three-way mirror. Things didn't look so good anymore.

I put on a pair of low-rise jeans and looked not like a muffin but an exploding popover. I tried a plain white tank top and felt like a Hooter's waitress on an off day. I wriggled into a floral dress that was meant to invoke a breezy summer afternoon but conjured Eleanor Roosevelt instead. I felt like an idiot. Had I really imagined that my body would return to its former shape after all it had been through? Inasmuch as I thought of it at all, yes, I had.

Welcome to being an American woman in the twenty-first century, I thought. An American woman who's given birth. I felt like this for a while.

And then I started to feel differently about my new body. It started to become normal, to become mine. Not destroyed, but changed. I stopped cringing over my stomach and wincing away from mirrors. I focused more on the twin bodies I was caring for and on my own mind, thinking about things I might read or write, ways of living, and plans for the future.

I also started to think about shopping differently. It has become a less casual action, one I take more care with. Now before I try on a pair of pants, I check the waistline. Now I have to work harder to accentuate and camouflage, to find things my body feels easy in, not confined or strained or ashamed: a V-neck instead of a crew, skinny jeans instead of boot cut, a long linen tunic, a drop-shouldered swing T-shirt, an empire-waist dress made of voile instead of jersey.

I am already a new person as I try on that dress—I am a mother now. I am also still me, the me that reads and writes and walks and people-watches, the me I feared lost but was only waiting for the weight of pregnancy and all its foreboding to lift.

But I find that I am still shopping for answers: Where will I go in these new trappings? Who will I meet? What new life is about to unfurl before me? Who will I become from here?

SAVED BY THE HOME DEPOT

Laura M. André

early in the morning, when I walk into the Home Depot, the air redolent of fresh lumber, the rush I get is better than any therapy or psychiatric drug: My thoughts sharpen, my body straightens, and my whole being begins to hum at a higher frequency. While *shop 'til you drop* typically summons images of women laden with shopping bags filled with clothing, makeup, and other trappings of femininity, I have six hammers, and none of them is pink.

As I confidently maneuver my oversize, bright orange shopping cart through dozens of aisles, wheels skidding across the shiny concrete floor, my eyes scan a potentially overwhelming array of products, tools, hardware, raw materials, appliances, and signage, until, laserlike, they zero in on the thing I need. I load the item into my cart and feel a deep sense of satisfaction—even giddiness—as the serotonin courses through my brain. I consult my shopping list and the whole process starts again. This is my Prozac.

I get my mood-stabilizing lithium when I'm in the middle of a project and I've made my fourth trip of the day to Home Depot. Xanax? There's nothing better than a research trip to the Depot, where I can alleviate my anxiety about an upcoming project by learning about how it's all going to come together. And then there's the occasional dose of an atypical antipsychotic, where I'm not actually looking for something; rather, I'm just browsing through the store, thinking *What is this thingamajig for? How do you use this doodad? Wow, there's a tool for that?* And I can do it all in relative anonymity, starting at 6:00 AM most days.

The time is an important factor, since I also suffer from agoraphobia in the truest sense of the word. I fear the *agora*, or marketplace, and especially the social interactions that are inherent in most shopping endeavors. (As it happens, the shopping center closest to my house is named the Agora.) My phobia manifests as an avoidance of all social interaction in commercial exchange. The self-checkout line at the Depot is a godsend. The best local hardware store in Santa Fe has a veritable posse of cheerful staff members greeting you as you enter. It's impossible to walk into the store without being approached by at least three red-vested guys peppering me with questions: "How can I help you?" "What's your project today?" "Can I help you find what you're looking for?" Bless their hearts. Many people love this kind of attention while shopping. Not me. I want to discover things on my own, and, if I have to tour the store just to find the right kind of screws, so be it. I will have learned the store's layout and probably picked up a few things I hadn't come for in the meantime. At the Home Depot, I can browse for hours without anyone asking me what I'm doing. I can go in with a list a mile long and nobody wants to see it. I can shop without it triggering my agoraphobia.

I do take real pills, too, to fend off recurrent depression, social anxiety, and a tendency toward bipolar disorder, but my Home Depot drugs have fewer side effects and are more productive and fun to take.

In 1999 I was in graduate school at the University of North Carolina at Chapel Hill, making little progress on my art history dissertation. My beloved grandmother died that year and my sweet dog had serious medical issues. I was in a moribund relationship, and in the throes of a deep depression that medication and psychotherapy weren't helping. I spent my days staring at the walls and contemplating suicide.

A university therapist suggested that I solve jigsaw puzzles as a way to alleviate the depression. I found the idea to be horrifyingly lame. But then my partner Ann suggested something not all that different. "We need a shed," she said one day. And we did. We didn't have a garage, and our single storage room was a disaster. At first, the idea struck me as overwhelming, and I resisted. Plus, getting a shed would mean having to call someone to build it. Oh, the horror! My telephone phobia was worse than my agoraphobia. If only I could build it myself. Gradually, as I thought through the possibility that the shed could be a kind of architectural folly—a miniature version of our colonial-style house, with cute white trim and gray siding—my spirits began to lift. I went to the Home Depot and bought a book about outdoor structures, which demonstrated, step-by-step, how a single individual could, in fact, build a shed from scratch. It was a different kind of puzzle.

It helped that I had a degree in architecture, but my education was theoretical and conceptual—it hadn't prepared me for the actual labor or skills needed to construct a shed by hand. Buoyed by my newfound passion, I dove into the project. "It's all about having the right tools for the job," Ann added. What I lacked in knowledge and experience, I could gain by learning about how tools make it possible to do almost anything. I acquired a mitering table saw, a hammer drill, and a carpenter's protractor.

I researched the needed raw materials and how they went together. Piece by piece, my puzzle began to take shape. With Ann's help, I dug the foundation, mixed and poured concrete, and built a platform. Then came the walls and roof, followed by a window and a door, and siding and roofing. I was amazed that I was accomplishing something I had never dreamed of. And I didn't have to call anybody on the telephone, or ask for anyone's advice.

I smashed my thumb with a hammer more times than I care to admit, but my swollen, dirty, splinter-ridden, cut-up fingers and bruised arms and legs were a small price to pay for the brightness in my emotional state. I was so proud of it. My dog and my grief eventually healed, and I even made better progress on my dissertation, all because I threw myself into the project.

I furiously worked on that shed every day for a few months, from early in the morning until sundown. It may have been my first episode of hypomania, but the manifestation was both benign and productive. An intensely pleasurable bout of productivity, creativity, and boundless energy supplanted my dark depression, and I received a ton of kudos for the work I did, which made me feel even better.

About a year after the shed was finished, we ended up moving to a bigger house closer to Chapel Hill and Ann's job. I took on a part-time gig working on a museum catalogue, and I was teaching at two universities while working on my dissertation. The depression came back in 2001. I was listless and despondent about my future and I felt that I had no purpose.

"We need a bigger laundry room," Ann observed. Back to the Home Depot, where I bought another book. I purchased a demolition saw and began recklessly hacking away at a wall. I learned about plumbing and electricity, about drywall and tile. I crawled under the house and into the attic, went through three pairs of overalls, threw out my back, and ruined my hips and knees, but I built a wonderful laundry room. While working on that project I thought about my dissertation and came up with new insights, and wrote at night.

I finished my dissertation in 2002 and took a job teaching at the University of New Mexico. Ann and I moved to Albuquerque, where our house was perfect and didn't need any projects. I was still unaware that I needed home-improvement projects to stave off the depression. I tried to turn my dissertation into a book and to focus on my teaching while my relationship continued to suffer and the depression came back. We broke up. This time, I had no life-saving projects in which to immerse myself. I moved out and eventually quit my job and my book. I was horribly depressed for six years and, instead of unintentionally hurting myself while working with tools, I bought scalpel tips and began to cut into my skin words and phrases that expressed my increasingly desperate feelings: *I'm sorry, forgive me, disorder, empathy, loser.* My therapist and psychiatrist tried to help me, to no avail.

Then, by the grace of powers far beyond my understanding, I met Candace. She not only gave me hope and showed me what true love is but also helped me find a new psychiatrist, who immediately put me on a different medication regimen, based on his suspicion that I was suffering from a not-otherwise-specified type of bipolar disorder. The depression began to lift, and I made huge progress in therapy. Candace and I moved in together in 2010, and, although I was not completely out of the woods depression-wise, I felt like a new person.

"I think I'd like a deck," Candace said. "A kind of floating deck, like a boat dock, with a ramp leading to it." Done! It's not perfect, but I never smashed my thumb with the hammer. I had a blast building it, working with my hands in the sun each day, and in the process we both realized that I really do need to have productive home-improvement projects in the works to stay mentally healthy.

A Facebook friend once asked me, "Why don't you hire someone to do these projects for you? Think of the time you'd save!" I replied, "Because then I'd have to call someone on the telephone, meet them in person, and spend more money than if I did it myself." And I'd be depriving myself of my Home Depot self-medication.

I'm aware that my shopping habits tend to reinforce a different stereotype: the tomboy lesbian who prefers to shop for tools rather than makeup. This used to cause me a great deal of anxiety, as if I were somehow letting my people down by not being a more girly consumer, but, in the nearly twenty years since then, I've learned to get over myself, and I'm proud of the skills I've acquired. Most women who venture into the Home Depot hang out in the window treatment or garden departments, but thanks to robust employee diversity training I've never once encountered a *but-you're-a-woman* attitude in the electrical or plumbing aisles.

Lately I've learned to head off my depression with smaller, less intense projects, like installing a water heater and resurfacing the bathroom cabinets. Still, whenever I'm feeling down, a trip to the Home Depot cures me, even if I don't buy anything. But right now I'm thinking about building a linen closet.

THE TRUE EVIDENCE OF
MY CONTENTMENT

Candace Walsh

When it comes to accoutrements, I am no minimalist. I have dozens of pairs of shoes, a bordering-on-overstuffed walk-in closet of clothes, a whole drawer devoted to workout wear, and enough lingerie to kit out a bordello. But if you really want to see my intimate inner workings, open my kitchen cabinets.

My everyday plates are hand-thrown Mamma Ró, from Italy, a generous gift from my former husband's stepmother. My wine glasses are Riedel, which were an extravagance only before Target took them on and offered them at a reasonable price point. My pots and pans come from E. Dehillerin in Paris: Emile Henry, Le Creuset, first honeymoon booty. After two nuptial go-rounds, I have a surfeit of bridal shower gifts from Pottery Barn, Crate & Barrel, Sur la Table, and Williams-Sonoma (affectionately referred to in our house as Willie Sóno). My utensil drawers are filled with an assortment of tools sourced from Ikea, KitchenAid, even a funky little Australian company named Dreamfarm. I have three manual can openers: my first red KitchenAid one that always misses a spot; the black KitchenAid one that works perfectly, which my wife Laura contributed when we moved in together; and a funny German one that removes can lids laterally. The flatware drawer is wide enough to accommodate two flatware caddies: One holds the elegant architectural set Laura had before we moved in, adjacent to the Crate & Barrel Dune set that I chose when I was engaged and twenty-seven in Manhattan, walking around drunk on my concupiscence, shooting stuff with the registry gun. (I just went to the website to see if it had been discontinued, as my first marriage was, but nope. I am heartened to see that it endures.)

I know. I sound like an obnoxious bourgeois twit. The Imelda Marcos of Food Prep. The Candy Spelling of Tabletop. I'm neither. I just love to cook, bake, and entertain—nothing makes me happier than a dozen friends at my table, enjoying the smorgasbord stemming from my latest cookbook crush—and when it comes to that, I don't like to "make do," even though I know how to, and can if I must.

Growing up in a wobbly family, I learned to seek out comfort from the familiar items in my kitchen, no matter how imperfect they were: the avocado-green rice cooker with the white switch that popped up with a ding to indicate that the rice was finished, scorched the bottom layer every time, dried out the top, and rendered the middle sticky. But when my Cuban grandmother Migdalia simmered leftover rice in hot milk and served it to me sprinkled with salt, all of the rice maker's sins were forgiven and forgotten. The rice maker sat on the counter, unplugged when not in use, and I often plinked the button with my fingertip, as if playing a one-note piano.

On steak nights, my mother called my father into the kitchen after the meat had rested for a few minutes on the wooden cutting board. My father got out the electric carving knife, plugged it in, and showed the London broil who was boss. Why, in the 1970s, did people plug in kitchen knives and click them on like mini–chain saws? They were just slicing a piece of steak, not hacking through firewood. Yet there he stood in our small kitchen, in his white singlet undershirt and dungarees, sternly dispatching the meat into serving sizes while my mother receded, watching reverently as he did his manly-man work within her otherwise feminine sphere, a rare tableau of symbiosis in their embattled relationship.

Unlike many families, we didn't have an electric can opener, that humming-crunching block of machinery with the footprint of a small cinder block. *Overkill*, thought my mother (and I agree). But we had the handheld manual one that gouged tender fingertip pads with its heedlessly painful, unnecessary circular stamp-outs. The vegetable peeler was dull, nicked, un-ergonomic—although my mother was so deft with a paring knife that she never needed to use it.

I loved the manual egg beater that whirred so *clickety-ʒen*. Even that was a bit dated in the 1970s, when handheld electric beaters were ubiquitous and buzzed with the danger of clipping the fingertips of careless children going in for a swipe of batter, *Struwwelpeter*-style. But the one time I used the manual beaters to make meringue, my wrists wailed from the sustained exertion, giving me a time-travel hit of how much convenience and ease were once not priorities for kitchen tool design—and how much hardier my ancestral matriarchs were. My Greek great-grandmother and her two sisters used to soak, swirl, massage, and dry pounds of their garden's savoy spinach for the spanakopita, every few days, in large tubs outside in all kinds of weather. Their hands were their tools, and I have to say that the one time that I made her spanakopita recipe, the massaging-in-cold-water thing got unpleasant pretty fast (although it was the best spanakopita I've ever had).

The rice cooker and electric knife were given to my mother at her first bridal shower, along with this piece of advice from a ribald aunt: "The secret to a good marriage? Keep him well-fed and well-fucked." She did her part, but reductive axioms only go so far. The remnants of her registry flatware set were mixed in with all sorts of exuberantly rococo mismatched forks and spoons, also from yard sales, their curlicue, floral-embossed handles at odds with the registry set's smooth colonial simplicity. Plates were also mismatched, as were the pots, baking pans, mixing bowls, and drinking glasses. In search of a fresh start, a magic new launching pad, my parents moved many times when I was young. Things got broken, got lost, or were replaced piecemeal. My mother took us kids and left my father multiple times, and came back. I didn't know on any given day when we would next leave or return, but eventually her leaving took.

At one point, things in my childhood home matched. And then, they did not. Along with the lost consistency of forks and knives and plates, chaos rushed in from every corner, the linen closets, kitchen cabinets, silverware drawers filling to the brim with mishmashes of goods as my childhood flooded with unpredictability and upheaval.

I like wandering through big, focus group–tweaked upscale chain emporia, but my favorite places are the offbeat. Kitchen goods outlet stores, with their unpredictable mix of discount-priced stuff from all over the world. Seconds and overstock. The passé stuff in Germany or Spain or Italy is my novelty-gilded stash, providing me with, say, hard-to-get glass storage containers years before the U.S. market responded to people's desire to move away from plastic, or to have ramekins that are larger than usual and, coincidentally, perfect for my annual Easter breakfast mainstay: baked eggs with polenta, ringed by a stout collar of applewood-smoked bacon, topped with gruyère and chives.

Kitchen supply stores in Chinatown have endowed me with steamers, stove burner diffusers, and small, heartbreakingly beautiful porcelain bowls painted with bounding rabbits and maudlin monkeys. An industrial baking supply store in Manhattan dazzled me with dozens of different shapes of baking pans, not to mention sprinkles and sculpted sugar flowers.

At yard sales and secondhand stores, I've scored a crepe maker, nesting colored Pyrex bowls, a cocktail shaker emblazoned with recipes for vintage stiff drinks, squared-off tin canister sets with black plastic lids, and a little wooden treasure chest that housed a smoked glass decanter and two shot glasses—in case I ever wanted to tipple with a dashing pirate.

Although my family life was chaotic, we were culturally strict. I grew up in a blue-collar Long Island family with restrictive beliefs around religion, sexual orientation, vocation, and race.

If I hadn't looked so much like my parents, I would have thought I was switched at birth by a careless nurse. My second semester of freshman year at college, I threw over Campus Crusade for Christ for libertine pantheism. I've been in love with men, and with women. I married a man, had two children, and, years after that ended, married Laura, the love of my life, legally, in my home state of New York. We live in New Mexico and dig that white people are in the minority here. And my children, along with absorbing that culturally diverse vibe in their daily life, have three moms, if you count my ex-husband's partner.

Through the changes in my domestic life, I avoided the kitchen mishmash I remembered from childhood. I left my registry plates (Pottery Barn's Emma ware) and flatware with my ex at first, because their symbolism broke my heart in ways I couldn't face at every mealtime. But my kids and I needed to eat off something. So I went shopping in a secondhand store in Albuquerque and bought both a vintage yellow metal hutch and a set of plates to put in it: 1960s milky turquoise, with an insouciant daisy motif, edged with a silver line.

As my two young children and I tentatively moved forward, navigating jagged-edged feelings, the wrenchings of change, and the exhilaration of the new, I found myself feeding us the thrifty comfort food of my childhood: roast chicken with mashed potatoes and gravy; my grandma Marie's chicken fricassee; homemade pizza; turkey soup with rice.

We also played with new gadgets that had no bittersweet associations. On weekend mornings, I pulled out the Ebelskiver pan to make round griddled doughnuts filled with jam or melted chocolate; and I bought a plug-in waffle iron that my daughter came to commandeer, setting the foundation for her own confidence in the kitchen. We even made salt ceramic dough, rolled it out, used cookie cutters to punch out gnome and animal shapes, and then painted them with watercolors. Those doggies and gnomes still pop up occasionally in different places around the house, reminding me of the fragile tenacity of that time.

When Laura was courting me, she bought me a matching pale turquoise KitchenAid mixer. Today, Laura's parents' registry plates (Franciscan Atomic Starburst), from their wedding in the 1950s, mingle with that stab at resilience and recovery in the hutch. It's the kind of mismatch that doesn't irk me in the slightest; my post-divorce dishes and her parents' registry set each have their own shelf, and their midcentury designs work well together.

And every Thanksgiving, Laura and I host a houseful of people: her parents, my mother and husband number four, our dearest friends and colleagues. We pull down the Mamma Ró, the Emma ware, the turquoise daisy plates, and the Atomic Starburst. From the cornucopia of our authentic, consciously created domestic bliss, the results of days of cooking and baking spill out and nourish our beloved crowd.

At last year's celebration, I caught my mom telling my coworker's boyfriend, who was expertly disassembling our heritage bird with Laura's family heirloom carving set: "I think a man should carve the turkey. Call me old-fashioned. . . ." Although this heresy was being said in the heart of our same-sex domicile, I let it go, reasoning that at least she wasn't pressing an electric carving knife into his hand.

After Thanksgiving, I sometimes page through the Williams-Sonoma catalog and consider getting a set of dedicated, tasteful turkey-motif toile dishes, on sale. I mean, if I had to choose something. But here's the true evidence of my contentment: I don't think my kitchen needs one more thing.

SHOPPING STORIES

Marni Hochman

Shop • ping

Noun

The purchasing of goods from stores.

Goods bought from stores, esp. food and household goods.

—*Oxford Dictionaries* online

1. For some, shopping is an art; for others, it's a sport. It can be a vice and it can be a cause. Some love it. Some hate it. Rarely is someone indifferent.

—PAMELA KAFFKE

ying in bed together under the red comforter with white polka dots, a pile of pillows behind our backs, I am all wide-eyed anticipation. We snack on crackers and the chopped liver I helped chop in my great-grandmother's wooden bowl, which would normally not be allowed in bed, but this is a special occasion. The Sunday edition of *The New York Times* is spread out on top of us. My grandmother finds the big spring fashion section and we peruse the pictures and discuss the latest styles. After we devour both the chopped liver and the fashion pages, we make plans to go on a shopping trip to New Jersey, where there is no sales tax. "Is Mommy going with us?" "No, not this time," my grandmother responds. *Mommy doesn't like to go shopping*, I think. I can't imagine it. I look over to one of my grandmother's closets filled to overflowing with a rainbow of beautiful clothes neatly organized with blouses on top and pants underneath.

Boxes of shoes are stacked neatly on the floor. Her clothing has taken over both hall closets and the closet in my uncle's former bedroom. "Can I try on the Cinderella shoes again?" I ask, referring to a pair of clear-heeled and clear-toed mules painted with gold stripes and swirls. They are the most beautiful shoes I have ever seen. "Tell me the story of the shoes again," I command, and, as she does so, I put them on and also a glittery black dress that is way too big for me despite my grandmother's petite size. And I feel like a princess.

2. *Shopping is a woman thing. It's a contact sport like football. Women enjoy the scrimmage, the noisy crowds, the danger of being trampled to death, and the ecstasy of the purchase.*

—ERMA BOMBECK

My mother has agreed to take me shoe shopping at the mall. We enter the shopping center in a suburb of Washington, D.C., and pass by the Orange Julius and the arcade without stopping. I am like a hound on the hunt. My mom is just trying to keep up. As I approach one shoe store I glance in and don't see anything I am interested in and we keep going. We pass Spencer's, but that is a place to go with my friends, not my mother, so I don't even slow down. We stop at another shoe store. I hold up a shoe and ask the sales clerk if they have a size 5. He shakes his head and says the smallest they have in that style is a 6. A little exasperated sigh escapes me. It is not easy to find shoes that I like in my size. I really hate shoe shopping. We continue the chase. I try on a pair of shoes at another store, but they are uncomfortable and I don't like any of the other styles. My mother looks tired but is not impatient. This time we have left my father at home rather than snoozing on a J.C. Penney couch. If my mother doesn't like to shop, my father abhors it, with a combination of loathing the actual act of shopping and detesting the thought of spending his hard-earned money on what he considers frivolities, especially when money is tight, which it always seemed to be. "Why would you want some other person's name on your butt?" he inquired when my mother finally agreed to buy the one pair of Calvin Klein jeans that I owned. My mother asks me, "What exactly are you looking for?" "I'm not sure, but I'll know them when I see them!" I answer. Somewhere around the fifth store, I do see them. Black, lace-up leather booties with a zigzag of black suede under the laces, across the top, and around the outside. They are perfect, so different from all the other black lace-up booties that my friends wear. I wait in jittery anticipation while the salesperson heads into the back to look for my size. When he returns with a box, like a dog that knows it is about to be let outside, I can barely sit still while I wait for him to fish them out, lace them up, and hand them over. *Oh, please, let them fit. Please let them fit.* I get them on and do a couple of laps around the store and then a little victory dance. They fit! My mother twists her mouth in contemplation. "Your father won't be happy if I buy these for you." The shoes are expensive and, as the wife of a podiatrist, she knows they are not good for my feet. I roll my eyes. I won't be happy if she doesn't. Finally, she reasons out loud that we might never get out of the mall if she doesn't buy them since it is so difficult to find a pair of shoes for me that are both comfortable and fashionable. I wear them out of the store. I am ecstatic. The frustrations of the previous two hours melt away. "This is way more fun than, like, shopping for matching Garanimals, don't you think, Mom?" She laughs despite her exhaustion. The ankle boots are so unique and so . . . me. And I can't wait to wear them to school on Monday.

3. *When I was younger, shopping helped me discover many new places and many new things.*

—MIUCCIA PRADA

I stop and look around me. I can't believe I'm in Paris, France. It's so very much like I had imagined and nothing at all like I expected. A fleeting feeling of gratefulness to my paternal grandmother for funding this high school trip passes through me almost unnoticed. My best friend Lara, another friend we have made on the trip, and I are giddy for the chance to be let loose to shop in *Paris*. I have already bought the one thing my mother asked for while we were in London, so now I am free to use my spending money as I like. We stop in at a perfume shop, all glass and mirrors. Perfume in *Paris*! We smell everything but buy nothing because the prices are high, as one might expect in a perfume shop in Paris. We practically skip from store to store in our excitement, talking and giggling all the way. We enter a hat shop and I immediately see the perfect thing. A Parisian chapeau! It's a pink straw hat with a thin pink ribbon around the crown, holding a little spray of pink-and-white flowers in place. I put it on. Lara says, "So cute!" And, I think, cheap enough to afford. I attempt to use my third-year language skills with the cashier, who has no patience for this silly American girl with bad French. Embarrassed, I look behind me for my best friend, whose language abilities are the only reason I am passing third-year French, but she is not there and I switch to English. I wear the hat out of the store and we continue on. There is a slight wind picking up and Lara tells me to hold onto my hat. "It's fine," I say. "It fits me perfectly and it's not going anywhere." But sure enough, and like a scene out of a version of *Sex and the City* for adolescents, just as we are crossing a small but busy side street, my hat flies off and is put down right in the middle of the street. I run to get it, Lara trying to catch my arm but missing. As I stoop to pick it up, a car comes out of nowhere, or so it seems, and I grab the hat and jump out of the way, narrowly escaping by only inches. My best friend is pale as I return to her and she hits me, yelling, "You are going to give me a heart attack!" "But I got my hat!" I exclaim triumphantly as I feel the buzz of adrenaline electrify my whole body. Shopping and danger, a heady combination. Still I think, *Boy, that was close. The parents wouldn't be pleased if I died in Paris. Better hold onto this hat.*

4. *A couple of weeks ago, I was shocked to discover a survey that said half of British women hate shopping, I don't know how this can be. I love shopping. It's the most relaxing, pleasurable activity I can think of.*

—LINDA GRANT

The little bells on the ends of the strings tying my obligatory long skirt around my waist jingle lightly as I walk barefoot along the chaotic rows of campers, vans, and cars, scanning the wares that are being sold. It is a typically hot, humid Virginia summer day and I am glad that I decided to wear my mother's thin, pink-and-purple-flowered, old hippie blouse. After waiting in line all morning, we finally had our concert tickets and now have time to explore. This is my first Grateful Dead experience, unfortunately about as close as I am ever going to get to what my parents experienced in the 1960s, and I can't believe what a show there is in the parking lot before the concert. We pass what seem to be hundreds of tie-dyed T-shirts, long skirts similar to my own, jewelry, tour books, and food. Clearly there are other things being sold and bought as well. I see papers with small dots on them trading hands and catch whiffs of sweet, pungent smoke. But I am focused on the endless array of multicolored goods peeking out of all manner of colorfully decorated vehicles. I am aware that all of the items on display are being sold by Deadheads hoping to make enough money to travel on to the next show. And I am more than happy to oblige. I start with a bag of homemade trail mix. Music surrounds and follows us as we walk on. The bright hues and swirls of a vividly dyed T-shirt catch my attention and I decide to purchase it. I pull it over my other top and we continue to slowly wander. I am attracted to a small table full of friendship bracelets. My boyfriend buys the one I am eyeing and gently ties it around my wrist. Staring for a moment at the purple-and-blue converging diamond pattern, I think that I must be as happy as any new bride. I look up at him into the same blue as the bracelet and clearly see my own feelings looking back at me. Refusing to acknowledge any end to this summer when we each head off to colleges in different states, I am all smiles and sunshine even when the rain begins. My boyfriend grabs my hand and we run laughing to find cover.

5. *The thing about shopping is that you never know exactly what you are going to find. A shopping experience can be filled with joyous surprises or unexpected pitfalls. No matter how hard you try, you cannot plan every detail of a shopping trip, and you never know exactly how it will end up.*

—Amanda Ford

As we stroll through the shopping arcade, shop owners call to us to come inside and take a look. Small stores filled with every sort of bric-a-brac line both sides of the walkway. Merchandise spills out onto the pavement, sitting on tables or hanging on racks, enticing buyers to stop and look. The heavy, blistering mid-day air of Bangkok is oppressive. I am not used to this kind of heat, coming from a cooler, rainy July in Yokohama, and I am dripping with sweat, but despite my discomfort I press on. There is so much to see. I glimpse a beautiful royal blue at the corner of my eye and turn toward it. The richly colored silk tank top almost shimmers in the heat and I am dazzled. I take it off the rack and pull it on over the thin shirt I am wearing. My husband-to-be smiles and nods his head in approval. Sold! Earlier in the week when we went to the Sunday market, we bargained with the merchants because it was expected, but I'm not very good at it and my heart isn't in it. For me, the sport of shopping is in finding a good deal, not in making one. I don't know if this is the type of place where you can bargain over price, but I don't even attempt it. *What's the point in haggling over a couple of dollars when that extra money means so much more to them than to me?* We continue our leisurely pace along the storefronts. I pause occasionally to take a closer look at something—a pretty raw silk skirt, a silver necklace, a celadon mug. I am disappointed that the graceful wood carving of some Asian goddess that I instantly fall in love with is too expensive. I pout as we walk on. Then I stop suddenly with a sharp intake of breath. "What's wrong?" Terry asks, looking concerned. I don't answer him but run toward a small table with a turning jewelry display and pluck off a pair of earrings. They are thin brass and each one has been shaped into a spiral. He looks at me quizzically. I explain that I had bought a pair exactly like these in a night market in Thailand a few years before, when I was on a break from teaching English in Taiwan, but had sadly lost one. What luck! "We're going to have a great trip," I say to him.

6. *Shopping involves more than just economic considerations like the relationship between material quality and price. There are social, ethical, and political*

issues embedded in shopping decisions as well. Yet most of us do not give a lot of conscious thought to what can be called the politics of a product.

—MICHELE MICHELETTI

We have arrived in Houston, but our luggage hasn't. I am practically in tears. My brother's wedding is in two days. The airline assures us they will find our bags and get them to us before then, but right now we have none of our things. We head on to Galveston anyway. Once we arrive and check into the hotel, I call my brother. "Looks like we need to do a little shopping," I say, trying not to sound too upset because he probably has enough to deal with. "Well, the only place to do that around here is Walmart," he responds. "Walmart?!" I half scream into the phone. "There isn't even a Target or a K-Mart? What kind of place is this?" "Sorry," he says. I can't remember the last time I stepped into a Walmart. The "Evil Empire" is what we call it. But at this point we are desperate. My three-year-old daughter is already clamoring to go to the beach and we have no swimsuit, not to mention clean underwear or children's toothpaste. "We are only going to buy what we absolutely have to and not one thing more," I command as we head into the superstore. Unless pressured by time or children, I am not one to rush through even the most mundane shopping trip, preferring to explore the shelves or racks for any new goodies or sales that may have appeared since my last visit. But today we zoom through the aisles, grabbing what we need as quickly as we can. The place is overwhelming and I feel nauseated. On the way to the checkout line, my daughter sees a huge tower of fenced-in beach balls. Her eyes get wide and she runs for them. I yell, "NO, NO, NO!" But she grabs a hold of one and wraps her small, chubby arms around it before I can get to her. "PLEEEASE, Mama. PLEEEASE!" "No, no," I say again. But it has been a long trip from Indiana and she is tired and grumpy and my daughter is not ever easily swayed. I am tired and grumpy, too. I stand there weighing my options. We are careful with our money, but not in the same fashion as my parents, or at least I do not think so. Perhaps my children will. I like to think that I stick to my one guiding principle, "Everything in moderation," which I say over and over to my daughter as we walk through stores filled with every imaginable child fantasy and go to birthday parties where there are enough sweets to give an elephant a sugar rush. I feel my mouth twisting just as my mother's did. I make a quick mental list:

Reasons Not to Buy the Ball

1. She doesn't need the ball.

2. She can't have everything she wants.

3. I don't want to give the Evil Empire any more of my money than I absolutely have to.

4. I don't want to give the Evil Empire the satisfaction of falling prey to their marketing scheme of placing the balls directly in front of the checkout lines where all children will see and run for them.

Reasons to Buy the Ball

1. The ball will keep her occupied for hours and we don't have any other toys except for those we brought on the plane.

2. The ball is cheap and will not add much to the Evil Empire's empire.

3. We will be able to leave the Evil Empire much more quickly and without incident if we buy the ball.

4. We are all tired and grumpy.

And just like my mother, I relent. My daughter is all light and laughter now and I can't help but smile, a guilty little smile, too.

7. *When women are depressed, they eat or go shopping. Men invade another country. It's a whole different way of thinking.*

—ELAYNE BOOSLER

I go to the bathroom and cry while I sit on the toilet. I am exhausted and overwhelmed. I don't want to be here. I want to go home to Bloomington, Indiana. It is cold here and I don't have any friends. My nine-month-old son is movement personified. My four-year-old daughter is still getting used to five full days of school at her new Montessori preschool and comes home impossible to deal with every day. My husband spends hours working on the coursework for all his classes because this is his first real position as a professor. And I am left trying to do most of the unpacking myself. After three months here, I am not getting very far. I come out of the bathroom, no longer crying, but my red eyes and nose give me away. My husband looks up from his work and knits his brows. "I think you need a break," he states matter-of-factly. I sigh and say that I know he has to get this work done. "I think it's more important that you get a little break," he responds, "and a couple of hours won't make a difference." "Well, okay," I answer hesitantly. I grab my coat and purse and walk toward the door, looking back for reassurance. He waves. I get in the car, shivering, turn the heat up full blast and head for the thrift store that I still haven't gotten the chance to check out. I find the store, relieved that I didn't get lost on the way, and make my way inside. I pass the clothing section and find a room with what looks like their prime merchandise, where I glance around for something Japanese that my new Japanese-history-professor husband might like for Christmas. Not seeing anything, I walk through the doorway at the other side of the room, continue by the shelves filled with kitchen gadgets and dishes, and turn right. Eventually I come to the children's area, where a disorganized jumble of games and toys stock the shelves. Aha! Cute little purses for almost nothing. Deliberating between a sparkly red purse and a little white purse decorated with purple flowers, I finally choose one. I also snap up another baby toy that has lights and makes noises and that will keep my son occupied in the car. My body starts to relax and I can feel myself growing calmer, the focus on the task at hand leaving no room for the stress and worries of home. I trace my steps back toward the kitchenware and spy the bookshelves beyond. Books! I can easily spend hours anywhere there are books. And now I have the luxury to look uninterrupted. I peruse the shelves and pull out anything I might be interested in, making a nice stack on top of the little table beside me. *Hmmm. I'm sure I don't need all of these.* I go through the pile, read several of the backs and dust jackets, and return some of the books to the empty spaces I have left. Then I move on to the children's books, going through the same routine: taking books from the shelves, looking through them, putting some back. Just as I am about finished, I see a familiar-looking spine. I pull the book out and realize it is one that I read as a child, and, by the looks of it, the very same edition. *The Secret Garden*! I hadn't thought of the book in years, but, holding it in my hand, I remember how much I loved it. And it smells deliciously of old book. Score! My find of the day! Just the thing I didn't know I needed. I will write something in the cover and give it to my daughter for Chanukah. I pay for the items in my cart and drive home. When I walk in the door, my daughter runs for me and encircles my waist. My husband turns to welcome me, my son in his arms. He sees the bag I am carrying, frowns a not-so-serious frown, and shaking his head says, "I don't get it, but you look much happier." And I am, at least for the moment.

8. *Whoever said money can't buy happiness simply didn't know where to go shopping.*

—Bo Derek

My two-year-old son is standing in front of me with his belly hanging out of a shirt that has grown way too small, way too fast. "Time to go shopping," I sing. I push him out the door and strap him into his car seat. We arrive at the children's resale shop and I shield his view of the neighboring bakery, knowing that if he sees it, I'll never get him inside. I let him loose in the small store and cross my fingers, hoping that he doesn't crash into or break anything as I head toward the racks of boys' size 3 clothing. I search through the small clothes, my hands on automatic pilot, stopping momentarily only when I see the right color, price, and style. It's a good day and I am quickly holding a good-size pile of little boys' clothes. I head back over to the toy area, but my son is not there. In a slight panic, I search around for him and finally find him by the shoes. He has taken off his sneakers and is working hard to get his feet into a pair of sparkly pink Mary Janes. I find a pair of boys' shoes in his size and attempt a trade, but he screams, pulls the Mary Janes away from me, and goes back to work. "Don't you want these cool shoes?" I ask, holding them out for his inspection. "They have red on them and you love red." He shakes his head. "How about these cowboy boots?" He shakes his head again. "You really like those shoes, huh?" He nods. "Let me see what size they are." He hands one to me and I check inside. They are a size too big for him. "Hmmm. A little big." He grabs the shoe and pushes his foot into it. I sigh and bend down to help him put the shoe on. *Well,* I reason to myself, *maybe if I let him wear them for a little while, he'll be done with them when it's time to go.* So I head to the girls' size 5 clothing. Although my daughter is seven, she unfortunately, I think as I head to the right rack, takes after her mom. When I am done there, I check on my son, who is happily playing with a big truck. After purchasing the clothing, I go back to collect my son. "Okay. Time to go. Let's get your shoes back on." But when I reach out to take the sparkly shoes off, he again lets out that god-awful siren wail. "Let me see how much they cost," I coax. I turn the shoe with his foot in it over in my hand. $3.99. I remember how I felt in my grandmother's mules. I could imagine a whole world in those shoes with me at its center. Then I picture my daughter, not so long ago, clomping around the house in the same shoes, necklaces draped around her neck, and my pink French hat on her head, talking to her pretend cats, Chocolate and Vanilla, about all the places they will go and all the things they will see. *Well, why should he be any different?* I pull the price tag off, let his foot go, and return to the cashier to pay for the shoes. We go to the bakery in the sparkly pink shoes. We go pick up his sister in the sparkly pink shoes. He sleeps in the sparkly pink shoes. He wears the pink sparkly shoes for two more days. On the third day he picks up his sister's sparkly red purse and we go to playgroup in the sparkly pink shoes and with the sparkly red purse. "Thank goodness we live in Ann Arbor," I mutter to myself as we enter the house. My playgroup mommy friends are, as I expected, amused and very understanding. "If he feels like a princess or whatever in these shoes," I laugh, "far be it from me to take that away from him."

9. *Shopping: chore, sport, hobby, meditation, therapy, obsession; done alone, as a group effort or romantic activity; frustrating or fun, boring or exhilarating; accomplished thoughtfully or carelessly; to find yourself, lose yourself, or see yourself through someone else's eyes; it might be all about you or somebody you love. It has at one time or another been all of these things to me. But when a shopping trip becomes a story, it is perfection, and what I most love about shopping is that you never know when that will occur.*

My husband and I are sorting through the endless boxes of stuff we have accumulated in hopes of clearing a space in the basement to turn into a teenage hangout. It feels cathartic to make a small mountain of things to give away. But now I find myself lingering over the bins filled with children's clothes. Which to put back into the bin as keepsakes and which to pass forward? I remember them wearing almost every one of these pieces of clothing. I remember buying most of them, too. I reminisce over my joy at purchasing the purple-and-yellow-striped Hannah Anderson outfit I bought for my first child's homecoming from the hospital and I recollect spying the light blue crocheted sweater at a yard sale. I recall agonizing over which adorable baby kimono to buy in Tokyo to be worn for the yearly holiday cards and I laugh when I come across the cheap sneakers we had to buy my son at a small-town five-and-dime because somehow we had forgotten to make sure he was wearing shoes when we left our house. I see the red glittery purse I bought for my daughter at the thrift store that day I was at my wit's end and the lovely dress my daughter almost didn't get to wear to my brother's wedding. And then I spot the pink sparkly shoes and tears spring to my eyes. I don't know why it is these shoes that finally get the waterworks flowing, but I am back in the resale shop, and my son is a toddler again. I can smell his little boy toddler scent and see the determination in his sweet brown puppy dog eyes. It was just a normal everyday shopping trip to purchase needed goods from a store and the shoes bought that day were just one sundry item among many in a bin. I did not buy my first car or my prom dress, my wedding dress or our house, or even that first baby outfit that day. But these little stories that wrap themselves around the odds and ends of our life like layers of tissue paper are what become the artifacts of our existence. *If my son tells this story to his children, they will want to see the pink sparkly shoes and maybe even try them on,* I think. Or perhaps it will be the opposite. They will see the pink sparkly shoes in the box full of dress-up clothes and want to know their story. I place the Mary Janes on the same "to-keep" shelf as my grandmother's mules. When I remove my hands, they are covered with sparkles.

MONOGRAMMED

Meg Worden

Would you like to apply for the Nordstrom debit card?" the woman behind the counter asked me as she folded the thin merino wool sweater, the color of an eggplant, *aubergine*, and the two black tank tops.

"Would you like to apply for the Nordstrom debit card?" a different woman asked a few minutes later from behind the Chanel counter as she wrapped a container of lip treatment in white tissue and slipped it into a tiny, perfect, black bag.

"No, thank you," I said to them both. I knew what would happen. They would take all of my information and input it into the computer, we would wait for too long with nothing to talk about, and ultimately I wouldn't qualify. We would then stand there, awkwardly finishing the transaction with the credit card that was already on the counter. "No, really, thank you." I responded to her second request with a discount attached. No.

When it was over, I headed for the the Women's Lounge on the third floor. You may not know this, but the women's restroom in Nordstrom is much more than a restroom. Calling it a lounge isn't just a euphemism. Before you get to the toilets, you pass through a room with sofas, lamps, occasional chairs. I sat down in a striped wingback, tears backing up in my throat. Here in this hidden place, I was safe. I looked at the shopping bags at my feet; the soft fabric handles clutched in my palm, and felt the familiar press of relief and contrition.

Over the last couple of years, I had traversed a broad money spectrum. I didn't have it, I had it, and then didn't again. The numbers varied, but the turmoil around it was constant. At this point, my husband and I were living in a hotel in a new city, jobless, headed for bankruptcy and divorce.

And I was shopping for merino and Chanel at Nordstrom.

I was twenty-seven the final time I carried ecstasy pills, taped around my waist, from New York City to Springfield, Missouri. I was twenty-eight when my son, Aidan, was born, weighing nine pounds, three ounces, with thick black hair and nectarine cheeks. He grew fast and loud, making his own boy space in the world, reshaping mine into a mother space. Enough time had passed that I assumed my short stint in crime was left far behind me, until two federal agents knocked on the door of my Brooklyn apartment, the white noise of traffic on the Brooklyn Queens Expressway outside my window, the whir of boiled carrots in my tiny food processor, designed especially for making baby food. I was thirty when I was sentenced, handcuffed, and led to a holding cell in the basement of the courthouse to serve two years for conspiracy to distribute five thousand hits of ecstasy. I was thirty-two when the bureau of prisons released me to my mother's house and back to my little boy, three and a half years old.

My mother was living near her parents in a farming community called Cassville in southwestern Missouri. This is a place where they pipe country music through the speakers at the gas station, haircuts cost twelve dollars, Walmart is the only option for everything, the local factories are the only option for working, and the hills that were once the majestic Ozark mountains roll on for miles of deep greens and great circles of gold. Much of my family on my mother's side had reunited here after my grandparents retired early from Lake Charles, Louisiana, trading bourré and the bayous for inexpensive land, a bucolic fantasy, and four picturesque seasons. A stark contrast from New York City.

The first week I was out of prison, my mother came home from the Walmart with a new digital camera. "I thought we could use this," she said, holding the laminate box to her chest. Still stunning at fifty-nine, her graying, naturally curly hair was cropped close at the nape, larger curls falling over her forehead, over the clear blue eyes she got from her father. "I couldn't really afford it, so I charged it," she said.

It was a familiar scenario. When Betamax fell to the wayside of the VCR, I was a freshman in high school. My single mother and I lived in a small, two-bedroom apartment in Spokane, Washington, where the winters were long and white, and the summers were temperate and swallowed by crisp sunshine. She worked for Alaska Airlines and I went to a tony Catholic prep school on a work-study program. Work study meant I had to stay after school and clean classrooms, come to school on the holidays and scrub the floors with steel wool puffs. The Suburban by Chevrolet was the most popular car driven by the doctor's kids that went to the school, but I didn't ride in those Suburbans. I took the city bus with all the other work-study kids who didn't ride in those cars that left the parking lots at the same time we started cleaning up after them. Naturally, we became the punks, the alternative kids. We smoked clove cigarettes; we smoked pot; we called the doctors' kids "preps" and decided that becoming a prep would make us boring, which was the worst fate that could befall us. If you can't join them, beat them, I guess.

One day my mother came home with a brand-new VCR. "It was four hundred dollars," she said. "I couldn't really afford it, so I charged it." We went to the brand-new Blockbuster Video to rent *Stand by Me*. The new of it all brought a familiar zipping through the veins, a spark of possibility. That VCR brought hope for a satisfaction we couldn't describe or fulfill. The camera she bought after prison didn't work out so well. We couldn't figure out how to get it to take more than seven photos before the battery would die, so she returned it. We probably kept looking; I don't remember. I do remember that taking care of my boy alone and working as a hairdresser in this country town—trying to build a clientele to come get the twelve-dollar haircuts, six for me, six for the salon—started to wear thin. Many weeks I brought home less than a hundred dollars. I worked to accommodate the clients, cutting their hair whenever they wanted to come in. My little boy spent too much time in day care.

William was one of my regular clients. He was charming, handsome, successful, and twenty-seven years older than I was. I was less bothered by this difference than I was intrigued. I had spent most of my sexual maturity mourning my nonexistent relationship with my own father and using sex with partners to fill that void. I longed to be objectified, filled up, numbed out. When William asked me to dinner, I had some reservations about the fact that he was older than my own father and that his own children were my age. Also, I didn't trust myself in relationships after the last one, the one in which I had a baby with a career criminal. I had hoped the next thing would be more normal, more mainstream, less scandalous. I didn't want to replace my father; I really wanted to finally do something he might be proud of. But it had been so long since I had let up on my rigid post-prison routine of trying to do better, and I really thought I should have a little fun, so I called him up and I said a final yes.

We ate spicy cauliflower and listened to B.B. King in the house on the lake, thirty minutes south of Cassville on the Arkansas border. The cedar house had Spanish-tile floors and fireplaces and a green roof. Stained glass surrounded the front door in classic California craftsman style. Sweeping lake views were framed by large windows and french doors. After dinner, we walked down to the lower deck, right at the edge of the cliff, looking out over the lake that stretched like platinum ribbons in each direction, reflecting the setting sun and the trees on the edges of the other side. We could hear the water slapping the rocks from where we stood and tears ran down his face when he talked about the things he had lost in his lifetime and the things he hoped to find. Later, over coffee, I was nearly knocked off my chair by the sensation that I was home.

Our favorite place for dating was Eureka Springs in Arkansas, only a half hour from his lake house. We walked the steep, twisted Victorian streets, slipping in and out of the galleries filled with eclectic jewelry, pottery, and other works by local artists. We ate crab cakes with spicy remoulade and seared sea scallops at the Grand Taverne Restaurant, and always drove to the top of the highest hill, crowned by the Crescent Hotel. This hotel was originally built as a cancer hospital, but later the doctor who ran it was run out of town for questionable practices and the hospital closed. The salon is now where the old morgue used to be. The Crescent's next incarnation was a girl's school and they added a bright conservatory for the darlings where, now, you can have your wedding reception. The story is that, at least one of the girls threw herself out of the top turret window of the current penthouse suite. In addition to those ghosts, a couple of fat house cats roam the corridors at night. The check-in desk, majestic fireplace, and old player piano that grace the lobby are the originals, and the view from the rooftop bar stretches clear across the valley to the Rio de Janeiro–style Jesus statue in white marble robes, standing fifty feet tall, arms outstretched, face to the sky. We sipped our ginger ales, William admiring his new steel bracelet and the turquoise necklace he had bought for me.

Being cared for made me feel high, grateful, and I was sexually excited by trying on clothes and jewelry for him, so I continued to accept his generosity with grace. He was a hero to me then. I smiled and thanked him. I took my sandals off on the long drive in his truck and tucked my bare feet under my legs in the seat.

We had been married for a year the day William held his credit card out with one arm, his other arm in a sling with a mobile Fentanyl drip attached, and we stopped at the imported furniture store after his shoulder surgery. He decided on the teak table as soon as he saw it. It was beautiful, and, after only minor hesitation on my part, I gave in and we laughed together. We joked for years about the Fentanyl table. Slipping a little out of control was comfortable for us. Making bad decisions was funnier than the tedium of practicality. When these shopping trips happened and we would laugh together, even though the pit of my stomach knew we couldn't afford it all, I surrendered with him. It was a relief knowing it was another decision I didn't have to make, another argument that never had to happen. It still brought up the feeling of being cared for, the VCR, another thing we couldn't afford but that we charged anyway because you can't put a price tag on hope.

Eventually, I took over the finances and saw, in black-and-white numbers, the reality of what was happening. The checkbooks weren't getting balanced, and only minimum payments were being made on credit cards, two car payments, the boat, the motorcycle, the mortgage, maintenance, shopping. Many months the statements showed over five hundred dollars in overdraft fees. The IRA account had been depleted and we owed taxes in the five figures for those withdrawals. Scared but determined, I got a new notebook; I crunched; I looked for a financial adviser. I was in way over my head. The black fear started coming in the night, accelerating my heartbeat, clipping my breath. I was a walking dichotomy. The way food can be a substitute for love—that's how shopping was. I had this proclivity; this craving for fullness, and the only way I felt like I could control it was to deny it. I would go from buying nothing at all—a zero spending budget—until my craving for hope, or my desire to laugh with my husband would bring me back into complicity. A new mattress, organic wool blankets, a new watch for him, another new watch for him, some new clothes for me. I would be angry at his spending when I wasn't a part of it, but, when I could be, I would allow myself to slip into denial, to soothe my loneliness—even though the result was like falling. Alice down the rabbit hole. Our age difference put me squarely into gold-digger territory, and I knew there were more than a few people who suspected as much. Obviously, I would take the heat for any financial losses. Relationships are always so much more complicated, layered, than anyone outside them can see, and I cared too much what other people thought. Especially one person. I needed this marriage to be successful, because I figured if it was, if I could manage this sinking ship with some kind of panache, then maybe my dad would notice. Maybe then he would be proud of me. I know. It's so cliché it's boring. But I kept swinging from zero spending to not giving a shit.

We had just finished gutting and re-outfitting our newest house, a nearly hundred-year-old bungalow on a tree-lined street, using all of our capital and our savings from the one we had sold to be closer to Aidan's school, when we got the call about William's job. He was the vice president of sales at a prominent toy company that had just been sold and the new owners laid off everyone from the CEO down. An hour after the call, Fed Ex arrived with his final check, prorated with no severance. Just like that, his job was gone.

I started writing in a more professional capacity, started teaching more yoga classes, went about the business of staging and selling the house, landscaping, cleaning every day so it would shine just in case we got a call from the realtor for a showing. To relax, I got online: Free People, Anthropologie, Lululemon. I put digital things in digital baskets and left them there. In a way, I stopped caring. As my fear escalated and the money dwindled, it became, ironically perhaps, easier to say yes. More hope, please.

Sometimes I went back to the baskets, clicked the buy button, and hoped I would be able to intercept the mail. I would spend the week in a state of excitement and despair, half hoping the thing wouldn't fit so I could send it back and assuage my guilt, the other half hoping the leather and lace would be my panacea.

When the house we had just bought finally sold, the buyers requested a three-week close. Of course, we agreed, even though it meant we were three weeks from being both unemployed and homeless.

We laid the Rand McNally atlas flat on the Fentanyl table. William updated his resume and hired a headhunter, and we plotted interviews west of us. Only west. We had decided that Portland, Oregon, would be our final option because I had lived there before and we knew we would have good food, decent schools, good people, and, if we had to be baristas, plenty of opportunity. We fought during the day, clung to each other superficially in the night. We were losing ground and grasping. The fights were escalating. My ability to disappear into denial was waning. Unforgivable things were said. Unforgivable things were done.

I sold everything in the house I could sell and put the rest in mobile storage to be shipped to wherever we might end up. We lived in hotels, a decidedly more comfortable way to be homeless than living on the street, but homeless nonetheless. We traveled with our eight-year-old son in the backseat listening to music, playing Nintendo DS, asking, "Where are we going next?" "Are we there yet?" It was July and I prayed for a solid landing before the start of the school year. We were depleting and unsupportive of each other. I was starting to accept that I was only staying in the marriage long enough for him to find a job in a city where we could both find work. I hoped that we would end up somewhere where he would meet someone else and I could leave again and stay gone forever. No matter what I bought, I had lost all hope.

Springfield to Kansas City to Denver to Salt Lake City. Plains rose to mountains and a week traveling the wide, wide streets of Brigham Young. A town scrubbed white, water and bones, water and bones. We passed the Hoover Dam and every mile of the endless power lines heralding Las Vegas. We stayed the night at the Bellagio, saw Cirque du Soleil. I felt the hot desert air on my skin, the absolute improbability of a city that shouldn't exist but does anyway. After Aidan went to bed in that Las Vegas hotel, William and I started smoking again. We discussed bankruptcy over cigarettes and the ringing of slot machines. The inside of those casinos, a mirror to my brain—loud, labyrinthine, addicted.

While he interviewed in Phoenix, Arizona, I did laundry at the hotel and took Aidan to the pool and we all waited, tenacious but weary for news, praying he would get the job. Our sense of urgency was not felt by the company, however, and when the waiting stretched into another week and then another, and our credit was rapidly vanishing on hotel bills, restaurants, the leather wallet I secretly bought at the gift shop to protect my iPhone at the pool, we left for Portland, our plan D. A corridor of evergreen, the Columbia Gorge, welcomed us to our new home. Our shaking hands signed the lease on an apartment just two days before the first day of school.

Over the next year, William got a job as a fitness trainer, making a fraction of what he used to make, but he was happy. I started a business that I was extremely proud of. Our shopping habits decreased markedly, mostly because we just didn't have the money or the credit. We had had to file for bankruptcy and lost everything but the car. Also, at some point we stopped trying to connect to each other.

The divorce was mostly a mutual decision. At least after I brought it up, he agreed. Divorce is a complicated and messy business, the kind of thing you know is going to be excruciating, and it is, but in entirely unexpected ways. There are ways you can suffer a divorce that you didn't even know existed. You get married and then you are just going along with a shared life and your dynamics and denials, and, when it comes time to extract yourself, it is like an amputation. Everyone regresses into their worst possible, most primal behavior. I drank too much. His temper flared more often and hotter. He told everyone I used him for his money and now that it was gone I was leaving him. When you are twenty-seven years younger and the money is indeed gone, saying as much is the obvious and easy way out, though it wasn't the whole story and hearing it hurt terribly. I had worked too hard to hold it together; I'd gotten us through the crush, done more than my part with little help. Divorce is just sad. It reminds you that it's possible to lose the things you love, that maybe you will never find what you are looking for, what you know you deserve. We all start out just the same, as twenty-one grams with the potential for a tail, and then we spend the rest of our skin-covered lives getting up every day and making a play for a love that lasts forever. It's all tears and blood and intermittent moments of grace.

I didn't bother defending myself. I take plenty of responsibility for mismanagement of funds; I do. I took connection and comfort where I could get it. I was so lonely. I got tired. I broke. I was in way over my head and lip gloss helped.

His shopping habits no longer affect my life. I only have to contend with my own and I haven't been in a Nordstrom in over a year. I have come undone again and am slowly putting it all back together. I am running and breathing and gathering a stronger system of support than I have ever had before. I am practicing radical acceptance for the painful imperfections that make me feel so uncomfortable in the world. I like space more than things, breathing room. I would rather be loved in ways that are surprising and only as sure as these things can ever be, us being human and all, than be served by predictable salespeople. I don't need a dressing room to feel safe.

And I almost get it right. I don't know exactly how these things work, but my J. Crew card survived the bankruptcy, and, recently, in a fit of PMS, a fit of insolence, desperately needing a soul salve for some life stress, because those never go away, I got online with money I didn't actually have and ordered a new bathrobe. A beautiful white bathrobe made of the same broadcloth as men's dress shirts, with the prettiest sky-blue piping around the collar. It wasn't warm. It needed to be ironed. And for an extra ten dollars, I got it monogrammed.

SPRING DISHTOWELS

Nan Narboe

a day that new dishtowels can "fix" is a day that doesn't need much fixing. No one I love is sick, brokenhearted, or in trouble. I have my health. I love my work. The roof over my head even has a warranty. I am free, for the moment, of the sense of insufficiency that advertisers use to sell to women—and yet, I go shopping.

Throughout the long, gray, rainy Oregon winter, I drink tea and read library books, content to stay inside. Today the sun streams through the windows and illuminates the daffodils in the yard, as exuberant as the day itself: the first full-blown, blue-sky day of spring. I look and look and then decide to clean the kitchen, lest it distract from the day.

That's when I notice my sad, frayed dishtowels. My weary, wintry dishtowels. The hunter-gatherer in me awakes. I need new dishtowels. Spring dishtowels. Now.

Expert shoppers regularly find things that are beautiful or functional or distinctively "them," like the black leather band ringed with silver that a white-haired man I know wears on his tanned wrist. Their finds bring me pleasure—and sometimes the wistful awareness that, if I put in the hours, I, too, could find such treasures.

Instead, I admire shoppers the way I admire fencers: as practitioners of a demanding and athletic form I'll never master. I am an occasional shopper, a half-hearted shopper. Take, for instance, the Fitbit electronic pedometer clipped to my bra right now. I was sold on electronic pedometers years ago; I even phoned the local co-op to buy one. But something interfered. Maybe the clerk took too long, or my teakettle whistled. At any rate, my attention shifted. This is what I mean when I say I'm not a shopper: Shoppers have endurance, shoppers keep going. I solve the same problem—the problem of wanting and getting—by wanting something else, like a cup of tea. It's not that desires are interchangeable, but that I want so many different things.

Years passed before I thought about pedometers again, this time right before a cab arrived to take me to the airport, where I ran into delays and had to cancel the day's work. The only way to come out ahead would be if the airport Brookstone carried electronic pedometers. It did. Three brands. Better still, I got the clerk of my dreams: quick to understand what I wanted, willing to name the brand he preferred, and fast-moving enough to get me out of the store in twenty minutes, my outer limit. (Airport delays are not for shopping; they're for eating soft-serve frozen yogurt and reading paperback thrillers.) I bought the Fitbit he recommended and, at his urging, paid to insure it.

You could say he was a good salesman; you could say I was an easy mark. You could also say that we were successful collaborators. I surely thought so, particularly when I lost the pedometer and it was replaced at no charge. The Brookstone salesman was the opposite of the clerk I flee: the one who doesn't have what I am looking for and tries to convince me that what she has on hand will work. I go silent rather than say the snarky things I feel like saying. I remind myself that some customers—probably the ones who love to shop—would welcome an approach that widens their sense of possibilities. Not me. I feel put-upon, a state I work hard to avoid.

I knew it all too well growing up. Worse, it's a state linked to shopping. Tall by age eleven, I came to dread the words I heard most often from clerks: "We don't have what you're looking for in your size." Trying to help or make a sale, the clerk would then suggest alternatives. A pair of kelly-green lace-up oxfords I was coerced into putting on my suddenly size ten feet horrifies me to this day. Watching my feet (previously good feet, running and jumping feet, feet you could find shoes for) turn long and green and ugly made me cry. Whatever the other choice was—and in those days before the Internet, it regularly came down to a choice between two make-do options—those were the shoes I wore to school that year. It took subsequent generations of young women to make my height and shoe size normal, and for me to understand that I was tall, not misshapen.

Shopping meant scarcity. It meant rejection. It fueled my queasy suspicion that I'd never belong. Mostly it was hard: hard to have reached my full height, nearly five-foot-eleven, by the fifth grade. Hard that I couldn't afford the Jantzen sweaters and Pendleton skirts the girls I envied wore. Hard that Capezio flats weren't even made in my size. All exclusion is costly and mine came with an additional twist: My grandmother, who owned a high-end dress shop, sent me her cast-offs, as well as items from her stock. That meant I wore Italian knits and cashmere coats to high school: clothing too old for me and far more expensive than the clothes I wanted.

Shopping was too complicated for too long for the impulse to remain intact. (I think of Parker, the lithe blond thief on the TV show *Leverage*. She sees something sparkly and her eyes widen and her head swivels to track it.) What I have instead is observation. Noticing—in this case, noticing the gap between what I have and what I can imagine. Reaching for a coat, I picture one that would better suit my mood, the temperature, or the clothes I have on. (A friend gave me her well-loved blue Burberry trench coat, describing it as perfect to wear with jeans. It is.) Folding a dishtowel to put under a hot casserole, I think, *Trivet*. I could do with a trivet. I even bought a house this way, by picturing the view I wanted to see from the window. After trekking through what felt like an endless run of bad-shoe houses, I remembered that a friend went to open houses for fun. He ferried me around, bless him, providing the stamina and hopefulness I could no longer muster. Seven steps into the house I now own, I saw the view I had imagined.

I phone the friend I had invited for tea and ask her to meet me at a kitchen store instead. There I forage until I find a display table laden with April Cornell prints: runners, tablecloths, napkins, dishtowels. I start at one corner and work my way around, dismissing dishtowels that are pretty but not right. I'm down to the final corner when I spot a stack of daffodil-bright piqué dishtowels. I unfold one and crush it between my hands. It feels right. It looks right. I buy three.

All better now: I figured out what I wanted, I found it, and I got it. The week before, what did the trick was peanut butter balls, a treat from my childhood. Making them was a gamble. Every few years I try a donut or a milk shake, only to discover they aren't half as good as I remember. But with the initial taste of the first batch (peanut butter, agave syrup, coconut flour in place of the original recipe's powdered milk, and raisins), I was happy. You may not think happy is a taste sensation, but it is.

Weather and hormonal changes leave me yearning for something—if only I knew what that something was. Yearning itself is hard to bear and yearning without a discernible object can lead to cycles of spending, eating, and viewing that are cut off from desire. Popcorn and reruns, followed by disgust. The reverse is what pleases me about the dishtowels episode. Following a hunch led to satisfaction. Isn't that what shopping is? Wanting something and trying to locate it: first internally, then out in the world.

I interpret the sensation of wanting something as hunger, which it is—although not necessarily for food. Sometimes what I want is sleep or company or a movie other than the one I'm watching. ("Let's find something with a faster pace," says a friend, teaching me to gauge whether the movie we're watching suits my mood.) When a houseguest lingers longer than the recommended three days, I want my house back. I want silence. I want to pile dirty dishes in the sink and ignore the phone. Or I want the opposite: a lover to laugh with, the zing of hot and sour soup, the checkout clerks at the neighborhood grocery to ask me how I'm doing. Or something highly specialized, like the masquerade of strolling through a pricy boutique as though I belong there (best done on the West Coast, where the wealthy dress down). Searching for what I want makes me feel purposeful. Grown up. Cosmopolitan. Imagining the blue-and-black houndstooth scarf I wish I could find, I am alive to myself—as is, I imagine, the aboriginal hunter who sings to the animal he's tracking.

Market researchers divide shoppers into two groups, those who shop for objects and those who shop for experiences. They study which group gets the better payoff, whether objects or experiences add more to the shopper's quality of life. I am arguing a different premise: that effective shopping, shopping that leads to satisfaction, is aligned with desire. It doesn't matter whether the object of desire is a sunset or a nonstick skillet, laughter or a shiny new speedboat. What matters is finding a link between an internal desire and its outward expression. Ineffective shopping—the kind that leads to outfits that age in the closet, untried recipes, vacations spent at someone else's dream destination—is shopping unmoored from the self.

Lantern-print dishtowels? Sure, why not. Peanut butter balls? Good call. A houndstooth scarf? Not this season. Despite repeated forays, I return from the hunt empty-handed. What matters is staying close. Connected. Reading myself as well as I can, and following through, acting on those appetites I am able to decipher. A fluffy aubergine robe with big pink polka dots that made me grin when I saw it in an English clothing catalogue makes me happy each time I put it on—a stroke of luck, I figure, although I'm proud of myself for taking such an outlandish gamble.

Self-awareness is inevitably erratic, a work in progress, an etch-a-sketch that shifts with the slightest shimmer of movement. Doing the best we can is the best we can do. Who knew that I consider new dishtowels a rite of spring? I certainly didn't. What are the odds that the ooze and faintly umami taste of an almost forgotten peanut butter candy would satisfy my sweet tooth for weeks? It takes nerve to act on our desires—and stamina to withstand those yearnings that are too diffuse to decipher. (Something . . . there's something I want, but I can't identify it. Animal, mineral, vegetable? Colonel Mustard in the study with a candlestick?) Wanting is a primal force. Trying to tamp it down is understandable, as is going numb to escape the tension it creates. But most of us don't want the moon. We simply want what we want. Whatever that is.

A successful day is one in which what I buy and what I eat and the way I spend my time satisfies me. Sometimes I can't put a name to what it is I desire; sometimes I can't locate it. Frequently, I run out of steam. Wanting, not to mention getting, takes effort, stamina, and luck.

Experience helps. Had the dishtowels been out of my price range, I simply would have admired them the way I do textiles in a museum. If their pattern hadn't matched my giddy mood, I would not have unfolded one to take a second look. At long last, I know how to shop—that is, I know how to shop for who I am. I would regret buying a scarf that fell short of my fantasy or dishtowels that were merely serviceable. Nothing make-do for me. I'm better off doing without. That's how the previous batch of dishtowels got so frayed, come to think of it. It had been years since I had seen any, either internally or out in the wide world, that I truly desired.

MOTHERLODE

Nancy Rommelmann

bout a decade after a woman gives birth to a girl, she begins to know exponentially and unequivocally less about fashion than her daughter. I'm not talking about (what are for me) the classics; I've got a DVF wrap dress and a half-dozen Betsey Johnsons, and at thirty paces I can peg the best polyester hostess gown in Goodwill. I mean what's going on now: When did acid-washed jeans become "sand-blasted," and what's up with all the denim, anyway? Is Lenny Kravitz to blame for oversize accessories? Are we on the sixty-seventh or seventy-sixth resurrection of the peasant blouse? How would I know? Just as I realized that I hadn't read the last Martin Amis book when the next was being reviewed, at a certain point I stopped trying to keep pace. I chalk up my disengagement, and my twelve-year-old daughter's budding awareness, to some sharklike sartorial survival gene that knows it needs to keep moving if it's to stay alive. While Tafv likes wearing the geometric-print Emilio Pucci nightgowns I inherited from *my* mother, she'll also shoot me looks of abject terror when I try on outfits that seem timeless to me, the Charlie's Angels pantsuits, the Dead Kennedys T-shirt. . . .

"No, Mama, you can't!" she'll shriek, tossing the blouse with the ruched sleeves back in the closet.

"But I wore that when I was pregnant with you. . . ."

"Mama!"

Embarrassment factor for Tafv if I wear the blouse: 704. Luckily, I still understand humiliation. And so, although it may be true that I was stranded in the fashion undertow two years ago, I also unwittingly did something brilliant, which was go online and order from Delia's.

For those unfamiliar with Delia's, it's a catalog of hip-huggers and bikinis, prom dresses and accessories, draped on teenage models who, with their navel rings and tank tops imprinted with dangling cherries, wear expressions poised between "I love sleepovers!" and "I just did the gym teacher." The opportunity to dress like naughty girls (as opposed to actually being naughty) has proved enormously appealing to 'tweens, and Delia's exerts a pull not unlike J. Crew, the defining yuppie catalog perused less for clothes than for clues as to how to look as though you, well, shop at J. Crew, whether you plan to get into a canoe with a Labrador or not.

The Delia's home invasion (a new catalog arrives about every three weeks) has proved to be all things to all two of us: Tafv can choose outfits at breakfast or in bed; I never have to set foot in a mall (a trip that for me ranks right up there with standing in line at the DMV in August); and, a boon I really couldn't have foreseen because she was ten at the time, and tiny: as soon as Tafv tires of or outgrows the clothes, she gives them to me.

"Your mom is so hip," her friends tell her, staring at my feet, at the black-leather-with-tan-stitching sneakers Tafv wore only once before I absconded with them (and that several acquaintances mistook for Prada's riff on bowling shoes). I think she likes to hear this because she knows that any credit for good taste is strictly hers, and because she never has to be embarrassed about my proclivity to wear the same outfit four days running.

Which means I say yes to about everything Tafv circles in the Delia's catalog, nudging her toward skirts with room for hips (which she does not have) and halters with built-in bras (which she does not need). Am I being practical? Economical? Fending off middle age? Death? Indulging my disinclination to own more than three pairs of shoes at a time? I make Tafv a grilled cheese sandwich and slap a few recent issues of Delia's on the kitchen table.

"How old do you think people should be to wear Delia's?"

"You mean, the limit?" she asks, turning the pages, it seems to me, in a bid to avoid eye contact. "They can be in the 20s, but over 20s, they can't wear them, Mother."

"Then how come you let me wear yours?"

"Because you can look good in them. The other mamas can't."

"That's very sweet. Does Delia's carry the current styles?"

"Well, there are different styles," she says slowly, in a try-to-follow-along-here tone. "Delia's will have themes. Sometimes it's clothes like Britney's, which I don't really like. This issue's kind of . . . leather/lace. Shakira kind of clothes."

"The model on the cover sort of looks like Shakira. I guess they do that on purpose."

"That is Shakira. See, 'Shakira,'" she says, running her finger over bright-blue type that reads shakira! and, next to it, in Tafv's girlish script, *Shakira*, complete with a penned-in arrow pointing at, um, Shakira.

"I don't like that," Tafv says, frowning at a girl in a floppy hat, a fringed suede belt, and a gauzy floral top. "What is this style called?"

"That would be hippie."

"Yeah, hippie, but in a motorcycle-gang kind of way."

"Honey, do you think there will come a time when I say, 'Hey, the Delia's catalog came!' and you'll think, *God, she's so uncool. . . .*"

Tafv laughs. "Probably," she says. "Abercrombie & Fitch is taking over. The style now is comfy but hip and sporty, like pants with a stripe down the side, and a little tank top with a 4 on it."

Both of which she currently wears, having borrowed them from a friend.

I look at the little top and wonder if it will fit.

It's a warm June afternoon, and I am walking to meet my husband for a drink, when I feel a car pull alongside me.

"We love your dress!" says a girl hanging from a passenger window. She and her friend are about twenty-three, the same age my daughter is now. The girl behind the wheel is saying something I cannot hear but do not need to. I can see, by the way she and her friend lean toward me, that they are as captivated by the dress as I am.

"Thank you," I tell the girls, and that I stole the dress from my daughter. They repeat that they love it as they drive on, and I silently thank Tafv again for leaving it behind after her trip home last summer.

It may be ten years since I absconded with her Delia's outfits. We may no longer communicate across the kitchen table. But I am still wearing my daughter's clothes, for the old reason—I am an erratic shopper who, like Steve Jobs and Buckminster Fuller, might prefer to wear the same outfit (almost) every day and get on with it—and a new and rather thrilling one: Tafv has grown up to be a young woman with impeccable taste.

There were stops along the way. By thirteen she'd ditched Delia's for Hot Topic, which within a year became anathema and led to a tomboy/skater phase: tight jeans, Vans, and ratty T-shirts, including my Dead Kennedys shirt, which I never did get back. By sixteen, she and her friends were thrift-store mavens, Tafv foraging for maternity tops and 1980s power dresses with shoulder pads. These she'd tailor, having taken up sewing, into outfits that were improbably chic. The sewing led to art school, which led to dropping out of art school, which led by age twenty to moving to New York to work in the art department for film companies, and then for one of the most famous editorial stylists in the world, where Tafv coordinates and shops for photo shoots for Louis Vuitton and Balenciaga and Lanvin. She will tell me to get this month's issue of *Vanity Fair*, of *W*, of *Italian Vogue*, to see the spreads she's worked on.

Do I marvel that my child is being paid to shop, that she is prized for her eye, whereas my father still occasionally asks me, "Did you get dressed in the dark?" I do marvel. I marvel that she can make an American Apparel floor-length tank dress look like couture, that she knows how to tie a scarf, that she is the epitome of grace whether she is wearing Converse or a buttery leather jacket from Top Shop or both together.

Talk about a tortoise giving birth to a gazelle. I don't know how Tafv got her ease, her confidence when it comes to clothes. I do know that with the dress she left behind last summer, she bequeathed some of it to me.

I found the dress—sheer, black, diaphanous, leaving one shoulder bare and having a simple string tie at the waist—in her bedroom closet, amid some old clothes she'd rummaged through while home. The dress did not look like much on the hanger, and perhaps I tried it on that first time less in hopes it might look good on me, than for momentary proximity with my child, now living three thousand miles away.

The dress slipped over me like mercury. Its engineering was precise if invisible—how else to explain that it—and I—looked stunning from every angle? I felt languid and ready and immediately wanted to board a plane. I learned, as the summer wore on, of the dress's other attributes: it weighs less than an ounce, it dries in minutes, it never looks or feels soiled. You might pack it and only it for a monthlong trip and look lovely and appropriate every day. I'm considering doing so.

Soon after I became one with the dress, Tafv phoned to ask if I would pack some stuff she'd left and ship it to her. I felt a bit of panic but told her, of course.

I did not mail back the dress. I did not tell her she'd left it. I did not tell her until summer's end, after I had worn the dress in San Francisco and Miami, to book parties and business meetings, after I'd slept in it after too much wine.

"Baby," I confessed one morning on the phone, "I have your dress."

"What dress?" she asked.

"The *black dress*," I said and described it. I pleaded my love for it. I reminded her of my lameness when it came to shopping, how I never would recognize the perfection of a piece like this unless she did so first.

"Um, Mom?" Tafv said. "You bought me that dress."

"What? When?"

"Remember, that store on Alberta Street?" she said. "I didn't really want it but you said I could wear it anywhere, if I went to Cuba again, or in New York at night, or to the beach. . . ."

That was *this* dress, I asked? And remembered Tafv standing before me in it, and my saying I had to buy it for her, that it was everything you could want in a dress.

Well, I told her, I did remember. But might I keep it a little longer?

"You can have it, Mom; I never wear it," she said. "I think you were probably buying it for you."

about the contributors

Allison Amend is a graduate of the Iowa Writers' Workshop and author of the short story collection *Things That Pass for Love*, which won the Independent Publisher Book Award. Her novel *Stations West* was a finalist for both the 2011 Sami Rohr Prize for Jewish Literature and the Oklahoma Book Award. Her new novel, *A Nearly Perfect Copy*, was published in April 2013. Allison lives in New York City, where she teaches creative writing at Lehman College and at the Red Earth MFA. Visit her on the web at allisonamend.com or facebook.com/ AllisonAmendAuthor.

Laura M. André is a former university professor who makes her living as a freelance editor, writer, and fine arts consultant. She is the editor of *It's All in Her Head: Women Making Peace with Troubled Minds* (itsallinherhead.com), an online anthology on women writing about mental health challenges, and was the coeditor (with Candace Walsh) of *Dear John, I Love Jane: Women Write About Leaving Men for Women* (Seal Press, 2010), a Lambda Literary Award finalist. Her writing has appeared in the anthologies *Ask Me About My Divorce: Women Open Up About Moving On* (Seal Press, 2009), *Queer Girls in Class: Lesbian Teachers and Students Tell Their Classroom Stories* (Peter Lang, 2010), and *Madonna and Me: Women Writers on the Queen of Pop* (Soft Skull, 2012). She lives in Santa Fe, New Mexico, with her wife Candace Walsh, two children, and two dogs.

Jennifer Finney Boylan is the author of thirteen books, including *She's Not There*, the first best-selling work by a transgender American. Her latest book, *Stuck in the Middle with You: Parenthood in Three Genders*, is about the difference between motherhood and fatherhood. Jenny is a professor of English at Colby College in Maine and is also a member of the board of trustees of the Kinsey Institute for Research on Sex, Gender, and Reproduction, as well as a member of the board of directors of GLAAD, Inc. Her website is jenniferboylan.net.

Emily Chenoweth is the author of the novel *Hello Goodbye* (Random House), which was a finalist for the Oregon Book Award and was named one of the top ten Northwest books of 2009 by *The Oregonian*. As a ghostwriter, she's penned eight young adult novels, several of which have been *New York Times* bestsellers. She lives in Portland, Oregon, with her family.

Janet Clare attended the University of California at Berkeley, Skidmore College, and the UCLA Master's Writing Program. She's written two novels and is working on a third. "With Mom" is her second published essay. The first, "Into Africa," was published online. Her flash fiction "Old Friend" appeared on First Stop Fiction. She is a New York native, now living and working in Los Angeles.

Wendy Staley Colbert's personal essays have been featured in publications such as *Salon*, *Whole Life Times*, *ParentMap*, and *This Great Society*. Her essays are also included in Theo Pauline Nestor's anthologies *We Came to Say* and *We Came Back to Say*. For more, see wendystaleycolbert.com.

Monica Drake is the author of the novels *Clown Girl* (Hawthorne Books, 2007) and *The Stud Book* (Hogarth, 2013). Her stories and essays have appeared in the *Paris Review Daily*, the *Northwest Review*, *Oregon Humanities* magazine, *Threepenny Review*, *Beloit Fiction Journal*, and other publications, as well as on the radio show *Live Wire*. She's an associate professor at the Pacific Northwest College of Art, in Portland, Oregon, where she has recently launched a bachelor of fine arts program in writing.

Ophira Eisenberg is a comedian, writer, and host of NPR's weekly trivia comedy show, *Ask Me Another*. She has appeared on *The Late Late Show* with Craig Ferguson, *The Today Show*, *Comedy Central*, and VH-1. Selected as one of *New York Magazine*'s Top 10 Comics That Funny People Find Funny, and featured in the *The New York Times* as a skilled comedian and storyteller with a "bleakly stylish" sense of humor, Ophira's debut memoir *Screw Everyone: Sleeping My Way to Monogamy* (Seal Press, 2013) is in stores now. She is also a regular host and storyteller with *The Moth* and has appeared on their award-winning podcast, radio show, and audience favorites compilation. See ophiraeisenberg.com.

Traci Foust's first book, *Nowhere Near Normal: A Memoir of OCD* (Simon and Schuster, 2011) was featured in *Marie Claire*, *The Nervous Breakdown*, NPR, KGO News Talk San Francisco, *VIVA* magazine, and MSNBC Today. Her fiction short *The Cruelty of Children* was nominated for a Pushcart Prize by *Echo Ink Review* and will be released as a short film in July 2014 by Sedona Productions.

Ru Freeman's creative and political writing has appeared internationally. She is the author of the novel *A Disobedient Girl*, which was translated into several languages. She blogs for the Huffington Post on literature and politics, is a contributing editorial board member of the *Asian American Literary Review*, and has been a fellow of the Bread Loaf Writers' Conference, Yaddo, and the Virginia Center for the Creative Arts. Her new novel, *On Sal Mal Lane*, was published by Graywolf Press in 2013.

Gloria Harrison's writing has appeared on *This American Life*, *The Nervous Breakdown*, and *Fictionaut*, as well as in *Bear Deluxe Magazine*. Gloria doesn't have much time to write anymore because she's a single mom raising dazzlingly brilliant and spirited middle school–age twin boys and has an impossibly uncreative day job. However, when she does find time to write, she works on a novel, a memoir, and essays for various sites around the Internet. You can follow her on Twitter @gloriaharrison, or like her author page on Facebook.

Marni Hochman is a small business owner, literacy volunteer, and mom. When she isn't working, tutoring, mothering, or shopping, she is writing. Her work has appeared in the online magazine *Role/Reboot*. She lives with her husband and two children in Ypsilanti, Michigan.

Aryn Kyle is the author of the novel *The God of Animals* and the short story collection *Boys and Girls Like You and Me*. Her new novel, *Hinterland*, is forthcoming from Riverhead. She lives in New York City.

Gigi Little's essays and short stories have appeared in anthologies and literary magazines. She's also the graphic designer for Forest Avenue Press. By day, she works as lead visual merchandiser for Powell's Books in Portland, Oregon, where she lives with her husband, fine artist Stephen O'Donnell. Before moving to Portland, Gigi spent fifteen years in the circus, as a lighting director and professional circus clown. She never took a pie to the face, but she's a Rhodes Scholar in the art of losing her pants.

Jessica Machado is an associate editor at *Rolling Stone*. Her work has appeared in *Bust*, *xoJane*, *The Awl*, *The Rumpus*, and *More Intelligent Life*, among others. She also writes about the kind of grownup she is at baggageclaimed.tumblr.com.

Abby Mims's story "The Way They Loved The Dead" was nominated for a 2012 Pushcart Prize, and her writing has appeared in a gaggle of lit mags and anthologies, including *Salon*, *The Rumpus*, *The Nervous Breakdown*, *The Normal School*, *The Santa Monica Review*, *Swink*, *Other Voices*, *Women on the Edge: LA Women Writers*, and *Cassette From My Ex*. She currently resides in Northern California with her family, where she is at work on a memoir about her mother's illness.

Jenny Moore writes and edits fiction and nonfiction. She is also an instructor at the Writer's Center and has taught at Grub Street and other venues. She earned her MFA from the New School and has been a resident at the Helene Wurlitzer Foundation. Jenny now lives near Washington, D.C.

Nan Narboe writes ThePracticeBlog.org, which she created to give away mind-body experiments like those she designs for her psychotherapy clients. She was the cook behind L'Auberge restaurant and cofounder of Cascade Valley School, both in Portland, Oregon. As a finalist in *Vogue* magazine's Prix de Paris writing contest years ago, she met the legendary editor Diana Vreeland—who reminded her of her grandmother.

Randon Billings Noble is an essayist. Her work has appeared in the *Modern Love* column of *The New York Times*; *The Massachusetts Review*; *The Millions*; *Brain, Child*; and elsewhere. She has been a fellow at the Virginia Center for the Creative Arts and the Vermont Studio Center and was named a 2013 Mid Atlantic Arts Foundation creative fellow to be a resident at the Millay Colony for the Arts. You can read more of her work at randonbillingsnoble.com.

Stacy Pershall is the author of *Loud in the House of Myself: Memoir of a Strange Girl* (W. W. Norton, 2011), chosen for the Barnes and Noble Discover Great New Writers program. She is originally from Prairie Grove, Arkansas, but now lives in New York City. She teaches writing at Gotham Writers' Workshop and the Johns Hopkins Center for Talented Youth and is a member of the Active Minds speakers' bureau. Stacy is currently at work on a young adult Southern Gothic novel about Chernobyl (really).

Robin Romm is the author of two books. *The Mother Garden* (short stories) was a finalist for the PEN USA Prize. *The Mercy Papers: A Memoir of Three Weeks* was a *New York Times* Notable Book of the Year, a *San Francisco Chronicle* Best Book of the Year, and a Top Ten Nonfiction Book of the Year according to *Entertainment Weekly*. Her work has appeared in *The New York Times, The Atlantic, The UK Observer, O Magazine, The Sun, Tin House, One Story*, and many other publications. She's spoken widely about writing and grief—at Columbia Medical School, the Jewish Theological Seminary, Red Bird Grief Center, and in private workshops. She's a frequent contributor to *The New York Times Book Review* and teaches at the low-residency MFA program for writers at Warren Wilson. She currently lives in Portland, Oregon.

Nancy Rommelmann's work appears in *The Wall Street Journal*, the *LA Weekly, Byliner*, and other publications. She is the author of The Bad Mother, a novel (2011), *The Queens of Montague Street*, a digital memoir of growing up in 1970s Brooklyn that was excerpted in *The New York Times Magazine*, and the story collection, *Transportation* (Dymaxicon, 2013). *Going to Gacy*, about her trip to interview serial killer John Wayne Gacy before he was executed, was released as an ebook in 2014. She is currently at work on *To the Bridge*, a book of narrative nonfiction about a filicide in Portland, Oregon.

Elizabeth Scarboro is the author of the memoir *My Foreign Cities*, an unlikely love story set on the frontiers of modern medicine, chosen by *Library Journal* and the *SF Chronicle* as one of the Best Books of 2013. Scarboro is also the author of two novels for children. Her work has appeared most recently in *The New York Times* and *The Bellevue Literary Review*. She lives with her family in Berkeley, California.

Susan Senator is an author, journalist, disability rights advocate, and the mother of three boys, the oldest of whom has autism. Susan has appeared on the *Today Show*, MSNBC, NPR, and CNN. She is the author of *Making Peace With Autism, The Autism Mom's Survival Guide*, and *Dirt*, her first novel. Susan has written articles and essays on disability, education, and parenting for *The New York Times, The Washington Post, The Boston Globe, Exceptional Parent Magazine, Family Fun*, and *Education Week*. Her writings took her to a state dinner at the White House, in honor of the Special Olympics, in 2006. She currently works as director of autism adult services and outreach at the Community Colleges Consortium for Autism and Intellectual Disabilities (CCCAID). Susan also teaches English at Suffolk University in Boston. Susan's publications, events listings, and blog can be found at susansenator.com.

Rachel Sontag is the author of *House Rules*, a memoir. She received her MFA in creative nonfiction from the New School and currently works as a social worker in Chicago, Illinois.

Kelly Shire is a third-generation native of Southern California. She received her MFA in in fiction from California State University, Long Beach; has published short stories in several small journals; and is now writing a memoir about family, pop culture, and growing up in Los Angeles County. She lives with her family in Temecula, California. You can find her at kellyshire.com.

When she's not writing, **Kristin Thiel** edits for a growing company she owns. She spends most of her time in Portland, Oregon, and online at kristinthiel.com.

Candace Walsh is the author of *Licking the Spoon: A Memoir of Food, Family, and Identity* (Seal Press, 2012, lickingthespoonbook.com) and coeditor with her wife, Laura André, of *Dear John, I Love Jane: Women Write About Leaving Men for Women* (Seal Press, 2010), a Lambda Literary Award finalist. She lives in Santa Fe with André and their two children. Read more about her at candacewalsh.com; follow her on Twitter @candacewalsh.

Mel Wells bikes, surfs, and works her dream job at Literary Arts in Portland, Oregon. Her writing has appeared in *Salamander*, *Pathos*, and *Boneshaker*. She is working on a book about her past life as a Mormon missionary in Belgium. She eats rain for breakfast.

Meg Worden has stories and essays online and in print at MariaShriver.com, *The Nervous Breakdown*, *Elephant Journal*, and *Moon City Review*, as well as her professional blog. Her prison essay, "The Visit," won first place in *Ascent* magazine's text writing contest in 2008. She is currently shopping her memoir project about the two years she spent in federal prison. Meg lives in Portland, Oregon, with her son.

K erry Cohen is the author of *Loose Girl,
Dirty Little Secrets, Seeing Ezra;* and the
young adult novels *Easy, The Good Girl,*
and *It's Not You, It's Me.* A psychotherapist and
faculty at The Red Earth MFA program, she lives
with the author James Bernard Frost and their
four children in Portland, Oregon.

HEATHER HAWKSFORD

Drinking Diaries: Women Serve Their Stories Straight Up, edited by Caren Osten Gerszberg and Leah Odze Epstein. $15.00, 978-1-58005-411-9. Celebrated writers take a candid look at the pleasures and pains of drinking, and the many ways in which it touches women's lives.

Goodbye to All That: Writers on Loving and Leaving New York, edited by Sari Botton. $16.00, 978-1-58005-494-2. An anthology for those who have loved and left New York City, with contributions from 28 talented writers.

The Money Therapist: A Woman's Guide to Creating A Healthy Financial Life, by Marcia Brixey. $15.95, 978-1-58005-216-0. Offers women of every financial strata the tools they need to manage their money, set attainable budget goals, get out of debt, and create a healthy financial life.

Hot & Heavy: Fierce Fat Girls on Life, Love & Fashion, by Virgie Tovar. $16.00, 978-1-58005-438-6. A fun, fresh anthology that celebrates positive body image, feeling comfortable in one's own skin, and being fabulously fine with being fat.

It's So You: 35 Women Write About Personal Expression Through Fashion and Style, edited by Michelle Tea. $15.95, 978-1-58005-215-3. From the haute couture houses of the ruling class to DIY girls who make restorative clothing and create their own hodgepodge style, this is the first book to explore women's ambivalence toward, suspicion of, indulgence in, and love of fashion on every level.

Body Outlaws: Rewriting the Rules of Beauty and Body Image, edited by Ophira Edut, foreword by Rebecca Walker. $15.95, 978-1-58005-108-8. Filled with honesty and humor, this groundbreaking anthology offers stories by women who have chosen to ignore, subvert, or redefine the dominant beauty standard in order to feel at home in their bodies.

Find Seal Press Online

www.SealPress.com
www.Facebook.com/SealPress
Twitter: @SealPress